SAVING ERNEST

A Family Mystery of Life, Death, and Destiny

PHOEBE TALLIS

WITH SPIRITUAL RESEARCH BY

INESSA BURDICH

First published in paperback by
Michael Terence Publishing in 2026
www.mtp.agency

ISBN 9781805881650

Cover design (AI)
Michael Terence Publishing
and Phoebe Tallis

Michael Terence
Publishing

The voice of the dead was a living voice to me.

In the Valley of Cauteretz, Alfred, Lord Tennyson (1864)

CONTENTS

FOREWORD

This book is both unique and fascinating. It is highly original because it tells the story of the author's extended family through the generations along the maternal line of descent. What makes it so unusual, however, is that the author, together with her close collaborator Inessa Burdich, is able, it seems, to locate these family members not only in their earthly lives but also beyond the threshold, in the worlds of soul and spirit. This is what gives the work its distinctive originality and depth.

It is not every day that we can read such an account—one that leads us from the world of physical existence into the spheres entered after death. In sharing these experiences with us, the author both challenges and encourages us to pursue our own enquiries. We are enabled to see the various states of soul after death and to realise that the situations and conditions of these souls are intimately related to the lives they have lived on earth. As we move chapter by chapter through *Saving Ernest*, it becomes clear that the events, emotions, and choices of earthly life are the shapers and moulders of the soul's early experiences in the afterlife. This insight is of great importance for us all to know, or at least to consider seriously.

Because it means no less than this: that the life we will lead after our deaths, when we depart our physical earthly bodies, will be determined by our lives whilst living in the body. Moreover, it shows that we can, here and now, begin to shape and fashion the life to come, when we ourselves cross the threshold. This is profoundly empowering. We are not simply passive recipients of whatever fate may throw our way, but rather the actors and agents in a creative process that starts already—each day—to build the worlds we will inhabit after death. Just imagine that!

We are not, then, puppets on a string, but the very beings who move the strings that determine our destiny. This is one of the deep lessons that *Saving Ernest* offers, provided we approach it with open minds and open hearts.

It is a heartfelt book, born of love and selfless service, written with the intention of helping those souls who may be delayed or hindered on their journey toward the light of the spiritual world. In this sense it is a book of healing—a labour of love in the truest sense.

Its narrative unfolds as a kind of detective story, tracing the sources of inherited wounds and the gestures that redeem them, but its deeper aim is revelation: to remind us that we are all, in truth, children of God, spiritual beings learning through experience. As we live on earth, we wear the personalities our karma has formed for us; after death, we gradually shed these garments and move closer to who we really are, our divinely inspired Higher Self. This is something which today, in our 21st century, we are in need of knowing. Namely, the realisation that our true being is God-inspired and not merely the limited earthly self that we know in our daily life.

And we are all of us on this journey of knowledge, whether we realise it or not—a "journey of souls".

This book can teach us important lessons. Though grounded in one family's history, its implications are far-reaching and of great significance. It shows how understanding, love, and consciously offered service can transform both the living and the dead. We can be deeply grateful to share in its insights—and I thank Phoebe, her family, and Inessa for allowing us to do so.

Dr Bob Woodward PhD (2025)

Spiritual researcher and author; publications include
Karma in Human Life: As Received Through Spirit Guides (2022)

AUTHOR'S NOTE

Questions of life, death, and destiny shaped my outlook since childhood. My parents introduced me to the work of Rudolf Steiner, whose insights into the spiritual world offered me a framework for understanding existence beyond the physical. Yet it wasn't until I lost my husband that these ideas became deeply personal. Faced with grief, I turned to Steiner's writings on the afterlife, seeking guidance not only in relation to my own sorrow but also with a view to supporting my husband's journey beyond death.

It was then that the unexpected began to happen. As I worked spiritually with my husband, I sensed that others—many others—were gathering around me, each with a silent request for recognition. Why were they here? What did they want?

At this point, I began sifting through an old family archive of photographs—a treasure trove I inherited from my great-uncle. Now, the past stirred to life before my eyes. Faces I had never met gazed back at me, their expressions holding quiet invitations to look deeper. And as they reached towards me, I started to explore their histories.

This book is the result of that explorative journey. In a sense, it is a family history, but more than this, it is an investigation into the mysteries of family legacies—drawn from real lives, lives that continue beyond their earthly endings. It does not seek to provide final answers, but rather to offer a way of seeing: an opportunity to witness the journeys of those who have gone before us and to glimpse the continuing connections between their world and ours.

The stories that follow draw upon both historical research and direct spiritual enquiry that reaches beyond what we usually call the physical world. Readers may take them as they will.

All that is asked is a willingness to listen for meanings that may at first seem unfamiliar, but which reveal the twin realities of body and soul that shape all human life.

DEDICATION

To Lorenzo:

Once we were one, then death made us two.
Like chaff from wheat, I was cast adrift from you.
But soul called to soul, over time, and then—
You, whom I lost, was found again.

Lost and Found, Phoebe Tallis (2025)

INTRODUCTION:

THE KARMIC DETECTIVE STORY

"It's destiny that we met!" cried Caroline.

"Ah yes," replied Felix, with an enigmatic smile,
"but destiny is really just soul-memory working in disguise."

Turn Left For Atlantis, Lorenzo Ebrio (2024)

A murder. A mystery. A story.

Not in the courtroom sense, but in the hidden world of the heart.

Here is a family—my family—woven through with love, sacrifice, tenderness, and grace. But also, like so many families, touched by tragedy. Somewhere in their midst, something was lost: the possibility of love, the gift of kindness, the delicate thread of artistic and emotional freedom.

In one of the book's earliest chapters, we witness what might be called a kind of murder. Not a legal crime, but a spiritual one—the quiet extinguishing of tenderness, the suffocation of hope, the death of a vital current between two souls. The story of Ernest and Beatrice Mallory stands at the heart of this book. It asks: *Whodunnit?*

Who—or what—led to such a loss, and where did it begin?

This book is, in part, a karmic investigation. With you, the reader, I move backwards and sideways through the lives of those who preceded Ernest and Beatrice, and through the layers of inheritance that shaped them. While the opening chapters frame a perplexing and often painful descent into suffering whose roots lie hidden, deeper meaning gradually emerges in the tales that follow.

We examine clues, recover lost contexts, and piece together the tangled legacies that formed one difficult marriage—and ultimately, a family. As we meet the cast of players, the stories shed light on how inherited trauma can both damage and, paradoxically, open a doorway to healing through the insight it yields.

But this is not a classic whodunnit, ending with a neat solution or a single culprit. As you read this book, you will see that each participant has an effect on others through their actions. Some of those effects are helpful; some are unhelpful. All have consequences, rolling down the years.

This is much more than a simple tale of ancestral lives. It is a layered history of interwoven generations, in which karma unfolds, characters sink and swim, intentions evolve. Each story holds invisible weight: unrealised destinies, unredeemed feelings, inherited burdens, and quiet redemptions.

What makes this book unique is that it does not end at the grave. Through meditative spiritual research, I have been able to continue the story of each character into the afterlife, illustrating—via the help of my colleague Inessa Burdich—how the soul continues its journey towards fulfilment, life after life.

It is in the afterlife that souls come to full spiritual consciousness. Here they seek understanding of their mistakes, and the meaning within life's seemingly random events. And they strive to right wrongs— often in collaboration with the living.

The twin concepts of karma and reincarnation are central to this exploration. Seen through their lens, these family lives take on a meaning that simple biography cannot reveal. They show us how our choices ripple through time, how even the smallest gestures create patterns that shape the soul's future.

To consider family history in this way expands our idea of inheritance. We receive not only eye colour or temperament, but also the unfinished tasks, wounds, and gifts of those who came before us. Reincarnation suggests we carry even more—experiences from former lives, layered into the soul's memory, shaping us from within.

Karma, often misunderstood as a system of reward and punishment, is far more subtle, more delicate a concept, even, than destiny, which has connotations of a fixed fate. No—karma is better understood as the law of inner consequence: the way our thoughts, deeds, and omissions echo across time. It is not retribution, but relationship—between who we have been, who we are now, and who we are becoming.

Seen in this light, our encounters are not random. Our families, our struggles, our capacities—all are part of a larger pattern the soul is weaving over many lifetimes.

How is it possible to explore such things? Through my collaboration with Inessa, I follow these ancestors into the realms of soul and spirit to discover the keys to their lives. This is not fanciful imagination, but a disciplined research practice using contemplative enquiry to access deep spiritual insight. What emerges is astonishing, intimate, and sometimes transformative.

These post-death stories are not tangents; they are the heart of the book. They show us how karma unfolds, how both pain and tenderness can persist beyond death, and how healing becomes possible when the living and the dead work together in love and awareness.

Although these are the stories of one family, they echo the shape of every family. Their patterns—love given and withheld, talents nurtured and thwarted, wounds passed down and finally mended—all these are familiar. Each of us is part of such a tapestry.

And so, this book is, in its way, a mystery—a whodunnit of the soul. A tracing of what was broken, and how it might be restored.

In seeking to solve this inner murder mystery, I hope to pour light into the darker corners of suffering—in my own family, and, by example, in others. Ernest, in many ways the central figure in this story, becomes the symbol for this redemptive odyssey. By 'saving Ernest'—that is, enabling Ernest and all other members of the family to reassert their spiritual strength in the afterlife—I work across the bridge of death to restore order and brightness to the family story.

A murder, a mystery... we turn the page to begin.

I:

THE SUITCASE AND THE

GATHERING OF SOULS

For there is nothing lost, that may be found, if sought.

The Faerie Queene, Edmund Spenser (1590)

My husband's death arrives like a tidal wave, crashing into my life and pulling me under. I struggle to stay afloat, grasping for meaning. Then I begin to read.

I plunge into literature on life after death, but it is the spiritual-scientific research of Rudolf Steiner (1861–1925) that speaks to me most clearly. He lectured widely on the afterlife during the First World War, offering comfort to thousands of grieving families. His words resonate deeply, providing not only understanding but a path forward—a way to connect with my husband in a new way, soul to soul.

In spiritual science, the so-called dead are understood to be as alive as we are—if not more so. I study accounts of their passage into the worlds of soul and spirit, learning how they continue to grow and evolve. Just as we miss them, so too do they miss us, and they benefit immensely from our loving thoughts. I also discover that it can be a true gesture of service to the dead to read spiritual texts to them, for this may offer guidance as they navigate their journey.

So, I begin. Each day, I read aloud to my late husband, picturing him beside me, listening. Then something unexpected happens. One morning, as I sit with my book, I sense another presence. It is our recently deceased friend, Pam—jaunty, cheerful, eager to listen in. The impression is so vivid, so startling, that I laugh aloud.

If Pam is here, why not invite more? Before long, my reading group expands. My grandparents, aunts, uncles, and others who have passed all take their places in my mind's eye, forming an invisible circle around me. It is an odd gathering. I can't hear their discussions or even tell for certain who is listening, but a quiet certainty keeps me committed to the task. In time, my hunch proves correct—some of these souls will later reveal just how much our gatherings have helped them.

At the same time, I sense my mother's life drawing to a close. I feel the need to help her reflect on her past, to bring her a sense of completion. But she is not one to reminisce easily. How can I encourage her?

The answer waits in my attic.

For years, an old suitcase has sat there, left to me by my great-uncle Jimmy. When I received it, I found it filled with family photographs and memorabilia, carefully annotated in his familiar hand. But life had been busy, and I had never taken the time to truly examine its contents. Now I hear an inner voice urging me: *Do it now. Digitise the photos. Make your mother an album of her family's story.*

Clambering into the loft, I pull down the suitcase and drag it into the light. Little dust clouds puff as I snap open the locks and lift the lid. The old fabric and cardboard yield with a sigh. Inside, the family waits, holding its breath. *At last*, they seem to murmur. *Here she is at last.*

Out spill sepia-toned portraits from the late nineteenth century, dog-eared packets of snapshots, medals wrapped in tissue, scrapbooks and notes. The faces in these photographs stare back at me—men with pristine collars and slicked-back hair; women in graceful dresses with elegant hairdos and misty eyes. Children blur like ghosts, fidgeting through the long exposures. Each face is a puzzle to be read, and I search them for resemblances, drawn irresistibly into their stories.

I pluck out, at random, a large cardboard-mounted photograph of a wedding and scrutinise it.

The suitcase spills out its secrets Tanto my living room floor.

Stylish frocks and hats grace the wedding-party group. Faces that are serious, happy, careworn, or youthful jostle for my attention. Three generations of ancestors are here, gathered to celebrate the marriage of my grandfather to my grandmother. Excitement stirs in me. Who are they all? What can I find out about them?

Beatrice Gwyndaf marries Ernest Mallory. They are pictured at Birmingham Botanical Gardens in 1922. It is clearly an elegant and fashionable event.

I find several beautiful portrait shots as I delve into the suitcase. Each person is dressed with pride. They pose with the careful dignity required of their time, when photography was an expensive event meant to flatter. I recognise some faces—my great-grandfather, my great-uncle, my great-aunt. But some people are unknown to me.

One young man draws my attention. There are two shots of him. The first I assume to be pre-war, while the second is evidently taken during his war service, as he is in uniform. The contrast between the two photographs is painful, giving me pause. I identify him as my great-uncle Eric, who died so young during the Dardanelles campaign in the First World War. I contemplate him and wonder what became of him after he died.

Now I find some intriguing portraits of my grandfather, Ernest Mallory, prior to his marriage. He's in his naval uniform. He looks superficially confident, and yet there is something nervous about his demeanour that intrigues me.

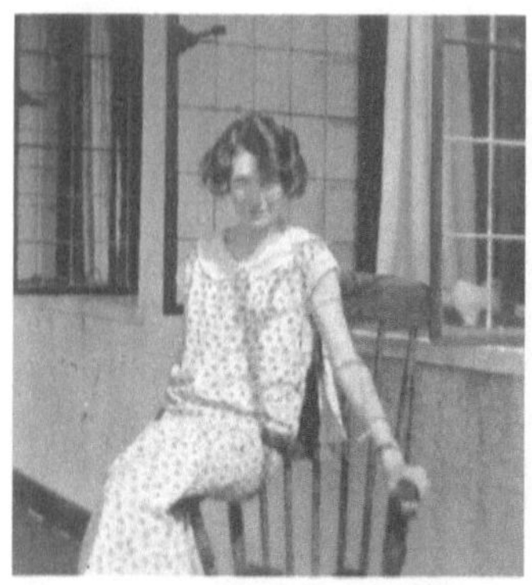

Beatrice and Ernest: snapshots. Location unknown c. 1925.

Ernest enjoyed taking pictures throughout his life, and his snapshots of himself and his new wife Beatrice have a carefree feel. They seem to capture the real-life moments of early married years in a candid, honest fashion. Beatrice perches here, poses there, smiles and laughs. She sports flippy curls and bohemian outfits, while Ernest lounges casually on the beach in rolled-up trousers. They look young and happy, although I'm aware that clouds gathered around them later on.

The Gwyndaf family appears next. They are clearly people of means. Emmie Gwyndaf, my great-grandmother—a beautiful woman—is pictured gazing adoringly at baby Beatrice. Another portrait shows baby Beatrice alone, little legs stuck straight out as she sits for the camera, bundled into a fluffy cape and feathered bonnet. She looks like a little chick.

But the true stars of this suitcase are two extraordinary glass photographic plates from 1912 and 1916 in full colour, still nestled in their original envelopes. They are made using the Autochrome Lumière process, which employed a mosaic of tiny potato-starch grains, dyed in different colours, to filter light passing to a photographic plate coated with black-and-white emulsion. After processing, the plate became a full-colour, transparent image that could be projected to dramatic effect. As an early colour transparency technique, Autochrome Lumière created luminously ethereal pictures that led to the process being dubbed the 'Colour of Dreams'.

These are rare artefacts, and they draw me in with their strange beauty.

Infant Beatrice pictured as a ball of fluff, with bunny c. 1897.

The first plate, from 1912, shows Beatrice and her sister Marion as teenagers, posing attentively with their mother in their Edwardian villa garden. By 1916, Beatrice has transformed into a poised young woman with the strong and clear face of an angel. (See chapter 5 and the book's back cover for reproductions of this photograph.)

The plates are so vivid it feels as though the family might stir, breathe, or brush a wisp of hair from their eyes. Roses cascade around them— a timeless setting. On Google Maps, I find the street on which they resided, and discover it still lined with lovely Victorian villas. I imagine Beatrice promenading along the street, parasol in hand, holding fast to her hat against the breeze.

The last layer contains photographs from my great-uncle Jimmy's side of the family.

The Gwyndaf women, mother and daughters, standing in their garden in Edgbaston, Birmingham, 1912. The women are all dressed in shades of blue, and they are surrounded by yellows, pinks, oranges, and greens. The colours remain true and strong, after more than 100 years. Autochrome Lumière glass plate.

Having no children of his own, he entrusted these gems to me too. A hand-tinted portrait of his father in colourful cavalry uniform strikes a glamorous note, and numerous pictures of the young Jimmy in panto costumes point to his exuberant personality as both child and adult. Some faces—such as in wedding photos—are strangers, but Jimmy's careful annotations guide me as I piece together his family tree.

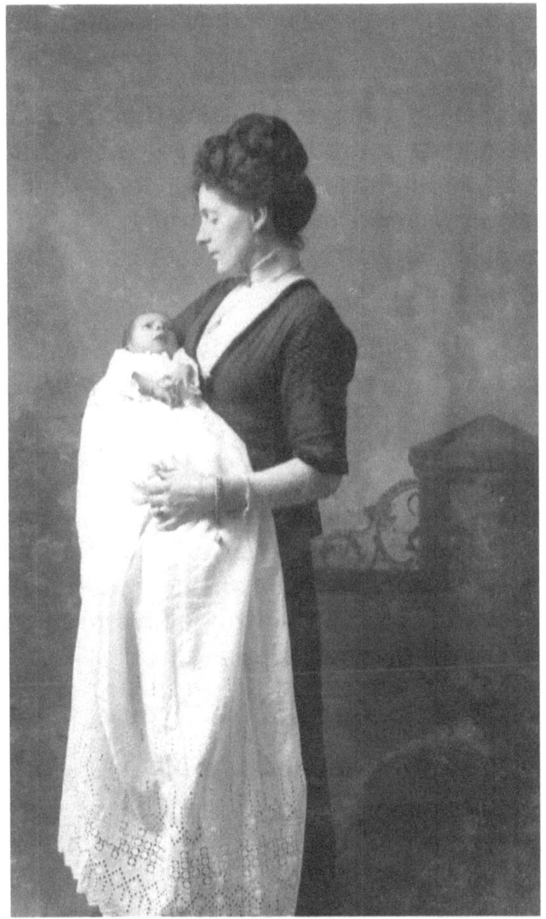

*A painterly photograph of mother and baby:
Jimmy Ruggles' mother, Polly, cradles
newborn Jimmy—1915.*

In doing so, I uncover a strange coincidence: two unconnected women, one in my family and one in Jimmy's, share two names—and those names are unusual ones. It is a striking coincidence, given that neither family knew of the other's existence. The story attached to this happenstance is presented in the very last chapter of this book.

As I sift through these lives, it strikes me how much families are impacted by the actions and experiences of their ancestors. A marriage here, a birth there, a youthful death, a domineering parent—these ripples flow across generations, shaping destinies in ways seen and unseen. The jigsaw of my family story awaits me. I feel my curiosity growing.

While I digitally scan each image, adjusting the colours and resolution to bring out the details, something strange begins to happen. These long-gone family members seem to come to life beneath my gaze. More than that, they begin to approach me. It is as if they gather behind me, stepping forward, their breath on my back, their light fingers tapping my shoulder.

The sensation is not unpleasant. It is warm, familiar, and oddly hopeful. It feels as if these souls are asking to be found. And that is an odd sensation, because who says they are lost? But that is the sensation I have, all the same.

I begin to think of them within my daily routines, pausing from time to time to silently address them. Are you here? How can I help you? What do you need? I share, in my imagination, the sights and sounds of beauty in the world around me—the robin's wild song, sweet rose perfume, the hush of a snowfall, blazing sunset skies.

Does this reach them? Does it help? I'm not sure.

I sense that some of these souls remain at a distance, waiting for something more. Although I do not yet know what that is, I resolve to find out. I suspect, though, that I will need some help to understand what is being asked of me.

And that is when I meet Inessa Burdich—and the world of spiritual research.

2:

MEETING SPIRITUAL RESEARCH

There are more things in heaven and earth, Horatio,
Than are dreamt of in your philosophy.

Hamlet, Act I, Scene V, William Shakespeare (1601)

Everything changes when I spot an advert for a course on *supersensible perception*. Intrigued, I scrutinise the details. The course is led by Frank and Inessa Burdich—internationally recognised practitioners who work within the traditions of spiritual science—and promises to explore methods for perceiving realms beyond the physical, an area I have longed to understand more deeply.

One session in particular catches my attention: *Working with the Souls of the Dead*. It feels as though this opportunity has been placed in my path at precisely the right time. I take a deep breath and book my place.

The course is a revelation. Over several days, we work to expand our awareness beyond what we can see and touch. It is meditative, contemplative work, requiring deep concentration—but it captivates me. The presenters speak with clarity and integrity, reassuring me that their work is not speculative but grounded in careful methodology and seriousness of intent.

On the final day, I encounter the insight I have been waiting for. We explore the spiritual journeys that unfold after death, examining the different stages a soul passes through, the challenges it may face, and how these challenges might be mitigated with support from the living.

One concept strikes me profoundly: some souls may become *stuck* in their journey through the spiritual worlds. I have never considered this possibility before. Could it be that the group of souls I have been

17

sensing—those whose presence feels so tangible—need specific help to move forward?

But it is the practical exercises that truly shift my perspective. Frank and Inessa guide us to perceive the presence of deceased souls within our gathering space—souls who, like us living participants, have gathered to gain insight and comfort from the lectures. These souls, Frank and Inessa explain, exist in different states, and we are invited to engage with them not through imagination, but by attuning to the subtle vibrations they emanate.

Each soul occupies a distinct space in the room. The first soul I encounter fills me with an unexpected weight of heaviness and sorrow. An odd tipping sensation unsettles me, as if I am standing on the deck of a tilting ship. Frank explains that this soul is *earthbound*, unable to release his attachment to his earthly existence. Many souls, he notes, arrive beyond the threshold of death in confusion and fear, clinging tightly to the familiar—to their former lives on earth.

Stepping into the second soul's space, I feel an entirely different energy: restless, agitated, almost electric. My limbs seem to vibrate with uncontained emotion. This, I am told, is a soul in the *realm of purification*—or *soul-realm*—the period after death when we review our earthly life from the perspectives of other people we have encountered. Souls spend varying lengths of time in purification depending on the weight of their earthly life. During the sojourn, souls experience the full impact of their actions—both for good and for ill— and process unresolved emotions such as anger or jealousy.

I imagine how illuminating, but at times painful, this process could be: to witness oneself reflected in the lives of so many others. Inessa confirms my thoughts, explaining that this phase is why souls in the purification realm often radiate such intense activity.

Finally, I step into the last space. A wave of expansive happiness overtakes me. It is as though I have stepped into the radiance of a sunrise, my sense of self dissolving into something greater, a vast space of light and love. Inessa explains that this soul is at the threshold of the *spirit-realm*, free from all earthly constraints. I think of the expectant souls I have sensed around me, and hope that they too will find their way to this place of peace.

These exercises reveal something crucial: a soul's journey is profoundly individual. What a soul needs depends entirely on where it is in the process—there is no single solution.

I leave the course with a feeling both of wonder and responsibility. The souls I have been sensing—those connected to my suitcase of photographs—are not merely lingering; they may be seeking intervention. And now, I have met someone who can help. I speak to Inessa, explaining my wish to support my family of souls.

"Yes, of course! How exciting! When shall we start?" she replies.

Great Expectations

I expect the souls I encounter to follow the familiar model of death I have studied. At death, I have read, the *life-force body* (which animates the physical body) and the *feeling-and-emotion body (or soul)* depart.

Many near-death accounts describe the person's departing consciousness passing through a tunnel of light and encountering a radiant being who prompts reflection on the life just lived. Some texts describe a panoramic *life-review* unfolding, after which the life-force body dissolves and the soul moves forward, carrying its memories. These memories are vital; they form the personal encyclopaedia from which a soul will shape its future development.

Texts go on to describe how the soul then enters the realm of purification (soul-realm), experiencing its life in reverse and from others' perspectives. Lessons are distilled and transferred to the *spirit-body*—the eternal aspect of our being that continues through lifetimes. Eventually, the soul dissolves, and the spirit-body, alone, journeys on through the spirit-realm, encountering other beings and preparing for reincarnation back upon the earth.

But the supersensible research course teaches me that this journey is not always so straightforward. Some souls become stuck; others face interruptions. As Inessa and I begin our meditative research, my expectations are reshaped again and again by what I start to discover beyond the threshold.

But how does one actually work with the souls of the dead? That question becomes the foundation of our research.

HOW CAN WE EXPLORE THE LIVES OF THE DEAD?

Only when we love something do we gain knowledge of it.

Theosophy, Rudolf Steiner (1904)

To tell the stories in this book, I have researched both my ancestors' earthly lives and their continuing experiences in the afterlife. Each chapter follows this investigative pattern: first, imaginatively reconstructed vignettes of the person's life—informed by both earthly and spiritual research—then the story of their existence after death, and finally, any assistance that is offered to them.

You may now be wondering—how have I conducted this research? And, most intriguingly, how is spiritual research and assistance undertaken? The answer to these questions is simple: I do not work alone. As mentioned in chapter 2, my research is a collaborative process with spiritual research colleague Inessa Burdich—of whom more below.

Investigating Earthly Lives

Reconstructing my ancestors' lives has been a fascinating and immersive experience. I have pieced together their stories using historical records—letters, postcards, newspaper articles, birth and death records, and reports on historical events. Family anecdotes and personal memories, both my own and those of my parents, have also provided invaluable insights. But even with these resources, gaps remain, especially the further back in time one goes.

This is where *intuition* and *imagination* come into play. I have spent hours studying the photographs from the suitcase that inspired this book, meditating on the presences I sense within them, and listening to the voices of the dead. My meditative reflections have yielded striking perceptions, offering glimpses Into the essence of these individuals beyond what is captured in documents or stories.

With an empty mind, I send out enquiries across the threshold, and back to me come delicate hints—ideas, suggestions, and motifs—that I sift through, considering each as it is given, openly and with gratitude. From these experiences, ideas are seeded that grow into an impression of the earthly-life stories of the characters.

Most vital of all are the spiritual perceptions of my research partner, Inessa. She brings a level of clarity that allows me to flesh out the motivations, emotions, and inner struggles of these souls. Through our combined efforts, their stories emerge in greater depth, bridging the known and the intuited.

Each soul has expressly given consent for me to share his or her earthly and post-earthly experiences—a permission I honour with the utmost care. I write their stories with sensitivity and respect—the details of my ancestors' lives are not merely historical facts but intimate experiences of living. Together their lives form threads in a much greater tapestry of spiritual evolution.

I am always aware that I am writing about real people, whom I wish to depict truly and compassionately. Each portrait is carefully painted to show a mix of strengths and vulnerabilities. In this way, their real humanity touches us all.

Investigating Life in the Spirit

How does one become a spiritual researcher? There is no one prescribed path. Each person comes to this work through their own unique journey.

Inessa's background spans an unusual combination of physics, psychology, therapeutic education, professional-level chess, and spiritual study. Among the many influences on her path, she has focused particularly on the meditative exercises of Rudolf Steiner, making her approach deeply aligned with my own interests and understanding.

As a physicist, Inessa applies rigorous methodology to her spiritual research. Her disciplined approach challenges me to refine my perceptions, striving for greater accuracy and clarity.

Our collaboration is both precise and intentional. We conduct our meetings by remote internet link—she in Germany, I in England—yet the soul-spiritual connections we seek are not bound by geography. In this way, modern technology has paradoxically expanded the reach of spiritual research.

All our enquiries are undertaken in full consciousness—without the use of trance states or mediumistic methods. Instead, we employ focused meditative techniques that allow us to extend our attention beyond the material world.

Before each enquiry, we discuss the individual in question. I provide background information, including photographs, which serve as a focal point for our exploration. Inessa finds that a photograph where the person is looking directly into the camera is especially useful, as it allows her to perceive the *soul pictures* embedded within.

We also consider the broader context of the family tree. Over years of work, we have built a repository of knowledge about my family, enabling us to recognise patterns and recurring themes across generations. This contextual approach deepens our understanding, helping us discern karmic connections and long-standing soul dynamics.

Although my own spiritual perceptions are considerably less refined than Inessa's, I have been intrigued by how often our impressions align—either in content or in symbolic resonance. Occasionally, Inessa perceives glimpses of a soul's karmic past or even their potential goals for future incarnations. These are never fixed predictions—free will remains central to a soul's journey—but rather serve as indications of tendencies, such as a desire to cultivate clearer thinking or greater open-heartedness in a future life.

The Meditative Approach

Our methods are rooted in contemplative practice. Inessa describes her work as "meditation applied as contemplative enquiry," an approach well-illustrated by the physicist Arthur Zajonc in *Meditation as Contemplative Inquiry*. Zajonc outlines a process that begins with the quieting of the mind—a deliberate cultivation of stillness, like an empty canvas. From this stillness, focused attention is directed towards the object of enquiry, allowing subtle insights to emerge over time.

When Inessa and I engage with a soul, we begin by holding their name and image in focused attention. Gradually, impressions arise, like ripples across a calm pond—sensory, emotional, or symbolic perceptions that offer glimpses into the soul's present state. As Zajonc describes it, this process involves "thinking the thoughts of the other".

But can these impressions be trusted? Interestingly, scientific research is increasingly exploring the validity of intuitive perception, and coming down firmly in favour of its legitimacy.

For example, researchers such as Dean Radin have shown, through large-scale statistical studies, that intuitive perception consistently exceeds chance levels. Similarly, reviews of parapsychological trials—like Etzel Cardeña's survey of more than a thousand experiments—suggest that evidence for such phenomena is now as strong as for many accepted fields of science.

Outside academic research, there have been other serious explorations of extended consciousness abilities. One instance is the US government-sponsored "remote viewing" studies, where trained participants learned to describe distant or hidden places with striking accuracy, suggesting that perception may indeed reach farther than the senses.

Intriguing?

Perhaps it is time to reconsider the role of intuition. As Einstein is often quoted as saying:

"The intuitive mind is a sacred gift, and the rational mind is a faithful servant. We have created a society that honours the servant and has forgotten the gift."

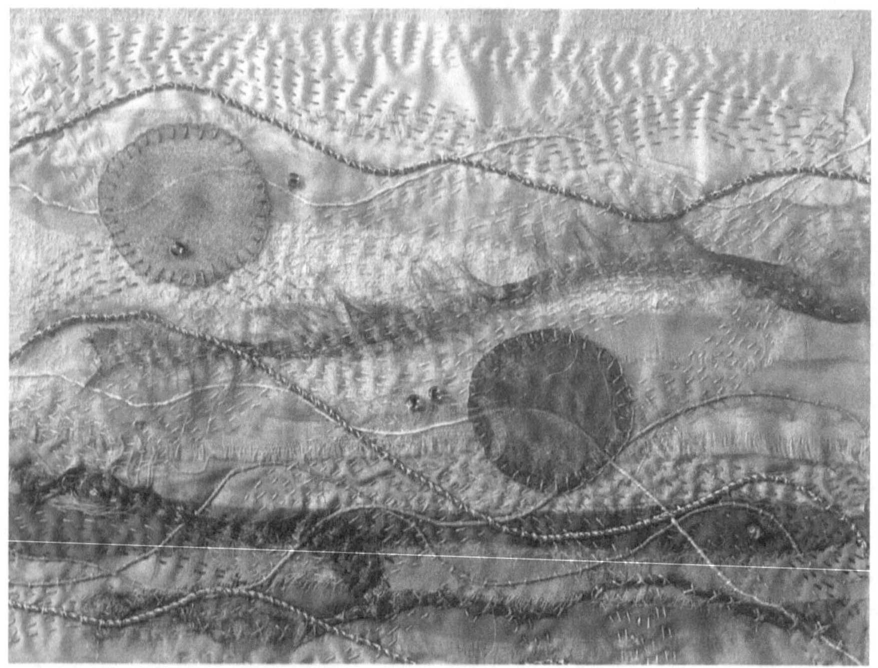

*Author's meditative impression of two connected souls in spherical form, travelling alongside one another in the realms of soul.
Souls may reveal themselves as spheres of light, or in a likeness familiar from earthly life—yet often softened by youth and even radiance, as though time has withdrawn its weight.
Media: Embroidery and collage.*

Interpreting Impressions

Once Inessa and I receive impressions intuitively, the next step is *interpretation*. This is where the intuitive and the rational mind must meet, engaging in a kind of internal dialogue until meaning emerges.

The impressions we receive often manifest as symbols rather than direct, literal images. For example, in one enquiry I perceived a soul sitting contentedly by a fireside. Initially, I thought this suggested he was stuck between the earthly and spiritual realms. However, Inessa's perception revealed that the soul was in fact in a period of peaceful reflection and learning in the afterlife. My initial image was not incorrect, but rather a symbolic representation of this deeper reality.

Language itself is often inadequate to fully convey these experiences. We rely on phrases like "it is as if…" or "it feels like…" to bridge the gap between spiritual perception and human expression.

Author's meditative impression of a soul appearing in human form
rather than as light or sphere (as in the previous illustration).
She sits quietly reading—a gesture which Inessa understands as the
soul's contemplation of the Book of her Life.
Media: Embroidery and collage.

Developing Inner Senses

This work relies on the cultivation of inner senses—sometimes called *organs of insight.* Such faculties develop through meditative practice and the disciplined quieting of the mind. Zajonc describes how repeated cycles of focused contemplation lead to a state of *contemplative knowing,* in which understanding arises from an inner resonance with the subject of enquiry.

Respect, openness, and love are essential to this process—Zajonc echoes the view expressed in the chapter's epigraph in asserting that nothing can reveal itself to us that we do not love. True spiritual research requires a selfless interest in the subject and an attentiveness beyond ordinary sensory perception. If one approaches with pure intent, results are far more meaningful. As Ralph Waldo Emerson put it: "All becomes poetry when we look from within."

A Shared Gift

The insights presented in this book are the result of a shared effort—between myself, Inessa, and the souls who have allowed us a glimpse into their journeys.

In the meditative tradition I work within, spiritual existence reveals itself in the form of *imaginations*—not as external, physical impressions but as living, intimate experiences. These imaginations are invitations to perceive the inner reality of another soul, provided one is open and quiet enough to receive them. Other researchers speak of an *expanded mind* that stretches beyond ordinary sensory confines, allowing such perceptions to emerge.

This work is an immense privilege, offering small steps towards bridging the divide between the living and the dead. As interest in the afterlife grows, perhaps our time is ripe for healing this divide—so that souls on both sides of the threshold may work together in the service of spiritual progress.

Turning the Page

So let us now turn the page, introduce the players in this tale of lives and destinies, and begin our spiritual detective work to solve the mystery of Ernest's life.

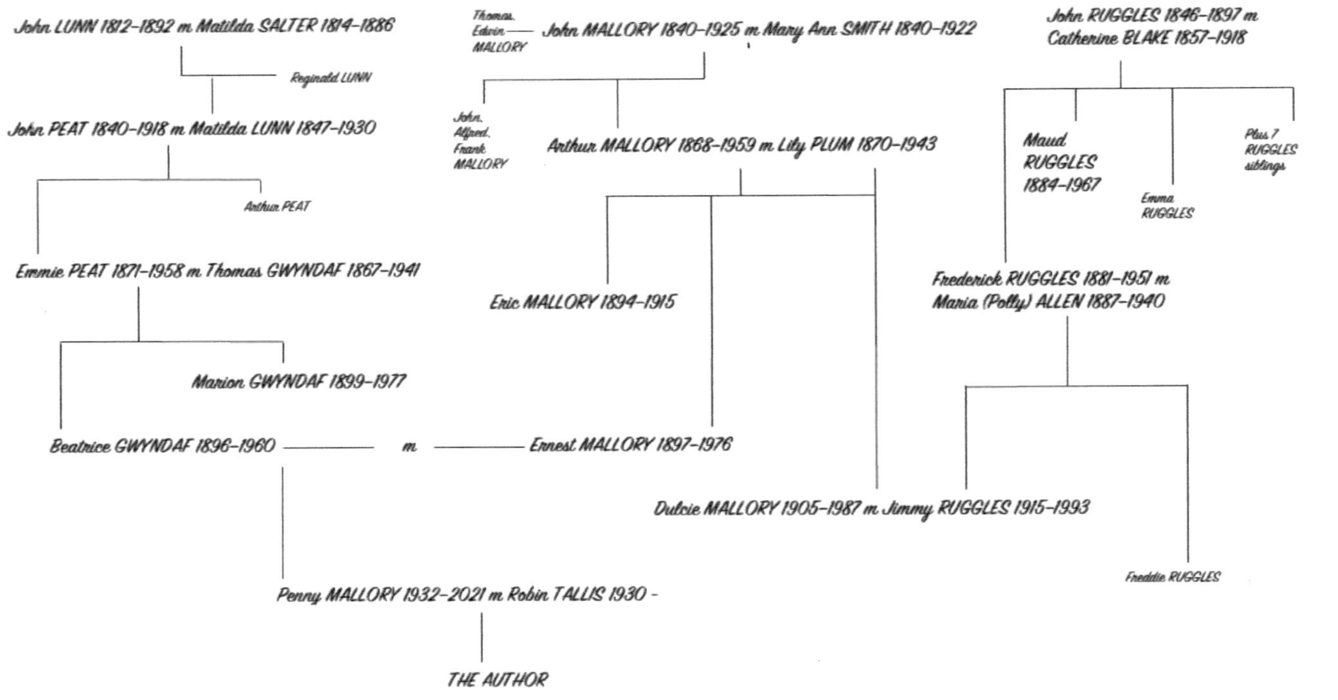

FAMILY TREE: Phoebe Tallis: Maternal Line

Phoebe Tallis

The Lives

Step now with me, from research into story—
from the contemplative to the incarnate.

Here begin the lives of my ancestors:
their fears and hopes, their moments of beauty
and of failure.

Travel with me, as we pass through their earthly days,
and onwards... into the realms of soul and spirit.

Come with me to watch the unfolding of karmic paths,
witness the workings of inheritance,
and enjoy, as guests, this banquet of experiences.

Here is the wound, here the pain—
and here the love that works to heal
what once was broken... and begins to mend again.

4:

THE FORGOTTEN SOUL

ERIC MALLORY 1894–1915
My Great-Uncle

His wounds were lacerating.
Indeed, he thought he could not survive.

Yet his gentle soul called again and again, until she heard.
And then, how brightly his happiness burned, to be safe again,
to be loved once more.

Upon Sands of Sorrow, Lorenzo Ebrio (2013)

*Eric photographed prior to volunteering for wartime
service. He is eighteen or nineteen years old, and
living in Erdington, Birmingham c. 1913.*

*Eric photographed during
wartime service c. 1915.*

11th July 1915: Gallipoli: 40th Field Ambulance

The small wooden boat, packed with troops, approaches the beach of Cape Helles, Gallipoli. It slops sideways in the heaving waves. Eric's knuckles whiten as he grips the sides of the boat and prays that he can hold down his rising bile. His Field Ambulance is attempting to land with their unit, 13th (Western) Division, to relieve 29th Division in the battle against the Turks. As the boat is cast loose from the steam tug, the navy lads start rowing for shore. Thirty yards to go, and then all hell breaks loose. The water churns with bullets as Turkish riflemen up on the cliffs overlooking the beaches let rip at the unprotected soldiers huddled in their boats.

Oh God, thinks Eric, *how can we get out of this alive?*

Screams erupt from all around him, blood blossoms from limbs, heads, and bodies; men leap for the cover of the water, their faces full of terror as well as resolution. Some drown with the weight of their equipment, some are wounded and sink without a trace, some clamber over the bodies of the fallen and struggle onto the blood-marked sands, making for the meagre shelter of rocks. Somehow Eric makes land, and gasps with relief as he shelters with others of his unit.

He checks his medical supplies are still intact. His hands are shaking, but he finds it calming to go through his pack—water purification tablets, disinfectant, tourniquets, bandages. Yes, it's all there. Even the blank sheets marked *Field Ambulance: Casualty Return*—as if he'll ever find the time to fill them in. *Ridiculous*, he thinks, *but how the army loves its paperwork*. Another bullet spatters the sand near his feet.

Men bound for Cape Helles, Gallipoli, May 1915. The soldiers have just disembarked from their transport ship to the small trawler, where they stand packed in, ready for the landing on the beaches.
Ernest Brooks, Public domain, via Wikimedia Commons.

Landing at Gallipoli, Anzac Cove 1915 by Charles Dixon. This depicts New Zealand troops landing in Gallipoli, and gives a clear impression of the dangers facing troops as they come into land.
Archives New Zealand from New Zealand, CC BY-SA 2.0
creativecommons.org/licences/by-sa/2.0 via Wikimedia Commons.

A few days later and the elation of the landing is clouded in his memory. It's been a drudge through horror ever since. Eric's useless bicycle was left on board ship. As a bicycle orderly in the Royal Army Medical Corps, he was expecting to be rushing up and down the lines in France or Flanders, carrying medical supplies and helping out wherever needed. But who can cycle on these dreadful narrow beaches in Gallipoli? Even the hospital tents are crammed onto a tiny strip of land. Water sucks in and out of them at high tide. The conditions are insanitary, disgusting, and there is so much sickness and pain. Eric is weary of it already. He's deployed as a stretcher-bearer, a ward orderly, a surgeon's aide, and an emergency medic—for everything from missing limbs to cholera. It's all well beyond his short basic training.

At eighteen he had volunteered for the army. As a clever young man, educated at King Edward's School in Birmingham, Eric had been speedily recruited to be in the Royal Army Medical Corps. Quick wits were what was needed in the RAMC to absorb the training and to use initiative in life-threatening situations. At the time, he was glad of this role; it suited his ideals. He was a creative, sensitive lad, secretly reading poetry in his bedroom in the quiet hours when his family had gone to bed. He wanted to do his best, to shine, to make his father proud. He wanted to help the war effort and do good at the same time. A medical appointment sounded good.

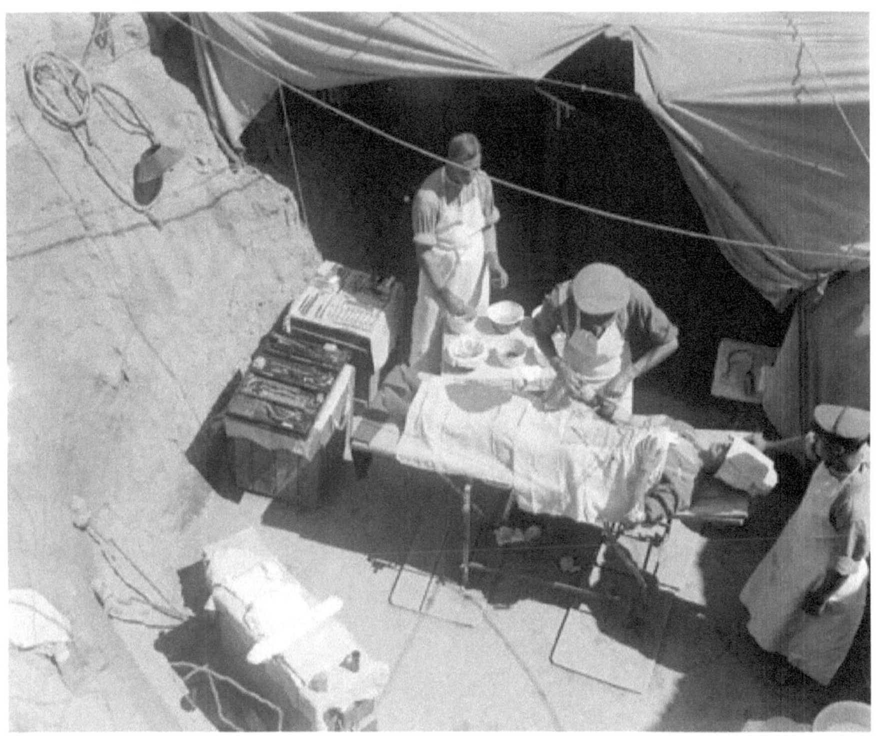

Field surgery, Cape Helles, Gallipoli, almost certainly a staged photograph, as many were in the First World War.
Ernest Brooks, Public domain, via Wikimedia Commons.

Eric cringes as another sniper bullet whizzes past his head. Today he's on stretcher-bearer duty. He grips tighter to his end of the stretcher and stumbles on, eyes down, willing his feet to tread gently for the sake of his patient, a young rifleman writhing in pain and swathed in hastily applied blood-soaked bandages. One, two, three paces... just a few more yards to the medical tent.

How far away this is from the war he thought he would fight. He lugs the groaning soldier the last few feet and deposits him gratefully on the grimy floor of the hospital tent. Part of him smiles wryly at the memory of his father, Arthur, all bonhomie and elegant moustaches, slapping him forcefully on the shoulder and booming "Make us proud, my boy!" as he, Eric, stepped onto the embarkation train in Birmingham.

Dressing station at Gallipoli 1915, from the photographic collection of Lieutenant Colonel G.J.S Archer, RAMC. Wellcome Images via Wikimedia Commons: creativecommons.org/licences/by/4.0.

Eric's poor younger brother Ernest, standing beside Arthur, was the picture of misery as Eric disappeared into God knows where, to fame and glory or perhaps oblivion. But Eric's little sister Dulcie grasped his hand firmly, fixed him with one of her adoring looks, and kissed his cheek. "Don't forget us, dear Eric. I will make you daisy chains for remembrance, to keep you in our hearts," she declared, and he had felt a tear bead his eye. Little did he know that her promise of daisies would echo long after his death.

His mother, Lily, small and determined, waved a little handkerchief until his train was way down the line, and she was just a dot in the distance.

Rifle fire rips through the medical camp, snatching his attention back to the present. "Cover," roars his officer commanding, and he dives for shelter behind a small rock, shuddering with fear and the sheer, wearying stress of it all. A snatch of *The Charge of the Light Brigade* comes into his head. "Into the valley of death..." echoes in his tired brain. Not that he rates Tennyson. Eric's more a modern poetry man, but that poem seems to him to sum up the utter futility of this suicidal war in which he finds himself trapped.

Eric worries about germs; he fears he will catch some illness or other in the filth and squalor. The men were always being told not to drink at the local cafes in Alexandria from where they embarked. Syphilis is the reason—you can catch it from cups. Still, he went drinking with his pals anyway—to blazes with it, he'd thought! He wrinkles his nose. Typhus, cholera, dysentery—they've got it all here, thanks to the flies, the dirt, and the lack of medical supplies. What a hole.

He notices that his hands are shaking all the time now. Why is that? His head hurts and his stomach churns incessantly. He has to run to the khazi several times a day. What if he's got dysentery? It can be deadly if not caught early. Better see his officer in charge. Back to work now. The shower of bullets has stopped. He stumbles down the rough steps into the tented hospital ward, dug down into the sand to try to shield it—uselessly as it happens. It's regularly strafed with gunfire, just to add to the suffering in there.

The tent reeks of blood and sweat. It's packed with the wounded and dying. He's put to feeding a man whose face is smothered in bandages. Poor fellow—a shot to the face took out his eye and shattered his cheekbone and jaw. Eric's hands shake so much he can hardly spoon the soup out of the tin mug and into the man's mouth, but he cares about this poor soul, who cries for most of the day. He strokes the man's hand once the soup has been consumed, and offers him some weak words of reassurance. Time crawls, the flies are pervasive, the heat oppresses everyone. Sweat runs down Eric's face and into his eyes as he cleans festering sores and bathes wounds that are too gruesome to describe.

*Royal Army Medical Corps stretcher-bearers carrying a wounded
soldier through the trenches at Cape Helles, Gallipoli, 1915.*
Ernest Brooks, Public domain, via Wikimedia Commons.

Why are we fighting these Turks, he asks himself, ten times a day?
What's it all about? He ponders lines from Stephen Crane's harsh anti-
war poem *War is Kind*, which he read in a magazine just—oh when
was it? Years ago? Last month? He can't tell. He savours those burning
words:

> *Swift, blazing flag of the regiment,*
> *Eagle with crest of red and gold,*
> *These men were born to drill and die.*
> *Point for them the virtue of slaughter,*
> *Make plain to them the excellence of killing*
> *And a field where a thousand corpses lie.*

His glossy ideals have withered away. War's not for him, medical care
seems to be futile, nothing makes sense anymore. The shadows close
in.

The next day, Eric has a fever. He shivers, vomits, has diarrhoea. By
the end of the day it's turned bloody. His stomach is like a griping pit
of pain. His skin crawls with fear but the doctor gives him emetine and

says he'll be fine. He vomits frequently now, each time he's given the emetine, which tastes bitter as hell. He's been in bed for a week, two weeks. He's enfeebled and his back is sore. He feels stalked by a demon that is going to consume him. Periods of terror intersperse with periods of depression and despair.

He wants to see his sister Dulcie's sweet, straightforward gaze once more. He'd like to give Ernest a hug and tell him to stand up for himself. He longs for his mother to give him a kiss on his forehead and smooth his hair. He yearns to have the chance to write all the poetry that's in his heart but has never yet got out onto paper.

Now they give him opium for the pain in his bowels and it makes him even more nauseous. A third week steals past him, and he feels the world shrink away, until he's in a vacuum of suffering. He is small as a pinpoint, then he is enormous as an elephant. He begins to see worms on his body. His fever becomes worse. He's so tired, he's so dried up, he can't hold down any water. Although Eric's a strong young man, his condition worsens with each hour. Now he's in and out of consciousness. He can't tell what they are saying to him. Does he hear the word cholera? They put him on a ship. It glides away with him. Are they taking him to heaven?

The ship hits choppy water and bucks and heaves. More vomiting. Oh God, when will it be over? A pretty nurse appears, from time to time, wavering before his eyes. She gives him something metallic—nitrate of silver? a small part of his brain wonders. And morphine. And more emetine. The nurse tries to tempt him into drinking warm tea or eating broth with a dry biscuit. "Soon be well, Private Mallory," she says, soothingly, "They'll look after you in Alexandria. There's proper hospital care there, you'll see." She pats him on his arm. But really, he doesn't care anymore.

Eric struggles back to consciousness to find himself in a clean-smelling hospital. The windows have fresh white curtains. *They are like clouds in a summer sky*, he thinks. But the beautiful curtains don't help him. He drifts away again, in and out of sleep. He doesn't know where he is, and sometimes he forgets who he is. Towards the end, he starts talking wildly about his stomach wound. It's full of worms, and they're eating him, he sobs. *Why won't anyone listen?*

"He's raving," Eric hears someone say, but he's not sure who they're talking about.

"He must have seen so many wounds, poor boy," says another voice.

Time flows on endlessly. Eric is still, now. His breathing is shallow. He thinks of the green grass of English meadows, when he can think at all. His mother's beds of roses float before his memory, perfumed and velvety soft. He reaches out to pick one and it eludes his fingers. Somehow, he cannot quite touch it.

The next day, Eric dies. He is just twenty years old.

His death, at such a tender age, leaves a wound that will not remain his alone. Quietly, it will flow into the lives of those who follow him.

Afterlife Encounters
Eric: visited 2022-2025

The Enigma

In her later years, my mother would often say: "I wish I'd asked about my uncle Eric. But there's no one left now who can tell us about him." All we know is that he served in the Royal Army Medical Corps, died of dysentery, and lies buried in a lonely grave in Egypt.

Curious to discover more, I examine the cemetery layout and pinpoint the row and plot number where he rests. On Google Maps, the graveyard, although well-maintained, looks dry and exposed—a far cry from the peaceful English meadows that Eric might have longed for. My heart aches for him. Eric is a mystery, a blank space in the family story.

That is, until I begin my spiritual research with Inessa. What we uncover about Eric's life and soul is astonishing, revealing tragedy, resilience, and an extraordinary opportunity for healing.

Undead

"I have the impression he's standing by his grave," I say, in some consternation. After 100 years, that's not what one would hope for.

"Yes," Inessa confirms, "but he's not standing, he's lying. He's curled on his side, with his hands over his face. He's dry as a stick, something like a mummy. He's tied to his previous incarnation as Eric, and cannot move on."

What a sad state this young man is in. He believes himself forgotten by everyone. A century of loneliness has brought him to utter despair. He cowers into the dust, suspended in a limbo of sadness and fear— neither alive nor, in a strange sense, fully dead.

"He remains trapped in the *supersensible spheres* near the earth," adds Inessa. "His soul cannot travel forward. His four bodies are still present around the site of his grave."

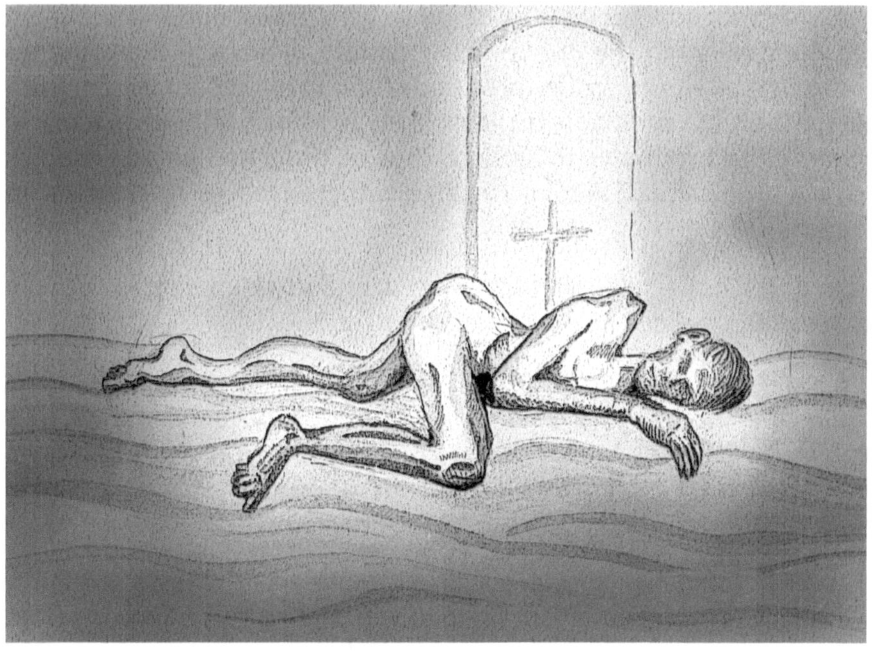

Author's impression of Eric lying upon his own grave in Alexandria.
Media: Acrylic, crayon, chalk.

Whilst we are on earth, we all possess these *four bodies*, as described by Rudolf Steiner. There is the visible, physical body—the form we can touch and see. There is also the life-force body, which animates us and gives vitality. Then comes the feeling-and-emotion body, sometimes called the soul, which carries our joys, sorrows, and all the shades of human experience. Finally, there is the spirit-body, the eternal essence that connects us to the divine.

Eric's predicament is strange and unsettling. Fragments of all four bodies remain clustered near his grave, holding him in an uncanny state of being. Though he is undoubtedly dead, he exists in a way that resembles life—a life bound to suffering, silence, and the weight of an existence that refuses to release him.

How did this happen? War leaves deep scars on the soul. But Eric's situation is extreme. The traumas he endured in life so damaged him that his feeling-and-emotion body (soul) split into two prior to his death—a rare occurrence where a soul fragments due to suffering—and prevented him from moving forward into the soul-realm.

This split soul now remains tethered to his physical body, which itself has mummified in the dry Egyptian climate. Alongside the tethered and split soul sits Eric's life-force body, bound in similar fashion. Even his spirit-body—ordinarily the least likely to remain behind on earth—lingers close by, unable to ascend. Thus *all three* non-physical bodies remain at the site of Eric's grave, like withered leaves stuck to a tree branch.

"It's a most peculiar and spooky sight," exclaims Inessa. "Very unusual. But we can help him. Let us begin."

We study the two photographs I have of Eric. In the first, he's a happy young man, his soft eyes exuding a dreamy quality. In the second, he's in uniform. His eyes are hooded, his face shadowed and closed off. It's as if the war has hollowed him out; the open-hearted young man is almost unrecognizable.

"His soul fractured during his army experience," Inessa explains, "when his youthful optimism collided with the horrors of war. As time went on his soul became absorbed into the anguish around him and he couldn't retain his sense of self amidst all the horrors. His inner spirit cracked under the weight of so much death and suffering. He couldn't cope with it."

When Eric fell ill with dysentery, he was still physically strong, but the treatments given him—opiates, alcohol, harsh emetics—overwhelmed his system. Instead of helping him, they poisoned him further, dulling his consciousness and leaving him vulnerable to darker forces.

"It's as if the machinery of war devoured him," says Inessa. "He lost his grip on reality completely, and he gave up his life."

A Healing Journey

Now we turn our attention to helping my great uncle. Eric needs love, warmth, and spiritual refreshment to recombine his soul and spirit, and be set free. I think for a moment, then suggest something simple: "Shall I give him a bath?" I ask.

Inessa smiles and nods, and in my imagination, I prepare a basin of warm, herb-scented water. I bathe Eric gently, imagining the desiccated figure softening under the warmth. To my astonishment, it works. He begins to stir, his curled posture loosening.

"That looks very positive," encourages Inessa, as she works to free him from the sticky forces of illness and medication that cling to him. "All things have a type of living energy," she continues. "Illnesses have forces within them that are negative and can stay with us long after our initial infection. It's the same with medications. Some are quite gentle, but some, such as opiates, are very powerful and their influence can be harmful to the soul."

Inessa can see, from her contemplative enquiries, that Eric was afflicted with not one but two types of dysentery—amoebic and bacillary. In addition, he has a syphilitic infection from local drinking vessels—the army was right after all! Finally, Inessa can detect that there is a shadow of cholera infection.

"No wonder he died," I say.

But Inessa answers, "He should not have died. He was very strong and it was not his karmic destiny to die in this war, despite how it appears."

It is intriguing to speculate about Eric's role, had he lived. I learn from Inessa that souls tend to journey together in groups, connected by previous karma and loving intentions. Family groups often fall into this category of connected groups.

Added to that, we choose to come down to earth at a time that is suitable for our karmic intentions. We hone ourselves, as souls, in the fire of life experiences that we've selected for ourselves, with the help of the divine world.

For Eric, the karma of war intervened, breaking the path of his planned journey on earth. This rupture poses a double problem for him. His early death lifted him out of his rightful era and away from his family group. In time, he must return to earth again under a new constellation of circumstances that will shape his next incarnation.

"It happens to many souls," explains Inessa. "Wars are a primary reason for such events."

It is not clear at present how a future incarnation might work out for Eric, but in any event, if we don't succeed in freeing him, he may never have the chance to reincarnate at all. We get back to work.

Concentrating hard, we continue with our meditative healing work on behalf of Eric. I sense that Eric longs deeply for English skies and landscapes, and I think of the lines: *Oh, to be in England, Now that April's there*, from Robert Browning's poem *Home Thoughts from Abroad*. I stream the poetic words into the warm bath of water, because of course anything is possible in one's imagination! For good measure, I let images flow around Eric—a soft English summer's day, green lush meadows, sweet roses. I swear that I hear Eric sigh with pleasure, and that he settles more comfortably into the warm bath of verse. Inessa is amused at my inventiveness!

Then, Eric's guiding angel appears. Light floods the scene as the angel approaches him, stitching up the imagined wound in his stomach and brushing away the worms Eric believes are consuming him. To Eric, who lacks spiritual beliefs, I sense that this divine intervention, clearly seen by both Inessa and myself, manifests as a hospital scene. Such an interpretation would be Eric's 'best fit' to help him understand the healing tableau of angelic beings that now surround him.

Eric sees himself in a clean, white room with plump pillows and crisp sheets. Competent nurses bustle around him, offering him water and a bowl of fruit—ah, so refreshing! A gentle breeze flows through an open window, carrying the scent of England. Eric smiles. For the first time in a century, he relaxes.

This double-view of events gives me a fascinating glimpse into how we, as souls, mould our individual perceptions of after-death experiences to be comprehensible to our own belief systems.

With Inessa's support, Eric's fractured soul reunites. The two halves of him—his broken wartime self and his original, hopeful spirit—come back together, like a rent garment that is woven once more into a whole.

Now Eric's soul makes a gesture towards me of gratitude. *You didn't forget me*, he seems to be saying. *Thank God, you didn't forget me*. For my part, I thank my mother for holding Eric in her awareness and encouraging me to find out more. It is fulfilling to me, to feel Eric's relief and peacefulness—a fitting step forward in his recovery.

Restored

After our restorative work, I marvel at the transformation in young Eric. The enigmatic young man in the family album is no longer a blank space. He is a presence once more, hopeful and vital in a way I never imagined. Though I mourn the life he could have lived, I feel joy in knowing he is finally free.

As we leave him to settle and integrate the healing, I feel deeply grateful for the experience. What began as a tragic story of suffering and confusion evolved into one of redemption. Eric, who has been lost in the pages of my family history, now stands as a testament to the power of spiritual healing—a soul that has endured the worst of human experience, only to emerge from it with renewed strength and potential.

In a way, I feel I have witnessed a spiritual rebirth, and this serves as a reminder that through love that is consciously offered, through meditation and prayer, and through spiritual intervention, even the most fractured soul can find its way home.

But as we shall later discover, Eric's journey is not yet complete. He will need a little more help to find his true way home, a story we will return to in chapter 7.

Turning the Page

Eric's story now gives way to that of his younger brother, Ernest, whose life unfolded in the long shadow of loss. With the elder son gone, Ernest as the surviving heir inherited burdens never meant for him—burdens that would shape his path, and draw his wife Beatrice into their weight as well.

5:

SHADOWS IN THE HEART

ERNEST MALLORY 1897–1976 & BEATRICE GWYNDAF 1896–1960
My Grandparents

"Surely you can understand my words?" he said to his bride-to-be. But she could not hear him, for the sweet, dreaming song in her head drowned his voice.

"Surely you can look after my heart?" she said, holding it out to him. But he could not see her, for the tangled boughs obscured his vision at every turn.

The Toy Soldier's Hand and other Tales, Lorenzo Ebrio (2014)

Ernest in Ceylon post-First World War c. 1919. He served in Ceylon as Paymaster Sub-Lieutenant and his role was Secretary's Clerk serving a Vice Admiral.

*Beatrice was a stylish dresser with a bohemian
twist to her personal presentation.
Studio photograph c. 1922, Birmingham.*

1903: Beatrice: Little People

Beatrice lies on the rug in the nursery, carefully snipping out tab clothes to dress up her paper dolls. Most girls she knows have ready-printed outfits that their mothers buy for them. But Beatrice makes her own. Mummy always encourages her towards artistry, and Beatrice excels at designing dolls' clothes. Her little people are the most fashionable, the most tastefully dressed, the most chic and unusual.

Beatrice spends hours leafing through her mother's fashion magazines—especially the gorgeous pages of *La Mode Illustrée*—poring over the fashion plates, tracing, and sketching. From her artistic fingers fall modish paper outfits—walking costumes with trim waists, ball gowns with puffed sleeves, and cloaks for all weathers— all topped with picture hats. She keeps her treasured outfits well away from the sticky fingers of little sister Marion, whose childish hands grab at all and sundry, including Beatrice's carbograph pencils and the watercolour paint set Daddy gave her for Christmas.

Emmie, Beatrice's mother, pops her head in. "All right darling?" she asks.

"Yes Mummy, I'm drawing out Lady Sybil's new wardrobe. Look, here's her promenade costume."

"Oh, that's beautiful, Beatrice, and you have the frogging on the coat just right," encourages Emmie. "Now, do you think that her hat might need a big ostrich feather added to it? And she would need some mauve gloves, do you think, to go with her mauve pelisse?"

Beatrice nods keenly. She wants to get her dolls looking just right.

Emmie leaves, and Beatrice works on. Sara their elderly maid-of-all-work dusts and polishes around the room. She pants a little as she bends to clean the skirtings.

"Sara," pipes up Beatrice, "what's a ne'er-do-well?"

"Why, that's someone who doesn't do right, Miss Beatrice. A man who gets himself into trouble—too much drink, too much gambling, and no good to his family. A naughty sort of person." Her feather duster flicks lightly around the toys on the shelves—two pretty porcelain dolls, a monkey with cymbals gripped in its paws, a Noah's Ark in shining wood. "Why do you ask?"

"Oh, I heard Mrs Salmon say it about Mrs Dobbs' husband at Mummy's coffee morning," explains Beatrice. "Mrs Salmon said Mr Dobbs plays cards and drinks. Isn't he a friend of Daddy's?" A pause.

"Is playing cards naughty, then, Sara? Only Mummy and I sometimes play solitaire. I don't think it's very naughty, do you?" Beatrice finishes, gazing at Sara for clarification.

Sara chokes and splutters out: "Never you mind, Miss Beatrice. Best not to go worrying about other folks. Little people like you should be seen and not heard! You mark my words, it's not a good idea to repeat gossip!" and she stumps out of the room, her shoulders shaking with mirth.

Beatrice is left puzzled. *What is naughty about playing solitaire?* she ponders. *Grown-ups have such silly notions.*

1912–1915: Ernest: Shifting Expectations

The ruler smacks onto Ernest's wooden school desk at Mr Wilson's detested crammer school. The fifteen-year-old flinches. He's been caught scribbling comic verse when he should have been reading his Latin. Ernest's father, Arthur, is stern when he sees Ernest's marks for his Latin exams.

Arthur is a brilliant, charismatic man, by turns irascible and jovial. To be a child of his is to sit in the firing line of Arthur's expectations and wince at the rapid-fire of his ambitions. "We need more study and less day-dreaming," he says to Ernest. "Knuckle down, my boy, and remember," tapping his nose, "there's no money in poetry."

Lily, Ernest's mother, is proud of both her sons' interest in the arts. She takes care to nourish Eric's and Ernest's souls with trips to the art gallery, concerts, and the theatre, despite Arthur's protests.

While Eric hides his love of poetry for fear his father will disapprove, Ernest writes verse for all the family, and even Arthur enjoys the comic creations flowing from Ernest's pen. "Where does he get it from?" laughs Lily, as she reads aloud Ernest's latest poem about the family's holiday in the Lake District.

> *In our macs we drip and trudge,*
> *With nowt to eat but Rydal fudge.*
> *Why are we so adventurous?*
> *Well, I blame our progenitors,*

quips Ernest's poem. Eric admires the rhymes, and Ernest glows. *There's nothing better than impressing your older brother,* he thinks.

War comes. Eric scrambles to enlist, under his father's approving eye. "They say it'll all be over by Christmas," Eric assures Lily, smiling his grave, beautiful smile.

When he leaves, the whole family waves him off on the train platform. Ernest, disconsolate without Eric, fears that the war may drag on, and that he, too, might need to join this alarming conflict one day.

But it turns out Ernest has his own war work to do. He's a bright young man with excellent mathematical skills, and it is Arthur's own boss who presses Ernest to take up a traineeship position, saying: "Anyone can be a soldier, Ernest, but only a very few can be good engineers. We need clever brains like yours to do war work."

And so it's decided. Ernest is now in a Reserved Occupation, and promising to be as inventive and meticulous as his father. Privately, Ernest is glad of the job. His weak eyesight may have precluded military service, and what a shameful thing that would have been. He feels the need to shine as best he can, so as to match up to Eric's splendid example. He grabs the offer of respectable war work with alacrity.

Ernest is so proud of Eric that it hurts. He writes a long letter to Eric every week, to which Eric replies, but less and less often. *Still, service letters can take a long time to arrive,* thinks Ernest, *and surely some go astray.* The family plan their next vacation to the Lake District, and cross their fingers that Eric might get some leave.

But suddenly, the wheels are ripped off the steady family cart. A telegram arrives in July.

Regret to inform... Eric Mallory... died of dysentery... buried in Alexandria.

In those few short words lives a world of grief. Ernest feels the anguish and the shock as an injury, a wound, a disfigurement of his soul. An image of himself, like a glass plate photograph, arises before Ernest's inner eye. He watches as tiny fractures appear on its glossy surface, chase one another across his own face and form, and threaten to break him into a thousand pieces.

Ernest's outer universe, too, shivers and dissolves. In its place, he stands on the frontline of the family's expectations, with no shelter from his brother's shadow. He feels the strain of this shift, amidst his own sadness, and bows his shoulder to the weight.

1916: Beatrice: The Colour of Dreams

Marion and Beatrice are close. Of course they argue, but they enjoy one another's company. With a three-year age gap, Beatrice should feel like Marion's protector, but strangely it feels like the other way around.

Marion knows when something is troubling Beatrice, and always winkles it out of her. "Is it the tummy ache, Beatrice, is it the poor cat next door who's left out in the cold, is it that your new dress looks wrong on you?" Then she offers a comforting hand clasp, or a practical solution—curl up in bed with a hot-water bottle, kidnap the cat, speak to Mummy's dressmaker.

Beatrice and Marion have discussed the idea of a second Autochrome Lumière glass colour plate for some time, just between themselves. Magazines call the glamorous colourised photographic technique the 'Colour of Dreams', and it is all the rage in fashionable society. "Do you remember we had a glass plate taken in 1912, Marion? You were quite young then," reminds Beatrice. "It looked like an oil painting."

The glass plates are designed to be viewed privately through a diascope case, or—at grander public exhibitions—projected by magic lantern. In the latter form, enlarged to the size of a portrait, they appear richly luminous and alive.

Marion chuckles. "Yes, I remember—I wanted to read my book, not stand in the garden for an hour squinting into the sun," she recalls.

"We could persuade Mother, I'm sure," says Beatrice, getting back to their present plans, "but what about Father?"

"We'll tell him it's de rigueur and that the Parsons and Clark families are having them done," decides Marion. Thomas is as socially conscious as the next man, and likes to follow the latest trends.

Now the family are grouped in their rose-kissed summer garden, waiting expectantly for the photographer's shutter to fall. *This photograph could travel down the years and be treasured by all our descendants*, ponders Beatrice, solemnly.

Marion fidgets in the warm June weather, but Beatrice herself breathes deeply, her calm, striking face framed by sunlight. *For all my children*, she thinks. And she crosses her fingers.

As they stand quietly, a gentle breeze wafts across the garden of the family's gracious Victorian villa in South Birmingham. The hellish happenings of the war, glimpsed in newspapers, seem far away indeed.

Autochrome Lumière glass plate 1916: Beatrice stands to the left,
Emmie in the centre with Thomas at the back and Marion to the right.
This mesmerising image drew me into the story of the family.
It is as if the souls of the people are captured here in this photograph.

At last, the portrait is done. In due course, the glass plate, carefully packed, arrives. It is spectacular, glowing with depth and light. Beatrice and her mother, Emmie, exclaim over it in delight. "It's even better than the one we had done in 1912," says Beatrice decisively, and Emmie agrees. Thomas remains behind his newspaper, making no comment beyond a grunt.

1917: Beatrice: Flytrap

The Gwyndaf women are interested in the latest art and often catch a tram to the Birmingham Art Gallery, to scrutinise the newest acquisitions and take refreshment in the tearooms.

Beatrice herself, though, loves nothing better than to walk to the lush paradise of the Birmingham Botanical Gardens and stroll the avenues of flowers. The glasshouses fill her with a sense of peace, the soft leaves of the plants somehow inviting her tender touch. One day, she vows, she will have a marvellous garden of her own.

It is here that she meets Ernest Mallory one day, as she and Marion stare, fascinated, at the fly-eating plants in the hot house. Beatrice touches one plant experimentally with her fingertip and—look, look!—it snaps shut. She snatches back her finger, and she and Marion laugh.

This is how Ernest first glimpses his beautiful Beatrice. Her face is glowing with merriment, her eyes shine. She is elegantly dressed, with all the poise of a fashion plate.

He pauses shyly—yet at last he cannot resist stepping into Beatrice's orbit. Sweeping off his hat, he introduces himself and informs the young women that he's here with his family on a little outing. It is the anniversary of his brother Eric's death, he explains. The family have visited the memorial stone in Erdington, and now they've come out to be together on this pleasantly warm August day and honour Eric's memory.

"Oh, Mr Mallory, I am sincerely sorry to hear of your loss," exclaims Beatrice. She extends her gloved hand and they shake. "Would you care to join us?" she says, with a smile.

Marion is intrigued. Here is a new Beatrice, placidly confident, basking in the rays of Ernest's evident admiration. The pair chat and joke.

Ernest can understand the Latin nomenclature on the labels, and Beatrice hangs on his words. *He's well-educated, then,* thinks Marion.

Taking tea in the Botanical Gardens Cafe, the two parties meet. The Gwyndaf girls and the Mallory family get along famously, it seems. Lily Mallory, mother of Ernest, is full of gossip and fashion news. She presses the girls to take coffee with her the following Tuesday morning when she will be 'at home' and promises to share some stylish new dress patterns with them.

It all goes very well.

1917–1918: Beatrice: Postcards and Poetry

As 1917 wends its way towards winter, the relationship between the two young people grows in familiarity. Ernest relaxes into the persona of a charming beau, and Beatrice blossoms into being his chosen girl. Ernest plies her with funny verses, romantic lines, endless quotations. She has to laugh. "Ernest, I never knew there were so many words that rhyme with one another in the whole world!" she chuckles.

Ernest loves to be teased by Beatrice. It's such a novel experience to be uncritically admired, that his passions run away with him. Before very long, he is down on one knee in the tropical house at the Botanical Gardens, addressing his passionately worded proposal to Beatrice.

Beatrice is not much surprised. She knows that Ernest is very fond of her, and she's been half-expecting him to press his suit. As he expresses his admiration for her, Beatrice is distracted by the tickle of a banana leaf on the back of her neck. It carries her away to a moment in childhood: she, snoozing in the garden hammock, Marion, tickling her awake with a feather. She drifts with the memory, then startles to attention as she hears:

"Will you make me the happiest of men?" And: "Say yes, Beatrice, do say yes!"

For Ernest, Beatrice is a catch. Beautiful, exotic, wealthy, and artistic, she is a girl to show off, a girl to call his very own. Beatrice is overcome with Ernest's amour, his romantic phrases, and long words. He's clever, handsome, and he seems to know how to guide and protect her.

"Yes, Ernest," she decides, "I will marry you." Ernest clasps a hand to his heart, closes his eyes for a moment, then slides a ring on her finger. It is a daringly modern ring, she notes, almost bohemian. Just like her.

Beatrice's dreams for married life feature an idealised domestic paradise. The house will be beautiful, furnished to her direction and taste. The garden will be impressive, artistically designed, and crammed with colourful plants. She will cook for Ernest, giving him all his favourite dishes, and she will polish the home into a gem of love and happiness. And of course, Ernest will adore her for her efforts.

She will, after a while, produce a nice little family: a boy for Ernest and a girl for herself. Or would that be the other way around?

She hopes that, once she is without her parents, out in the great wide world of married life, Ernest will soothe her unease. She imagines him spreading his wings around her, scooping her up, and cherishing her for the rest of her life.

The engagement is announced, but before any plans can be made, the war ends. Now Ernest apologises, explains—he feels he must volunteer to serve his country because his Reserved Occupation work no longer keeps him tied to England. "It will make no difference, dear heart. I am yours, here or in foreign lands. We can write to one another. And you know I remain devoted to you," says Ernest.

Beatrice feels that she cannot argue, although she is downcast at the separation and the delay to their plans.

Ernest is posted to Ceylon on naval duties, and Beatrice must be content to sit romantically on a bench in the Botanical Gardens, penning loving postcards to him. In return, Ernest sends funny poems. "Look how he rhymes my name with ventriloquist," laughs Beatrice to her mother and sister at the breakfast table.

Marion takes the thin blue paper and reads aloud:

> *Beatrice, sweet Beatrice,*
> *If I were a ventriloquist,*
> *I'd make the birds and blossoms cry,*
> *"How beautiful!" as you walk by.*

The rhyming is unexpected, the rhythm like a music hall song. It's clever. The family all chuckle, but Marion has a small stab of envy.

When will a boy ever write me a poem? she wonders. She observes Beatrice's glowing face on days when Ernest's letters arrive.

"Where is my own Ernest?" Marion sighs to herself as she stares into the dressing table mirror.

1919: Ernest: Disguises

The ceiling fan turns squeakily in the office. The monotonous sound gets on Ernest's nerves. He pores over ledgers, diaries, and charts. He is well thought of by the Flag Secretary he serves. His careful and methodical nature, his ready wit, and desire to please those in authority all stand him in good stead as Paymaster Sub Lieutenant in the Royal Naval Volunteer Reserves.

He's attached to *HMS Venus* and stationed in Ceylon, but fortunately he rarely has occasion to be on board ship. He hates that infested, sweaty hulk. No, he's mainly at the spacious Trincomalee House, sharing an office with Ted Jester, Ralph Billingham, and Jock Fraser. His desk has a view out onto the veranda, from where he can hear the susurrating breezes in the trees, and the crickets endlessly chirruping in the velvet heat of the evenings.

Almost as soon as the war had ended, Ernest had felt it vital to take a stint in the forces, for the sake of Eric's memory and his father's approval. But the prospect had filled him with dread. From somewhere he conceived the idea that he would never return. Even though the danger of war was past, he felt as if death were folded into his embarkation papers—pressed there like an official seal. Shaking with fear, he set sail towards what he was sure would be his utter destruction.

On arrival, and due to his grammar school education, Ernest landed straight off with a good posting, prestigious, and interesting. Arthur, delighted, sent him encouraging letters once a fortnight. He wired Ernest money, with instructions to: *Make sure you buy drinks for your fellow officers, my boy—you've got to get along with everyone, so that you can grease the wheels.*

It was Arthur's idea of good advice, but it pained Ernest, who would rather have hidden, reading, in the Trincomalee House library.

The fellow officers with whom Ernest was supposed to get along were rough and unfriendly. He'd been the butt of jokes because of his glasses and his bookish demeanour. On board ship, Reggie Mason stole Ernest's photograph of his mother and drew a moustache on it, then it was thrown from one man to another as Ernest strove to catch it. "Mummy's boy Mallory," someone yelled, and it stuck.

Ever since this episode, Ernest keeps his picture of Beatrice in his inside pocket and never lets anyone see it. He thinks of her often, this wonderfully kind girl from a nice family. The more he considers her, the more pleased he is. She is yielding, sociable, and just bohemian enough to be intriguing. Arthur is full of pleasure at the evolving liaison between Ernest and Beatrice. *A glow of approval from Father— what a rarity!* thinks Ernest, as he considers his intimidating parent. Though to be fair, Arthur wears many disguises, and benevolence is certainly one of them.

Shortly after Ernest's inaugural week at Trincomalee House, a small metal trunk arrives with his initials on it. It is packed with luxury dry goods and treats—tinned sardines, marmalade, condensed milk, and cocoa. Towards the base are linen handkerchiefs and some fine monogrammed writing paper. In Arthur's copperplate hand, a note says: *To get you started making friends.*

Ernest's face burns even as he feels the kindness of the gift. It's always the way with his father—a gift has conditions attached, or parental expectations slipped inside.

This afternoon the office feels hot, despite the ceiling fan. Two of the chaps go outside for a cigarette and Ernest follows for a breath of air, but they don't include him in their chatter. He stands for a while, hands in pockets, then goes back to his letters and charts.

On his next day off, Ernest walks with his camera to one of the temples nearby. He likes to send copies of his interesting Ceylonese shots to his mother and little sister, Dulcie. They write back in excitement at the wide world that Ernest is seeing. He's a kind brother and takes time to pen messages for Dulcie on the back of each photo.

Here is a temple with elephant carvings, he writes. *Do you think they will let me bring you one home?*

And: *You say you cleaned your bike with 'Nellie's help'. Is that a special new type of polish?'*

which makes Dulcie laugh. Ernest feels sorry for her, the sole child left to absorb Arthur's enthusiastic directives and edicts.

Ernest's photograph of a temple, Ceylon 1919.

Now Ernest concentrates for some time on taking light meter readings and adjusting F stops. He steps backwards to gain a better vantage point of the temple scene, and his foot knocks against something. There's a crash. He turns, to find a set of brushes and a sketchpad scattered over the ground. Ernest is full of apology.

"Please don't concern yourself," remarks the young British officer, retrieving his easel and brushes with an easy grace. The two young men strike up a conversation, soon debating the war art of John and Paul Nash.

The Nashes' excoriating images from the Western Front are stark, inhuman, and almost surreal, Ernest observes.

But of great spiritual accuracy, suggests Rollo Blount, who turns out to be a Paymaster Lieutenant in the Royal Naval Reserve.

Rollo shares his outlandish philosophical ideas without a trace of embarrassment: "What if all emotions are living things, like animals?" Rollo, wonders, smiling. "If you were quick enough, perhaps you might reach out and catch one by the tail!" Ernest laughs at the thought. He's bemused but intrigued. Now Rollo's suggesting that the Nash brothers have caught those wild beings of war and violence and imprisoned them in their pictures. "Those canvases capture the essence of emotions in the paint," cries Rollo with a grin, as he packs away his brushes.

It's poetic, thinks Ernest, *and very eccentric.*

Through Ernest's own lens in Ceylon, we glimpse his interest in the unfamiliar world around him. He captured street scenes rather than landscapes and had a careful eye for composition. We also see his habit of observing life from behind a camera, a way of seeing that would echo in his inner life.

Delighted, Ernest joins Rollo for cocktails at a bar, and their conversation never flags.

Rollo's charm and confidence draw people to him. Although he is somewhat older than Ernest, friendship blooms between them. By association with Rollo, a wonderful thing happens—Ernest becomes one of the chaps.

Now, though, Ernest becomes aware of something else, a secret that he dare not even articulate. He notices a subtle charge when Rollo brushes against him, a warmth of affection when Rollo hums as he paints, a happiness in his core when Rollo and he laugh together. It is a form of love, though Ernest neither names nor acts upon it. His feelings confuse him, but Rollo is relaxed about their strong bond.

"It's reincarnation, old chap," he says drowsily, as they lounge in the shade of a cafe. "Those Buddhists believe in it, and so do I. You and I were friends in another life, mark my words." Ernest shrugs, smiles, takes another pull of his gin, and marvels at Rollo's self-assurance in airing such perfectly mad views.

As Ernest becomes increasingly absorbed in his relationship with Rollo, he writes to Beatrice less and less. Her letters become anxious, prickly, bewildered. He rarely writes back. And he never writes to her, or his family, about Rollo. How could he? What would he say? Rollo is the blank in all Ernest's letters home. It is as if the substance of his letters is hollow. All the real content is in the margins, where lie invisible words that speak of his soul.

The end of it all is sudden and cruel. The staff car is returning from a supply run when the axle hub collapses on a bend. The crash can be heard a mile away. Twisted metal hangs quivering in the air, and smoke rises from the wreckage. "Get them out!" yells someone, and the men near the scene of the accident sprint towards the staff car, wrenching open the driver's door. "Careful now," mutters someone, as Rollo is hauled out. He's still breathing. They get him to the hospital ward where he's bandaged, bones set, drips applied. Ernest is traumatised. Rollo, his best friend, his soul mate, now hanging by a thread of life. Ernest feels his own life hangs likewise.

All the treasured evenings spent with Rollo in philosophical chat, discussions on art, enjoyment of cocktails, and playful experiments with hashish drift back to Ernest. He sits by Rollo's bed, squeezing

Rollo's hand and willing him to come back from the abyss. He reads to Rollo, wipes away his sweat, moistens his lips with water. He even prays, although he doesn't believe in God. But anything's worth a try.

Rollo dies within a week of the accident. The whole unit turns up for the funeral. Now Ceylon is too painful for Ernest and he puts in for his discharge papers. When he leaves, he packs away, carefully wrapped in tissue paper, one beautiful print of Rollo Blount gazing expressively at him. Ernest will keep this print for his whole life, and eventually it will make its way, via Dulcie, into the suitcase of family photographs.

Ernest's soul is riven by the grief and loneliness he endures. The cleft is depthless and dark. Into it creep shadows of shock, confusion, and guilt. He both sees them and tries to ignore them. He can do nothing to redeem himself from their grip. First Eric, now Rollo. It is more than his soul can bear.

The image of his inner being, that cracked glass plate photograph, finally gives way. This shattering creates a thousand fragments. They flee to the four winds, and he cannot call them back.

The destruction he foresaw for himself on embarkation to Ceylon is enacted, and its consequences will resound through the family line for years.

1920: Beatrice: Doubts

When Ernest returns from the Far East, Beatrice is overjoyed. She races down to the railway station to meet him, together with Lily and Dulcie. But the man who alights from the train is distant and haggard. Beatrice's heart skips and then drops to her boots.

What is wrong? Ernest is polite but absent. Attentive, yet nothing he says rings quite true. Like a cracked bell, the tone of his emotions is somehow—off. Shadows flit behind his eyes, but when he blinks, they are gone.

"Ernest seems a bit jumpy, dear," says Emmie, after Beatrice has ushered her fiancé out of the Gwyndaf home one evening. "But I dare say he's unsettled from the strain of his naval duties. I hear from Mrs Hollins that her son was nervy after returning from the army, but he's right as rain now."

Beatrice listens, nods. Marion agrees—Ernest seems more brittle in temper, less relaxed. 'Out of sorts' is how she puts it. "Why not wait a while before the wedding?" she suggests to her sister. "Give him time to get his land legs again!" Beatrice wonders what to do for the best. She loves Ernest and is excited about their impending nuptials. But if things are not right between them…

Ernest gradually re-emerges from his emotional absence. But to Beatrice, it is as if he puts on a costume of borrowed parts. It's Ernest, and yet not quite…

On the one hand, Ernest plunges back into his interests—music, photography, walking—with his customary enjoyment. On the other hand, he is overly-eager to comply with his father's expectations—back to work at Graham James Engineering, marry, start a family, acquire a suitable house. Ernest jumps at Arthur's recommendations for a new wardrobe of civvies. It is as if he cannot any longer find his authentic self, and so must build another from a different blueprint. Like Arthur, he takes to buying formal suits from Goldstein's on Sherlock Street, starched-collar shirts from Rosenbaum's on Corporation Street, Saxone shoes polished to a mirror shine. He looks good on it, and yet… it isn't quite him. A gentler, more affectionate, more creative part seems dimmed—the soft centre of Ernest, the Ernest that won Beatrice's heart, is elusive.

Beatrice lies awake at night, a faint doubt murmuring in her heart about the marriage. But surely it is too late now to call the whole thing off?

The following week, Ernest unexpectedly presents her with a small box. In its cushioned depths nestles the soft gleam of a pearl necklace.

"They're like you, Beatrice," he says, smiling. "You're the secret beauty in my life—and I am the oyster treasuring my pearl. Then he reads a charming little poem dedicated to this idea, which he calls *My Girl's a Pearl*. It is disarmingly sweet and rather reassuring. It feels like the most authentic thing Ernest has offered since his return.

It crosses Beatrice's mind that Ernest might be a true poet at heart. "He seems only able to express himself on paper," she muses to Marion.

"A bit like Thomas Hardy?" Marion suggests, thinking of the brooding, repressed worlds of Hardy's novels, and disliking the association.

Yet with her new notion, Beatrice experiences relief. Perhaps she sees again the 'old' Ernest—the romantic, dear young suitor who once fell at her feet. It will be all right, after all, she tells herself. She need not do the awful thing: cancel the wedding, return the ring, refuse Ernest. Her spirits lift, and the wedding regains its glow of promise.

The steady march to the altar begins. The couple are carried along on the wings of… love? Perhaps—or perhaps by expectation, and the soft intoxication of hope.

1922–1933: Beatrice: Baby Steps

*Ernest and Beatrice on their wedding day,
Birmingham Botanical Gardens, 1922—a
union full of promise.*

Beatrice, poised at the door of the church on her father's arm, smiles at the gathered crowd. She peeks through her eyelashes at her nervous fiancé as he stands and rolls the edges of his tailcoat in his hands. She feels proud and dignified. As her foot hovers to take the first step forward, she thinks again—*Yes, it will be all right. It will be glorious.*

The wedding is considered a social success. Firstly, there is the victory of the dress. A delicate, ankle-dusting silk-satin confection with lace detail. It looks chic, modest, understated, and individual. Then there is the setting. Birmingham Botanical Gardens, like an old friend, yields itself to the occasion as a blank sheet of paper welcomes a poem transcribed to its surface. Love is in the air, but more than this, social grace, rank, respectability. Beatrice floats on air, her dashing Ernest beside her. All his former tetchiness seems dissolved into urbanity. He is charm personified, warm, witty, and altogether winning. What a splash they make in the Edgbaston social scene. Emmie professes herself pleased, yes, pleased and gratified at the comments from guests. "Exquisite," they say, and "Perfect".

The best man is less than successful, but the bridesmaids comport themselves terribly well, and even, it seems to Beatrice, have one or two little flirtations of their own. But she is too busy to pay much attention.

As Ernest and Beatrice take their baby steps into marriage, it appears that they are well enough matched. Their honeymoon by the sea is filled with fun and it is as if they have launched a little, jaunty marriage boat that bobs happily along on merry waves. Beatrice flirts with her new husband. Ernest, as ready for levity as dry land for rain, teases her back with unguarded warmth. Their married life feels carefree. Beatrice is eager to please, easily contented. Ernest takes the lead, navigating their shared journey. They laugh, hold hands, and kiss.

"What shall we do tonight, Ernest?" Beatrice might ask, and he will reply: a meal, a walk, the theatre, the cinema. He always has a plan, and Beatrice gladly follows along behind.

Beatrice photographed by Ernest during the early days of their marriage.

Ernest takes great delight in Beatrice's family heritage, which adds to the quiet satisfaction he feels in these early years of marriage. He learns that his wife is connected to the legendary "Old, Old, Very Old Man" Thomas Parr, celebrated in a seventeenth-century pamphlet. Folklore claims that Old Parr, a farm labourer, lived to the age of 152, served under ten monarchs, and died soon after being introduced to King Charles I—his burial in Westminster Abbey sealing his fame. The story enchants Ernest, as does another marvel: Beatrice's great-grandfather was the inventor of a machine that transformed the Kidderminster carpet trade. Proud and fascinated, Ernest feels a glow of reflected glory in his wife's lineage and even begins a small collection of memorabilia about Old Parr—a gesture that touches Beatrice deeply. What a dear man her Ernest is, what a kind husband.

But as months pass, and then years, misgivings begin to creep into Beatrice's mind. Their early easiness has now faded, and they're entering choppier waters. Ernest's amorous advances have cooled. His attention is diverted towards his job. His free time is given over gradually to long and solitary walks. Beatrice starts to feel isolated within this marriage, even though Ernest shares her bed and eats at the same table.

She wonders if Ernest still finds her as attractive as he once did. He often tenses when she approaches him with romantic notions. He's tired, he says, or busy; he promises that tomorrow will be different. Beatrice's efforts to create a beautiful home go unnoticed. She lets her artistic interests slide, as she worries and frets about her situation.

Her heart aches when the babies she so desires do not come. "Do you think Ernest still loves me?" she worries to her best friend, Ella Myers. Her voice sinks lower: "If we don't—you know—then how will we ever have children?" Ella nods sympathetically—she, too, is still waiting for a baby.

"But we're young, Bee," says Ella, with confidence in her voice. "Ernest's just busy with his new position at work. It will all be fine, you'll see."

And it seems that Ella is right. After months of struggle at the Graham James Engineering Works, Ernest finally masters the nuts and bolts of his new role—Assistant Company Secretary. Beatrice's father, Thomas, is his boss. "What a taskmaster he can be," grumbles Ernest, "but I've got the measure of it now. I've just been distracted, darling— couldn't put my work down when I came home. It'll be better from now on…"

And certainly things begin to look up.

Because one day, after ten long years of marriage, it happens. At first Beatrice cannot be sure, but she waits… waits… then visits the doctor. "Why yes, Mrs Mallory, I can tell you that you are two months pregnant and looking very well on it too," confirms kindly Dr Palmer.

Beatrice could jump over the moon! She hurries home, hugging her secret, and awaits Ernest's return from work, too full of suspense to even cook the dinner.

The moment Ernest comes through the door, she flings herself into his arms. "Oh Ernest, Ernest, it's true, I'm expecting! The baby will be born in late November. I'm so happy!"

Ernest swallows. He is beyond words. Gratitude, joy, and relief all mingle. At last, he can prove himself a man. A son, a son to succeed him. It's a blessing indeed.

The little marriage boat hoists its sails, snaps its pennant in the breeze, and sets a course for contentment.

Arriving on cue, in November 1932, is a baby girl.

Beatrice and Penny with Ernest taking the photograph.
1935, Sutton Coldfield, Birmingham. Penny is Beatrice's
triumph and shield. Ernest observes and records.

Ernest is momentarily nonplussed. *A girl…* then—*Well, after all, it's wonderful. Sons can follow, and even if not, then little Penny is still the tiny miracle that makes the family complete.*

Beatrice's baby is her pride and joy. Little Penny bats her navy-blue eyes and smiles tirelessly with her cupid's bow lips, as proud Ernest takes shot after shot for the albums. As Penny grows, she becomes adept at teasing her grandfather Arthur, and charming her doting Aunts, Marion and Dulcie.

Ernest appears as proud as any father could be. But Beatrice remains a little anxious all the same. She watches for any flicker of disappointment that traditionally minded Ernest might feel in having a daughter rather than a son. *Is he truly happy?* she asks herself, from time to time. *And what if there's no second baby? What then? No son… how will that be for Ernest?*

She never voices the concern aloud but keeps it folded deep within— a small, furtive fear.

Unknowingly, by harbouring it, Beatrice lends the fear quiet strength. In time, it settles upon young Penny as a shadow, a sadness—never intended, never rooted in truth; but such things happen, such seeds grow where they are dropped.

1934: Beatrice: Blue Sky

Penny becomes Beatrice's complete focus. She sews exquisite, tiny outfits, conscious of her pleasure in her child with every stitch she makes. She sings to Penny, reads her nursery rhymes, and teaches her to look with appreciation at the world around her. Ernest beams at his daughter as she poses for him, twirls for him in a new dress, or sings him a song she's learned.

Beatrice, happy for the most part, still allows worries to nibble. She observes Ernest closely for traces of discontent, because there is still no sign of a son and heir. Arthur is bound to mind, and therefore Ernest will surely mind as well.

One afternoon, Beatrice and Ella sit together in the nursery, reading aloud a Winnie-the-Pooh story. The summer rain drums against the window. Penny giggles at the antics of Rabbit, Piglet, and Tigger, before dozing off.

Marion is downstairs, tinkering with ingredients in the kitchen. The sound of a pan clinking and the scent of onions and dill reaches up the stairs—ordinary comforts. It takes the strain off Beatrice, to have time out with her best friend, says Marion, but really, she is keeping her eye on her older sister.

Over the meal of salmon and dill croquettes, Beatrice asks, "Do you think men lose interest in their wives once they've had a child?" Her voice is light, but there is a trace of uncertainty, and her hand strays, doubtfully, to her pearl necklace.

Marion chuckles and says: "If that were the case, Beatrice, there would be a lot of only children in the world, wouldn't there? I mean, I wouldn't be here, for one thing!" Beatrice acknowledges the joke with a laugh and dabs at her mouth with her napkin.

"What do you think, Ella?" she enquires.

"I think husbands love their wives all the more for giving them a child," says Ella, who is now expecting her first baby. "I wouldn't worry, Bee. But why not talk to Ernest about your fears? I'm sure he'll reassure you."

Beatrice nods, but she suspects that neither she nor Ernest has much vocabulary with which to navigate such a conversation. Marion catches the doubt on Beatrice's face. She suspects that her sister's marriage is not doing as well as it might. Marion feels bound to offer support from her bystander's perch, but it's not clear what good she can do.

Later, after Ella has left, Beatrice mounts the stairs to check on Penny. She draws back the curtain, revealing a patch of blue sky. "Look Penny," she exclaims, "there's enough blue sky to make a sailor a pair of trousers! Up you get and we'll go to the park."

Marion declines to join them. Standing on the threshold, ready to leave, she wiggles her fingers and calls: "See you next week," then her signature joke: "If I'm spared…"

The door closes on Marion, leaving Beatrice feeling a touch bereft.

1935–1936: Ernest: A Sparse Toolkit for Domestic Bliss

Ernest truly admires his beautiful wife. Isn't she elegant? Isn't she graceful? Isn't she accomplished? What man would not admire and treasure her?

Why, then, does he feel there is a distance between them that is impossible to bridge? He dimly perceives that Beatrice yearns for softness and romance from a husband, but at the same time she leans on him for stability, guidance, and support.

It is a tricky combination Ernest cannot master. He tries and fails to meet her expectations. Instead of leading, he dominates. He hears himself overruling her quiet opinions and gentle ideas, and is reminded of his father. Not a good role model, he knows, for a happy marriage.

In trying to create romance, Ernest disappoints. It is as if he peers at his wife from beneath a carapace of bewilderment. His gestures of affection often miss the mark. He buys Beatrice a cookery book when she wants flowers. Or he offers work-based gossip when she's longing for a compliment on her pretty new dress. He feels Beatrice's gaze upon him—expectant, hopeful—and hears Arthur's voice, finger wagging as he speaks: "Now look here, my boy—attend to the small niceties and you'll keep the little lady's heart; get them wrong, and she'll soon lose faith in you."

Surely, thinks Ernest, someone else would have known what he should do. A brother, a friend—someone whose presence might have steadied him. But he has no one now, and his worries remain locked inside him, silent and anxious.

The trouble is that, in Ernest's heart, he cannot name what he feels for Beatrice. It is admiration, certainly. Fondness too, and perhaps even love, but it lacks the ease and certainty he once knew. Beatrice's interests are not his but... should that prevent a loving partnership?

At the heart of Ernest's struggles are two questions. The first is one of identity. He can no longer locate himself as he once was, can no longer glue back together those scattered soul fragments that flew away from him in Ceylon. Who, then, is he?

The second is the question of whether Beatrice can ever be his soul mate. A quiet voice tells him that such a status belongs to one person only. Unwelcome flashes of Rollo—his voice, his laugh, the way he looked that last evening—surface like images in a dream Ernest tries to forget. He pushes them away. They do not belong in this life.

Ernest honestly has good intentions to be a strong provider, a good husband, and a loving father, but he starts to avoid home life because his toolkit for maintaining domestic bliss is so very sparse.

It all results in long hours at the engineering works. An urgent job, a pressing problem, an important meeting—excuses that once were occasional start to become habitual.

One day, Beatrice expresses disappointment at the time she has to spend without him.

A minor exchange flares suddenly into a row. Ernest is hurt and frustrated by what he hears as criticism. He becomes irascible. "You silly woman," he shouts. "How do you think I'd pay for all this life we lead, without going to work?"

Beatrice looks at him with wide, shocked eyes. Her hand, almost without knowing, reaches for the cool thread of pearls at her throat as she swallows down her panic. Ernest's heart sinks. Guilt washes over him and settles, heavy, in his stomach. He's all apologies. He doesn't know what came over him. His temper is getting the better of him, these days, he explains. Inside, he's rattled. It's as if something ungovernable is living deep within him—dark emotions that lend him choler and harshness. It's unnerving. He vows to himself to be more careful, more patient, in the future.

1936: Beatrice: New Information

Beatrice leans heavily on her family when, the following year, catastrophe strikes Ernest in the form of a bout of measles. The illness leads to complications—tragically, Ernest loses much of his hearing. Beatrice and Lily nurse him devotedly but they cannot stop the calamity unfolding.

One day Beatrice comes upon Ernest standing next to the gramophone, trying to listen to a record. Tears roll down his cheeks. Music had been a real pleasure to him, and now, he says, it's just tinny noise through his hearing aid. Beatrice is deeply sorry for him, but her efforts to comfort him only seem to irritate. Deafness makes him increasingly withdrawn and angry. When Beatrice talks to him, he shouts at her for mumbling. When she raises her voice, he complains that she's bellowing.

There are compensations, though, she thinks wryly. She can talk for hours to Marion, Emmie, or Ella in the garden, without fear of being overheard. Beatrice's disappointments tumble into her confidants' ears more often these days. Marion and Emmie begin to look concerned, but Ella is comforting. "He's going to take time to adjust to being deaf, Bee dear," she advises. "Give him space, and make sure to praise him whenever he tries to build bridges with you."

Beatrice tries her best, although she finds the management of their newly constrained relationship exhausting. Ernest's temper seems to worsen by the day and one morning it hits a new note. During a petty argument, Beatrice is astonished to see him stamp his foot in a tantrum and pound his fists on the table in frustration. She's alarmed, steps back, cries out at Ernest to stop. His eyes blink, swivel towards her slowly—*he's like a man in a trance*, thinks Beatrice—then his expression clears and he seems at once calmer and more himself. "I'm sorry, my dear," he murmurs, and leaves the room.

"But it's not normal," Beatrice tells Ella later, "to be so volatile. Something's changed him from the man I first met, I'm sure of it. I do love him, and yet... I can't reach him. He won't talk to me."

"Perhaps he had an awful time in the Navy," suggests Ella, with a sigh. "My brother absolutely hated it, too. Said he couldn't get over it for years afterwards." Beatrice nods thoughtfully. Perhaps she should try asking Ernest about that period of his life. Hesitantly she tries a few innocent-seeming questions along the lines of: "I've often wondered what Ceylon was like..." or "Ella says her brother thought the Navy was awfully badly run. What did you think?" But Ernest clams up at once.

Still unmarried, Marion looks on, feeling less and less envious of her sister's domestic life. "Need you put up with his behaviour, Beatrice? Couldn't you strike out on your own?" she sometimes asks. But Beatrice cannot imagine it. She shrinks from social embarrassment, and clings to the status that marriage brings her. She cannot leave Ernest.

Beatrice's brave face sometimes slips, with her mother. One afternoon, the story of Ernest's outburst spills out. Her mother sighs and folds up her embroidery as the tale reaches an end. "Darling, marriage is never simple, is it?" she says, patting Beatrice's hand kindly. She stands, preparing to make them both some comforting cocoa. Then: "Sometimes we don't get the love we expect, dear Beatrice, but we can still find peace in what we have. It isn't always what we imagined, but it can be enough."

It sounds as if her mother is speaking from experience. Not for the first time, Beatrice considers her parents' marriage—formal, frosty, distant. Father looks like he's had the stuffing taken out of him these days, while Mother looks increasingly like the stiff-backed figure of Britannia on the pennies in Beatrice's purse. Emmie sits, in Beatrice's imagination, clasping a metaphorical shield and trident in defence of a life long-accepted, though never truly chosen.

Beatrice looks with an objective lens at her parents for almost the first time in her life. She realises that the simmering parental tensions she can vaguely recall as a child were probably extra-marital affairs—at least Ernest doesn't give Beatrice that sort of trouble—and the frigid lines of combat into which her parents ultimately settled were lines drawn in order to maintain face within society. *So that is how it is done*, realises Beatrice. Mother has become very strong; Father has lost his home ground and is now a guest within the marriage.

Beatrice views her situation through this new information. How much of the trouble between her and Ernest is inherited? How much is truly theirs? She glances sideways at Lily and Arthur's marriage. There it is again: another tense, unequal pairing. And then there is the shadow of the oldest boy, the one she never met. She senses that Ernest once looked up to him, and she wonders what kind of scar such a loss might have left behind.

It is as if scales have fallen from Beatrice's eyes, and a thin light now illuminates the family landscape. All around her, she now sees coolness where love should be, thoughtlessness where care might have blossomed, judgement shouldering aside forgiveness, introspection standing in place of intimacy. Beatrice begins to sense that she and Ernest are caught in currents older than themselves—patterns of loss and longing woven long before their own marriage began. She feels a brief stab of anger, quickly replaced by a mood of thoughtfulness.

Perhaps, like her mother, this adversity will strengthen her. In any case, she believes that she is irrevocably bound to Ernest. How could she leave him? What would become of her? And she could never bear to lose Penny.

Truthfully, she is very much afraid to be alone in the world, and so, perhaps, staying with the status quo, no matter the cost, is better than any other alternative.

1937–1938: Ernest: Courage and Cowardice

Ernest's life is destroyed. He believes this is so. His hearing has gone. The specialists were blunt: no hope of restoration. His hearing aid helps a bit, but it isn't the same; through it he hears only whistles and whines. Music sounds like screeching and crashing, voices cannot be heard over the hubbub of daily life. Already a loner, Ernest steps away from the world, and turns in upon himself.

Where once he was alert and curious, his conversations with people are now muffled, like the hooves of horses in a funeral cortege. His previous life is ashes to his touch, and he mourns its loss, silently, in solitude.

For a time, Ernest is overtaken by anger, depression, and misery. He takes it out on those closest to him—Beatrice in particular—at the same time knowing he is being unfair. She was an absolute brick, nursing him like that throughout the measles. He should be thanking her, but he cannot find any gratitude within himself at present.

There are brighter things happening, though, as 1937 bleeds away and 1938 arrives. His younger sister Dulcie seems to have met a suitable man at long last. Not too late for children, Beatrice comments, and mentally crosses her fingers. By the end of that year, Dulcie and Jimmy are engaged. The whole family is pleased. They all warm to likeable Jimmy. He's a handy sort of a person to have around, sparky, straightforward, generous.

And then there's Dulcie's friends, two 'bachelor girls' called Irene and Vera. They've appeared on the Mallory scene and now seem to be fixtures for the foreseeable future. Ernest suspects that Dulcie introduced them on purpose to shock Arthur, but it hasn't worked. Arthur flirts with Vera and hoots with laughter at the antics of the other, Irene, who used to be on the stage. Their presence has certainly raised dull family parties to being quite tolerable occasions.

Vera—pretty, charming, and graceful; Irene—boisterous and incredibly entertaining: the women intrigue Ernest. He sees at once that they're 'batting for the other side', as he delicately terms it to Beatrice. Beatrice is puzzled, then amazed, and finally amused. Her mother Emmie is scandalised when she learns the truth of it, but nobody is surprised by her disapproval.

Inside, Ernest hardly dares to ponder the girls' lives, the loneliness that must arise from their position, the difficulties their inclinations must cause them socially. Always in his quaking heart, he finds a question mark over his own preferences, because... Rollo. Does Ernest have his own brand of terrible weakness? Surely not, no, surely not.

He is mistaken, though, in what he fears. Rollo was not a temptation but a wound: the brother he lost, the subject of an adolescent adoration, the hero of his awkward naval youth. Unable to read his own feelings, Ernest will spend a lifetime torturing himself upon the horns of a doubt born from tragic misunderstanding. That fear will seep into everything—poisoning his tenderness towards Beatrice, shadowing his love for his daughter, and distancing him from his father. Yet he will not speak of it, and so it remains in the dark, along with his own insight into his tender emotions.

As 1938 draws to a close, and with much help from the womenfolk in his family, Ernest rallies. He re-engages with his job at Graham James Engineering Works, and all his colleagues say how well he adapts to the hearing loss. He's as sharp as a knife once more, discussing business plans and processes without missing a beat, lip reading, demanding things are repeated for his benefit or written down so he can fully absorb them. Even Arthur, who finds Ernest's disability hard to swallow (*"a son of mine, too weak to resist illness"*) has to concede a measure of admiration.

Yes, Ernest is a brave man. Everyone can see it. Only Ernest, in his heart, knows what is coiled inside: the fear of facing his demons, of naming, with honesty, his own vulnerabilities.

1939–1940: Beatrice and Ernest: A Javelin's Flight

War erupts again in 1939. Too deaf to volunteer for active service, Ernest at first believes himself to be useless in a war role. In any case, he is too busy, he tells himself, to take on extra work.

It is the shocking death of Jimmy's mother, Polly Ruggles, in an air raid, that changes Ernest's mind.

One evening, after Polly has closed up her small meat and offal shop in Sparkhill, she hurries homewards to treat herself to a movie at the local cinema. Tragically, she is one of many audience members who are caught in an air raid—an attack that crushes, injures and kills. It is horrible. Jimmy, away on active service, cannot come home for Polly's funeral. The family, who only met Polly once at the wedding, come along to support Dulcie who attends in Jimmy's stead. Jimmy's father, Frederick, is dry-eyed with shock. He shakes everyone's hand automatically, without looking at them, murmuring his thanks.

Jimmy's Aunt Maud, sister to Frederick, stands next to Ernest in the service. "They couldn't even find out who was who in some cases," she says to him in a stage-whisper. "Poor Pol—they never found her right arm, you know. She's had to go to the Lord without it. Awful, isn't it?" She knows Ernest is a former naval officer, and she assumes he is someone who can handle such detail. Ernest is appalled but unsurprised. One hears of such things; it's an obvious hazard of explosions.

He thinks long and hard about the victims of bombing raids and their families, after the funeral. Surely there is something he could do to help? He's able-bodied if deaf, and he's quick and clever. He's used to dealing with other men, leading them, taking decisions. He does it at work every day.

Ernest makes enquiries and finds that he could join the ARP as an Air Raid Warden, despite his hearing loss.

He registers straight away. It's only after he's joined up that he tells his wife.

"Air Raid Precautions services?" queries Beatrice. "What will you be doing?"

"I'll be overseeing the new barrage balloons they're installing in the fields behind us," says Ernest, a tinge of excitement warming his voice. "They expect wardens to enforce blackout, too, and keep people safe—informing, calming, patrolling, getting them to shelters. That sort of thing."

Beatrice's eyes widen. "Do you feel you can keep safe, dear, with your hearing as it is?" she asks, cautiously. Ernest is touchy about his deafness, she knows.

But to her surprise he considers her question carefully. "Well, I'm much better now at distinguishing sounds through the hearing aids, and I can lip read quite well. The training will give me a lot of knowledge about hazards and how to avoid them, so… I hope to be as safe as it's possible to be, in a war." He smiles, takes Beatrice's hand, and kisses it. Beatrice is astounded. Who is this man before her? Not her husband, that's for sure.

Enlisting in the ARP, having a sense of purpose and a chance to prove himself in action—something his Red List job during the First World War denied him—begins to change Ernest. From being a man whose temperament is like a ricocheting bullet, he develops into one whose focus and determination resemble a javelin flying cleanly towards its mark: the preservation of his neighbours' lives.

But the work does more than direct his energy; it offers him a vital chance to locate his true self at last—to realise himself as a man shaped by courage, competence, and legitimacy. For the first time, he is able to feel himself inwardly aligned with the man he strove to be all along. Fulfilment, at last, steadies his hand.

1941: Ernest: Big Bessie

It's a Monday night in March, cold, clear. A bomber's moon sails the skies. Everyone's nervous, waiting for news. Tepid tea sits undrunk as the ARP wardens busy themselves checking stirrup pumps, gas masks, stretchers, first aid kits.

Suddenly the telephone rings, ripping through the quiet night air with ferocious suddenness. Ernest jumps—sounds like that still unnerve him, coming through the crude amplification of his hearing aid. "A sighting of bombers, lads," says Alf's voice, down the line. "Get the siren going, get people under cover, and for God's sake ensure blackout. We don't want stray bombs being dropped on Streetly, do we?" The line clicks and goes dead.

The crew are galvanized into action. Spud and Titch grab their bicycles—off to patrol the local streets and herd people under cover. Most folk get under the stairs around here. Like Ernest, many men arranged to have their under-stair cupboards reinforced, instead of building air raid shelters. Beatrice and Penny will clamber into their hidey-hole, no doubt with cocoa, a couple of books and the battered but beloved Baba the teddy bear, whom Penny hauls everywhere with her.

Lofty Griggs looks across at Ernest. "Off to see our ladies, sir?" he grins, referring to his beloved barrage balloons floating at their moorings some half a mile distant. Lofty, a diminutive man, cares for the balloons like huge pets. He gives them names—Berta, Marta, Big Bessie—and fusses over them each day, checking for leaks to ensure they're ready to fox enemy aircraft by night. His son Horace is a bomber pilot. Lofty knows the importance of forcing the Luftwaffe up as high as possible—it reduces their targeting accuracy, his boy tells him. "You're doing a great job for England, Dad," says Horace, proudly.

Scratcher Pearson is packing his clip boards—three of them—securely in his bag. He's a terrible worrier, and can't be separated from his lists for a moment. Ernest understands this kind of nervousness. He's experienced it himself. He's reassuring towards Scratcher—or Ted, a retired bank clerk in civilian life—giving him firm leadership and just enough responsibility to keep him useful. Scratcher looks up to Ernest as a result, although he'd never say so out loud.

When the crew arrive at the balloon fields, they find Nobby, Dusty, and Dodger there already, on guard duty. All the men head for the winches, as Ernest indicates the chosen balloons to be raised. Other balloons will remain tethered below, bucking in the breeze like skittish horses. The men can hear the sirens wailing, and distant thrumming of aircraft engines. It's a race to get the balloons deployed.

A barrage balloon of Balloon Command floating just above the ground,
with others already deployed high in the sky: 1941.
They were designed to protect lives, were difficult to handle,
and deadly if loosed.
Bellamy W (Flying Officer), Royal Air Force official photographer,
Public domain, via Wikimedia Commons.

Tug Williams arrives—an ex-naval man who's calm under pressure. He and Dusty start checking the cables. "They're wound too tight," shouts Dusty. Scratcher's complaining about wind readings. The sirens scream, and the plane engines sound closer.

Suddenly: "Ernest, this one's got a fault on the main cable," yells Dodger, as the winch screams and the cable on Big Bessie vibrates. The coils of metal within the cable start to shiver and shred, then— ping, ping, ping—the shreds begin to curl backwards. The whole cable is disintegrating at the point nearest the winch. It happens so fast that Ernest barely has time for a breath before Lofty shouts a warning. Scratcher drops his clip board in alarm, and then the right corner cable goes, whipping away from its moorings and slicing through the air with enough force to decapitate a man.

"Bloody hell—watch out," yells Nobby, dropping his wrench and flinging himself to the ground.

Everyone moves at once. Ernest is already shouting directions.

"Dusty—grab the stabiliser rope! Lofty, take the east anchor! Tug—with me—steady her nose!"

He lunges, catching one of the handling lines that trail from the balloon's rigging. The hemp rope judders and burns against his gloved palms as the wind tears at the vast silver shape. "Hold her!" he yells, and Tug is suddenly beside him. Together they haul on the line, bringing the balloon down inch by inch while Lofty keeps tension on the anchor cable and the winch grinds them closer to safety.

In the dark, under pressure, the action is both terrifying and exhilarating. Ernest doubles over to catch his breath. There had been a moment, there, when he'd had to fight a distant memory, one that threatened to root him to the spot—crash of metal, screech of brakes, distant shouting. But he'd mastered himself, and now the memory has been put back in its box, the lid closed, the key turned in the lock.

"You all right, Beethoven?" asks Tug, hand on Ernest's back. Beethoven, Tug's nickname for Ernest, was born of Ernest's deafness and his fondness for music. It's a fine fit in the men's minds for someone educated and skilled. Ernest takes the ribbing surprisingly well. Everyone has a nickname in the ARP, and, having one of his own, Ernest fits right in. He's popular with his crew. They like his kindness, his no-nonsense approach, his decisiveness, and his ability to hold his nerve.

"Well, I think I've still got my head!" laughs Ernest, pretending to check, and the crew guffaw and slap him on the back.

After that, the deployment is straightforward, but Lofty spends the evening lamenting over Big Bessie's injured cable, and worrying that she's given herself a gas leak in the process. He'll check her over tomorrow, he says.

When Ernest gets home, he regales Beatrice with his story. Beatrice is impressed, admiring—Ernest glows. He's found his sweet spot in her regard once more, and he couldn't be more pleased. Later, Arthur comes to hear of the escapade and—"Well done, well done, my boy," he cries. Well, well, what a turn up. Ernest is the hero of the hour.

The ARP suits him very well. He might almost say he's grateful for the war, but that would be an awful thing to think.

1942: Beatrice: Flowers Still Make Her Heart Sing

Busy in the kitchen while Penny is at school, Beatrice concentrates on folding reconstituted eggs into the precious sugar ration, and the unappealing wartime margarine. Making the rations stretch is hard work. To ease constraints, she acquires some geese—fresh eggs for baking, and future Christmas dinner all rolled into one.

But when Penny gets wind of the Christmas dinner part of the plan, she bursts into tears and refuses to be consoled until Beatrice relents with a stay of execution. The geese, named Gert and Daisy after the popular radio entertainers, are now fully-fledged family members.

Beatrice smiles at the memory; it had been highly amusing, in its way—and Ernest had written a funny poem about it. She'd sent it round the family with great success:

> *Why should Gert and Daisy die,*
> *Just to be put in a pie?*
> *I will not eat them, no, not I,*
> *Says Penny, getting in a funk…*
> *We know that face, and we are sunk!*

Things between Beatrice and Ernest have improved. She thinks his ARP work is commendable and says so to anyone she meets. Ernest, pleased as punch, basks in the praise. Beatrice's admiration is sincere, and he laps it up like a cat lapping cream.

In turn, Ernest takes notice of Beatrice again. He commends her cooking, praises her clever Make Do and Mend dressmaking, and brings her home little gifts he acquires in mysterious ways. A pair of rayon-silk stockings is the best of presents, and Beatrice is effusive in her thanks. All is well for now.

Which is why Beatrice doesn't see what's coming down the road towards her.

Beatrice and Marion have organised a little get-together for Beatrice's knitting group—a home-front scheme to supply toys for children orphaned in the raids. Mrs Duncan, Mrs Rose and Mrs Baggaley are perched on the sofas, knitting and chatting. In between, they sip tea, nibble Beatrice's famous parsnip scones, Mrs Duncan's Anzac biscuits, and Marion's especially fluffy vinegar cake. The room is warm and smells of fresh baking; the atmosphere is light-hearted.

Penny sits on the rug, sewing bows onto knitted bears with grave concentration.

Then Ernest appears in the doorway. He's filthy, exhausted, fresh from helping to secure a bombed site in Wylde Green after the previous night's raid. "Another stray bomber," he mutters. His boots are caked in ash and something else that Beatrice fears to name.

"Oh darling, you're home," greets Beatrice, flustered. She's aware of the guests, Ernest's dirty boots on the clean rug, his tight jaw, his darting eyes as they take in the domestic scene. He's clutching his helmet in one white-knuckled hand, while the other hand opens and closes fitfully.

Mrs Rose rises to greet him. "Mr Mallory, I do admire your courage," she says kindly. 'You're doing wonderful things. I think we all feel safer knowing that you and your men are out there."

Ernest's face softens, and a flicker of pleasure steals across his face. Penny looks up, curious to hear about her father's night-time adventures, and wanting to capture a compliment about her teddy bear bows. So she sees it all, as does Marion, and all the knitting ladies.

Ernest mishears Mrs Rose's next comment. He catches 'married dragoons' instead of 'barrage balloons'. Confused, he launches into a short monologue about the rules on servicemen being married and unmarried. "It's all the same, whether they're dragoons, infantry, cavalry, or navy," he finishes. The knitting ladies rustle as they shift on the sofas. They're a little bewildered.

Beatrice steps in, not for the first time trying to rescue Ernest from the social awkwardness of his deafness. Ernest thinks he hears the slight hint of the school-ma'am, as she corrects him: "No dear, Mrs Rose was asking about the barrage balloons, not married dragoons.

You know, Fat Fred, Chubby Charlie, Big Bunion, and all those other ones." Then, to the room in general, smiling at her joke: "He has names for them all. The men love those big balloons. They treat them like pets—it's charming!"

There's a ripple of polite laughter. Beatrice reaches for a scone, splits it and heaps it with jam, before placing it on a small plate. She offers it to Ernest with a smile, which falters when she sees his furious face.

"Oh, Ernest, it was just a joke," she begins, but Ernest's hand is already arcing out—forward—down. The plate flies from Beatrice's hand; the scone lands on the piano lid, jam glistening. For a second, no one breathes.

In that still moment, Ernest takes a step forward, and his hand arcs back. There's a sound. Sharp. Sudden. Shocking.

Beatrice gasps and lifts a hand to her cheek. Penny cries out, dropping her teddy bear bows. Marion exclaims "No! No!," and the knitting ladies gape.

"You might think my war work's a joke," snarls Ernest, "but nobody else does." He looks dazed, his eyes are unfocused and the pupils dilated.

Silence. Even the geese in the garden have fallen quiet. The scone rolls, rolls, and finally falls to the floor, jam smearing down the piano leg and onto the rug. Then the spell breaks. Marion's on her feet, shouting his name. Ernest, flushed crimson, is swinging round and marching from the room, with Marion in hot pursuit. Penny's fleeing through the door after them, thumping up the stairs to her bedroom and slamming the door.

Beatrice sits, trembling and trying to maintain some shred of dignity. She begins to make apologies: "He...he's so tired and distressed by his work...I shouldn't have teased...it's just the strain of...he's under a lot of pressure...he never..." She glances out of the window and sees Ernest standing in the driveway, motionless, staring into space. Then Marion appears, shakes him, and he jerks like an automaton. Heated words follow.

Indoors, the knitting ladies pat Beatrice, sympathise with her, and exchange glances over her head. They leave shortly afterwards, tutting to one another and shaking their heads.

Beatrice is left alone, pondering. How can this be happening to her? To her, who dreamed of such a beautiful marriage. Stifling a sob, she climbs the stairs slowly to knock on Penny's door, but there is no response. She turns to leave, and sees something huddled on the landing. It is Penny's beloved, battered old bear, Baba, discarded like an old rag.

Later that evening, Ernest, wringing his hands together, apologises awkwardly to Beatrice. He doesn't know what came over him—it won't happen again, he insists.

On the surface, Beatrice accepts the apology and a truce is drawn. Inside, she feels something shift. Sadness and disappointment roll themselves into a hard ball in her tummy as she perceives that her youthful romanticism has finally passed beyond her reach. A chill steals over her. She feels like a boat holed below the waterline— tilting, foundering.

The following morning, with her face stiff from holding composure, she confides in Ella. "I don't know what to do with him anymore," she concludes. "He'd test the patience of a saint."

"Oh Bee, dear, I'm so sorry. Unhappiness taxes us all," says Ella, gently.

Now Beatrice is afflicted by an ever-present anxiety about further violence. She inhabits an edgy space with a man whom she feels she doesn't know anymore. Perhaps she never knew him.

She becomes careful. She weighs her words. The pliant stems of her love creep away from Ernest and cleave instead to Emmie, Marion, and Ella.

It flits through Beatrice's mind that she might leave Ernest, but she knows it is a thought that can never take form. Scandal, loneliness, social banishment — she cannot contemplate the risks. Besides, Ernest provides well for her and Penny. This is the bargain she must accept. She understands the transaction: security in one area, paid for by uncertainty in another.

Marion and Emmie hover on the periphery, protective and concerned. Lily watches, loving and disappointed—for Beatrice, for Ernest, and for the marriage she had hoped would be the making of her boy.

To comfort herself, Beatrice devotes hours to working in her garden amongst its fragrant petals and merry colours. With the blooms she gathers, she arranges dramatic, imaginative sculptures in large vases, and places them all around the house. Flowers are her consolation and her salvation; arranging them becomes her way of restoring order, however fragile, to a world that has slipped from grace. Yes. Flowers are her joy; flowers still make her heart sing.

1942–1945: Ernest: Breaching the Plimsoll Line

On that dread day in 1942, Ernest had felt wretched about his violence against his wife. Marion had torn him off a strip, then his father had done the same. To appease the guilt festering in his chest, Ernest raged at them in return—and won himself no friends.

He'd sat late into the night with a whisky, thinking: *Why did I do it? How could I have been so out of control?*

The night before the catastrophic tea party had been horrendous.

A lone bomber had jettisoned its load over a residential area of Sutton Coldfield, razing streets to the ground, crushing homes and people. Then followed the carnage. Innocent lives ruined or annihilated, futures smothered, memories obliterated.

For some reason, it's the bedrooms that wring Ernest's heart. Standing naked to the world with their walls ripped off, items of furniture still intact, these rooms look like intimacy invaded, the soft inner belly of family life ripped open to uncaring public view. Ernest is becoming increasingly oppressed by the human misery he sees.

That a small, armed metal cannister, dropped from 8000 feet can do this much damage... thinks Ernest's tired brain. He pictures the bombs, dropping like little eggs from the womb of a Heinkel, floating down balletically through the night mists, then—flash—rushing air— the crack of glass blowing from windows as the air pressure sucks at them—boom—crash—whump. Explosions, masonry falling, timbers crashing. It lives in his head—by day as imagination, by night as reality.

Ernest flexes tired muscles and grunts with pain as his shoulders crunch. He's not unaware of the paradox of his life.

Thanks to Arthur, Ernest's career is in engineering valves. Arthur himself won an MBE for his part in designing a valve to trigger explosives. As Ernest wades through the fields of slaughter and destruction that are bomb sites, he reflects on the utter irony of it all. By day, he manufactures a thousand little brass valves, tiny bits of brilliance that are critical components of bombs. By night, he staggers to and fro, extracting victims, brushing the soot from what's left of someone's arm, lifting shattered bodies from collapsed under-stair shelters.

Daddy's valves. Arthur's legacy. Life is bloody unfathomable.

He's working with Chalky Walker. That man's tireless, a serene sort of fellow who's good to have at your side. Suddenly, Chalky gives a shout. "Over 'ere, Beethoven, it's a spark-out or a goner." Either unconscious or dead, then. Ernest moves carefully over the debris.

In the faint light of their torches, they can see that there's a body lying trapped beneath a roof beam. He's a young man, and he has the look of a peaceful sleeper, his arm tucked behind his head in an odd gesture of relaxation. Unbelievably, in a distant corner of the debris-littered room, a clock strikes the hour from beneath a dusty cloaking of plaster, as it sits solidly upon the undamaged mantelpiece.

While Chalky feels for a pulse, Ernest moves the light to look at the boy's face. The beam of light trembles, flicks sideways, judders back to the face. Ernest freezes. The breath stops in his throat; sweat beads on his brow.

It's Rollo is his first appalled, anguished thought. The lad has the look of his friend. Handsome, dark, with high cheek bones. Panic crawls up his spine with tiny, skittering feet. Somewhere inside himself, the thousand fragments of the old glass plate—that inner image of himself, long since shattered—spin and turn.

Oh my God, he's been alive all these years and I didn't know—thinks Ernest—and—unendurably—*I've found him, and he's dead all over again...*

Then a voice in his head, irascible—his or Arthur's? He cannot tell. *Don't be ridiculous. This can't be Rollo. You're dreaming, get a grip man.*

Now Ernest looks more carefully, of course he can see that it's not Rollo. Rollo's face was leaner, older. This is a boy, with soft cheeks and a hard line to his mouth where Rollo's was gentler. Somewhere outside, laughter starts up, loud and raucous. On and on it goes. Harsh and hollow, jolting against the tragedy of death that lies before Ernest's gaze.

Ernest's breathing steadies and he can move again, but the shock has rattled him far more than he knows. For the rest of the shift, he works like a machine—dazed, slightly confused. Chalky watches him with concern and quietly speaks to the supervisor. They send Ernest home early.

On arrival, Ernest wipes his grimy boots on the front-door mat, closes the front door softly, and rubs away a dirty thumbprint from the door jamb. So much he does automatically, as if in a dream. He has the strange sensation that his consciousness hovers somewhere outside himself—just to his right-hand side—regarding him with dispassionate detachment.

Moving quietly, he crosses the hall rug, turns the living-room door handle, and steps into the tea party. He is startled. What is this? Who are these people? The sight jars everything in him after his exhausting night—the cosy room, the women, their bright voices rising around him, Beatrice pushing a scone towards him. His stomach turns. Then they laugh and laugh—what are they laughing at? Him? How dare they!

His hand arcs forward and down. Splat—there goes the scone. Smash—there goes the plate. Smack—and there is Beatrice, standing horrified and shocked.

What is happening? Marion is up and bearing down on him. He runs. Out of the door, stopping, hesitating—then she's on him, shouting. He shouts back, then he's away, gone, fleeing from the scene like a thief in the night.

Ernest's breath is tight in his chest as he remembers it all, silently knocking back whisky and soda in the quiet house, while the clock ticks and ticks by his side.

In the weeks that follow, Ernest comes about like a ship in the wind, and tacks blindly into the tempest of his feelings with full canvas aloft. Then he sets off once more on the choppy voyage of his life, with an unstable cargo of raw emotion weighing him down. He now rides well below his Plimsoll Line, safety precautions breached, and his ballast of shame slopping him from side to side as he tips and rolls in the waves.

1953–1955: Beatrice: Cascading Silks

Rationing, that soul-sapping constriction on every housewife, finally ends and Beatrice feels like hanging out the (unrationed) flags. Clothing coupons are flung in the bin. Ration books are torn up. Now she can buy as much butter as she pleases and make skirts from yards of material. Penny's wedding, gloriously free of restrictions, is a source of deep enjoyment to Beatrice—a gorgeous dress, a long veil, plenty of delicious food and drink, and a big marquee in the garden, which brims with Beatrice's carefully-tended flowers and shrubs.

Ernest continues unsteadily at home, but his ARP work did him credit, everyone agrees. He's a great asset at Graham James, too, where he's taken over from Arthur as Managing Director. He's as brilliant as his father, but his plans are often too convoluted for others to follow, leaving them scratching their heads and muttering about Pythagoras under their breath.

At home, he's unpredictable. Beatrice never knows, from one moment to the next, what might happen. It makes her tired and jumpy. She hears herself wheedling, manipulating, mollifying, and hates the voice that has become hers. But, like her mother before her, she is learning to manage a difficult man, and she does it as courageously as her tender character allows.

Emmie often comes to sit with Beatrice. They both enjoy hand embroidery, so they sit and sew in companionable silence or enliven the hours with chatter and gossip. The stranded silks cascade from their laps as the words fall, comfortably, from their lips.

"Have you seen Marion's new scarf? Italian silk?" Emmie might say. "She'll be wearing it to death come Easter."

Or "What about those new Bendix washer-dryers?" Beatrice might sigh. "Dulcie's friends the Hammonds have one. Imagine, all your washing and drying done in one machine. Just press the button and walk away!"

Or: "Did you see the embroidery on the Queen's robes at her coronation?" Emmie might ask.

"Lovely," Beatrice might agree, "but what a fortune they must have cost, and so much gold thread—that's no fun to stitch with!"

Emmie is Beatrice's companion, Ella is Beatrice's confidante, Marion is Beatrice's sentinel. Marion stands guard over her sister, never intrusive but always available. Beatrice often thinks that she is fortunate in more ways than she used to realise. *I have such a good family*, she reflects. *And Ernest is still generous and kind, in his way, although his illness has changed him so.*

Beatrice has come to realise that Ernest's struggles are about something deep inside him, something that he can seemingly neither recognise nor discuss. The medical world terms it neurasthenia, neurosis, a nervous breakdown, whereas to herself she calls it 'Ernest's troubles'. After much soul-searching, Beatrice accepts that Ernest will never regain his youthful lightness, that what is now ascendent in Ernest is the more anxious, depressive and defensive sides of his character. What can be done? Very little, it seems, but to find ways through. As the years pass, Ernest begins to offer little gestures of repentance. She feels them in the small, frequent gifts he offers her, the way she catches him staring thoughtfully at her as she sits reading, the times he supports her in the garden by digging or weeding.

She is both afraid of and compassionate towards Ernest, believing vaguely that he's experiencing some sort of trauma from his war work. But she lacks the tools to help. The culture has no language yet for post-traumatic stress disorder. So Ernest rides onwards through his sea of challenges, his wife breasting the waves alongside him.

Sometimes she hates him. When his moods boil over into tantrums, when he rages and shouts, when he beats his fists on the table and drums his heels on the floor in inexpressible frustration at the sheer unbearableness of life, she can feel her lip curl, and her heart beat hard with fear.

But she tells herself to remember that he's ill, not bad.

Oddly, sometimes, Ernest will then stop in the middle of his fit of temper, as if slapped.

Beatrice doesn't realise it, but as a wave of forbearance flows from her to him, Ernest's self-control awakens once more and delivers him back from the wilderness. Then he hears Arthur's disapproving voice in his mind: *Ernest, my boy, control yourself! Be a man!*

But Ernest cannot effectively turn his ship at this late stage in life.

1956: Ernest: Germs

Ernest admires the watercolours on his wall, the ones his staff gave him as a retirement gift. They're lovely pieces: a country lane with a lone walker upon it—"That's you, Mr Mallory," laughs the works foreman, Terry Rawlings—and a winter lake with birds rising into the setting sun. But they don't soothe the disappointment and bitterness inside. After years of careful leadership of the engineering works, Ernest's brilliant if sometimes intricate designs and ideas are rejected. Politics and small thinkers force him out. The blow is hard to bear. Ernest had expected to leave on a tide of respect—not rejection. True, retirement gives him time for his passions—poetry, photography, the ballet—but retirement hasn't brought him peace.

He's aware that Beatrice and Penny tread carefully around him; that he loses control of his temper and humiliates himself with angry tantrums; that he is both lonely and alone inside a maelstrom of emotions he cannot name.

Sometimes, he looks at his hands and they seem to be covered in germs. He locks himself in the bathroom and scrubs his skin until it's red and raw. He tells himself it's just a habit, but deep down, he knows he's trying to scrub away confusion, shame and grief. These feelings cling to him like mould, held down in the darkness of his soul where they proliferate for lack of cleansing light.

Confiding in someone might help, but by now reticence is a habit. Ernest can find neither the courage nor the capacity to voice his long-muted traumas. Silently, he soldiers on.

Often, he yearns for the soul-deep conversations he had with Rollo all those years ago—the only time that he felt truly at one with another, truly accepted just for himself. His soul is tired of its burdensome shadows. Thankfully, there are pleasant times—walks, holidays—but nervous illness dogs Ernest, and then he sinks into tempers and anxious ruminations. Beatrice encourages him into medical treatment when his preoccupations threaten to damage his health.

The treatment—electro-convulsive therapy—is unpleasant to receive. It leaves Ernest feeling dulled, with a type of synthetic peace which is both merciful and diminishing.

1956: Beatrice: Three Gymnopédies

Lately, things have been quieter, and Beatrice's optimism rises with the late spring weather. She breezes in from the garden, arms full of lilies, roses, and baby's breath. "Smell how sweet the scent is," she says to Ernest, offering a cautious smile. Ernest inhales deeply, savouring the intoxicating rose perfume. He recognises the gesture— a little bridge is being built between them by Beatrice—and accepts it gratefully. Moments like these are pearls.

Humming happily to herself, Beatrice arranges the flowers into displays for the sunroom and dining room. Dust particles float in the shafts of sunlight that grace the arrangements with spotlights of glory. Ernest sprints off to get his camera so that he can capture the beauty he sees. His photos reflect his own artistry and that of his wife. The flowers spike, froth, and jostle, their vibrant colours mirrored in the polished wood of the furniture, while soft shadows and light play across their forms. The arrangements are like quiet expressions of Beatrice's inner nature—they reach with open arms, they witness themselves as gently beautiful, they invite admiration, but they are silent and still as well.

*Ernest's photograph of a flower arrangement by Beatrice, 1950s—
Beatrice's vibrant inner nature has an outlet in her flower arranging.*

These days, Beatrice schools herself to think of her marriage as discordant rather than disastrous. It gives her breathing space—to hear only the smaller disharmonies and filter out the cacophony. Once, she and Ernest had hoped to share the same tune, but somehow, over the years, it was lost. Yet even quiet discord can, at times, resolve into harmony, as Beatrice discovers one morning.

On a bright Saturday in June, Ernest's friend Kenneth calls for a coffee, and the three of them fall to chatting about music. Kenneth, a keen pianist, waves his hands with excitement as he describes the challenges of mastering Satie's *Three Gymnopédies*.

"Play for us," begs Ernest, smiling kindly. Kenneth sits at once at the baby grand piano and begins.

The strange music uncurls slowly, dreamily—like a leaf unfolding, or a bird drifting on the breeze, reflects Beatrice. She feels herself light as air, the weight of cares fallen away, and as if she is rising upwards to a new liberty. Ernest, meanwhile, is leaning forward, rapt and alert. For him, the music quietens something so deep inside himself that it feels like his whole consciousness expands. He finds that his inner agitation stills; his spirit breathes. And look, what is this? For a moment, the scattered shards of his inner self seem to drift back and settle at his feet.

As the notes die away, Ernest blinks. "Extraordinary!" he says. "I cannot describe the feeling—such a peaceful composition, Kenneth, with a sort of mystery at its heart. I felt as if I were immersed in bliss, almost baptised by the beauty of the notes."

"You're very sensitive to the message of this music, Ernest," Kenneth nods appreciatively. "What did you think, Beatrice, my dear?"

Beatrice is silent for so long that both men look at her in puzzlement. "It is only that the words won't come," she smiles. "The piece made me feel so uplifted—light and free. Truly, it was like the passing touch of an angel."

Kenneth smiles at the image. Beatrice, meanwhile, is struck by the harmony between her husband's response and her own—his immersion, like a baptism; hers, the brush of an angel's wing. Yes, she thinks, we are both inspired by beauty.

Such a realisation warms Beatrice, in this little moment of shared enjoyment. The insight helps her live with the continuing saga of Ernest's inner turmoil, even as its challenges remain.

Yes, there are still pearls scattered through the days. And Beatrice gathers them when she can.

1960: Beatrice: Are Angels Real?

The fading happens gradually. Emmie's death in 1958 is a sorrow that unbalances Beatrice's hard-won equilibrium. She sinks a little, her spirits drifting downwards. Now she finds she is tired and her body is full of aches.

Almost it is no surprise to Beatrice when she is diagnosed with a cancer. She is fearful yet philosophical. What can one do, after all? It is the end of her life's efforts, she believes. She sinks beneath the waters of her fate. Marion cannot save her, Ernest cannot help her.

The treatment is a rotten experience, and carries little alleviation of the condition. Radiotherapy burns her skin, and the drugs cloud her mind. Ernest, deeply distressed, fusses around her, but his attempts to offer cuddles irritate and discomfort her. *Poor man*, she thinks. And: *Poor me.*

In her final days, Beatrice finds herself descending into the past completely. As Marion sits and holds her hand, Beatrice's happiest times roll out before her eyes—walking Penny's pram around the park, her heart brimming with pride. Tending her flower beds with the summer sun on her back and the scent of roses wafting on the hot air. Ernest's proposal of marriage when the world was her oyster. The day of the beautiful Autochrome Lumière photograph, which seemed to capture a part of her soul in its shimmering colours.

As she lies quietly in bed, she wonders—*Should I be praying?* But there has never been any spiritual presence in her life. She, Marion, and Ella sometimes speculated together about whether angels were real, but it all seemed a bit fanciful.

Beatrice feels a deep tug of regret for leaving her daughter behind, but the cancer will not allow her to wait. When Marion next calls, it is to find Beatrice gripping something tightly in her hand. With a wan smile, she presses it into her sister's palm. The cool pearls of Beatrice's old necklace slip silently between Marion's fingers, like a long-held sigh. Marion understands that she is being passed the memorial to Beatrice's marriage. "For Penny," whispers Beatrice, and a tear slides from the corner of her eye.

Carefully, then, Beatrice draws a promise from Marion to watch over Penny. It reminds Beatrice of another promise from long ago when she and Marion were girls, but she cannot quite recall what it was all about and the thought slides away from her.

Early one morning, Beatrice slips quietly across the threshold of death. Now she finds herself adrift in a strange world. Without spiritual signposts, she seeks a place of safe harbour and settles there, curling her remembrances around herself as protection and consolation. Flowers bloom endlessly, Penny toddles in the sunlight, and Ernest is always the charming, gentle man she first loved.

But this world is an illusion, a refuge created from her own longing. Nevertheless, Beatrice takes up residence, and holds tightly to her imagined paradise.

1976: Ernest: The Void

Ernest leans back in his garden chair on the little patio outside the sun lounge. Cherry blossoms drift around him. The four trees Beatrice planted make a haze of pink and white each spring, and he remembers her pleasure at their bloom.

Sixteen years without her, and the void she left remains. Their marriage had been fraught, yet a thread of loyalty and affection held firm. During Beatrice's final illness Ernest had sat for hours at her bedside, watching her suffer, unable to help.

His days are quieter now, filled with small family events and the consolations of walking and gardening. He reflects, remembers, regrets, weighs. Shadows linger, always, in his thoughts.

He worries for his family, in this fast-paced modern world, but it all feels increasingly beyond his control, even beyond his comprehension.

He sleeps more and more. Sometimes he considers what Penny told him—that life continues without pause beyond death. He isn't sure what to believe. Only that he's tired, and that another chapter must soon begin.

Rollo floats into his memory at that moment. "It's reincarnation, old chap," he hears Rollo say, and is once more transported back to Ceylon. "Those Buddhists believe in it, and so do I. You and I were friends in another life, mark my words."

Could Rollo have been right? Perhaps, somewhere beyond sight, his old friend waits. The thought moves Ernest more than he can say.

One evening Ernest goes to bed and does not wake. The housekeeper finds him still and composed, as if listening for something just beyond hearing. Death takes him, and he goes without argument. As he passes over the threshold, he looks back once, and there, following him, are a thousand tiny glittering fragments of a glass plate that once held a likeness of himself. They accompany him like a puzzle to solve, like a broken vessel to rebuild—or perhaps like a promise of salvation.

Afterlife Encounters
Beatrice and Ernest: visited 2021–2025

Wild Beasts and Cocoons

When Ernest dies, two things meet him. The first is his terror. The second are the wild beasts. They leap and snarl, dive and grab. There is noise, confusion, danger—so it seems to Ernest. What can he do? It is just like his horrible, taxing life all over again.

He's an engineer—he knows how to build. He throws up a shelter—a bubble—and steps inside. But before he can seal it, the beasts slip in with him. Now he's enclosed with what he meant to escape. He pounds at the wall; the sound returns to him. No one comes.

Time loosens. Ernest doesn't know how long he remains trapped; only that no help comes. He doesn't yet know that change begins only when he turns to face what he fears.

The first visit that Inessa and I make to Beatrice and Ernest in 2021 shows us Ernest's predicament. We then discover something unexpected: Beatrice, too, has created a shelter resembling Ernest's bubble, though it is born of an entirely different impulse.

Beatrice passes over the threshold in sorrow and pain. She glances around her. Nothing to comfort her, no one to greet her. So she decides to create her own after-death world. She builds herself a space of safety, spinning it with threads of favourite memory and lining it with happy hours. Here she rests, for sixty years, until Inessa and I find her, nested in a quiet cocoon.

"The two of them, in enclosed spaces!" I comment. "It seems unusual!"

Inessa agrees.

"Who should we work with first?" I wonder.

Inessa considers these two captive souls carefully. "I believe we shall begin with Beatrice," she says. "Her sanctuary is gentler than Ernest's, yet—paradoxically—it may be harder to open."

Beatrice

Celandine

When Inessa views Beatrice, she is intrigued.

"Beatrice is in a kind of cocoon that is positioned in a house, in an upstairs bedroom," she observes. "I believe it is a child's nursery. Her cocoon is filled with beautiful images that she gazes at, but none of them reflect the reality of her situation."

I catch my breath—I think I know where Beatrice is! Inessa's view aligns exactly with a 1933 photograph of my mother's childhood home, Celandine. Here, in Ernest's picture, Beatrice stands at the first-floor nursery window, gazing down at Penny's pram by the porch.

"Yes," exclaims Inessa, "this is the locus of her cocoon! Beatrice hasn't looked out of it for over sixty years. The trauma of her death drove her to retreat into memory, and lack of spiritual grounding now stops her progressing."

Beatrice's cocoon is spun from memory and fear. It shields her from pain—but traps her in timeless isolation. She is in a state called earthbound, like the soul I encountered during the supersensible research course. Now I learn more about earthbound souls.

They are not acting malevolently—only confused, overwhelmed, lost. A soul in this state might remain tied to a trauma, or bound to a place, person, or uncompleted earthly task. Emotions carried within the soul can cause this state—guilt, panic, shock, disbelief and denial, for instance. Beatrice's case is especially poignant because her cocoon is crafted from love—but it is a misplaced devotion that helps no one, least of all herself.

"She clings to the familiar, but it does her no good," says Inessa. "We should try to awaken her and persuade her to come out of her cocoon."

*Beatrice contemplates her baby girl from a
first-floor window c. 1933.*

Through our meditation, we send Beatrice light and warmth. I imagine a small window in the walls of the cocoon through which Beatrice might see us. "Hello," I say, "we're here to help. You can wake up now, Beatrice, and come out of your cocoon."

For a while, nothing happens. Then there is a shifting in the walls, some cracking—and like an egg breaking open, suddenly the cocoon reveals its interior world. Beatrice stands, silent and still, enraptured by her blissful memories. Behind her cocoon, Inessa sees her angel standing patiently, as he has done for the last six decades.

I now expect Beatrice to shake herself awake, open her eyes and step out into the light to take the hand of her guiding angel.

But no! Beatrice most definitely stays put. While she does, indeed, awaken, she remains rooted to the spot, fearfully peering out but refusing to step forward—because, what if stepping out means losing everything she's clung to?

"It's a good start," encourages Inessa, "but let's now leave her for a few weeks and revisit again. You might work with her in the meantime."

*Author's impression of Beatrice cocooned with her hands bound.
Her angel, unable to help at present, stands behind her.
Media: Acrylic and crayon.*

For the next few weeks, I think of Beatrice often, placing her in bright, colourful, spiritual light and sending her reassuring feelings. Slowly an impression comes to me that she has moved, and is now in a different space, though remaining motionless. Her fears still drag at her, I feel, like heavy weights.

Facing the Past

When Inessa next looks at Beatrice, she confirms progress. Beatrice has moved towards the 'door' to the soul-realm, but her heavy emotional state holds her back.

"What can you see?" I ask.

"Well, it looks like shackles at wrists and ankles," she replies. "They seem substantial, burdensome. Her angel shares them too."

So those must be the heavy weights I sensed before!

Happily, Beatrice's upper body is now bathed in light, though her lower body stands in some sort of murky substance—Inessa's image of the remaining pain and fear. Working together, we strive to dissolve these obstacles through meditation.

Then something remarkable happens in my inner vision (see the illustration below). Beatrice's bowed head lifts. Her arms fling skywards, shackles fly apart—and she jumps, light and unbound. Bliss and delight stream from her as she touches her angel's hand and walks into the bright space of the soul-realm.

"Yes," laughs Inessa, "that matches my perception too! We'll leave her to adjust."

Meanwhile Inessa reminds me that Beatrice's next step will be the life review—the soul's own process of seeing and learning. In the soul-realm, she explains, each person re-experiences their life in reverse order, feeling the consequences of their deeds. Through this, Beatrice will come to understand the aims her soul carried into life, set with angelic help before birth. "For now, these remain hidden from our earthly sight," adds Inessa, "but one day they will become visible to us."

When next we visit, I'm eager for news.

"How is Beatrice doing now?" I ask.

"Oh," chuckles Inessa, "she's having a good sort out!"

Apparently, every soul has its own gesture for its life-review process. For Beatrice, her soul expresses the soul-realm 'life-sorting task' as a tidying of her clothes and her house. Inessa perceives her as sifting through piles of clothes in her living room, discarding a garment here, admiring and folding away a garment there.

"It isn't literal," explains Inessa. "Her soul turns a familiar earthly habit into a symbol of inner renewal. The garments she keeps are her strengths—peace, kindness, courage. The ones she discards are the habits she's ready to leave behind."

Author's impression of Beatrice stepping free.
Media: Pastels and crayon.

Undercurrents of Karma

"I wonder what first drew Ernest and Beatrice together," I say.

"Something from another life," Inessa replies after contemplation. "They have shared history."

In that earlier life, Beatrice's frailty created dependence; Ernest's need to control was already a pattern. The same polarity reunited them—protector and protected—but now with potential to reverse these habits. Their marriage could have transformed dominance into care and dependency into strength; instead, they repeated the old pattern, and both suffered.

Into this difficult dynamic stepped Marion, drawn by unseen forces to be Beatrice's support and shield. Unable to alter the marriage, she nevertheless stood beside her sister, softening what she could.

The struggles of that life led Beatrice to withdraw inwardly before her death, and then to recreate that gesture in the afterlife—spinning her cocoon of memories from both love and denial. Marion, Inessa perceives, still lingers near her sister, quietly protective. "Perhaps we'll look later at Marion's role," suggests Inessa, and I agree; her story will shed more light on both women.

Reunion

As our final task, Inessa and I look to strengthen and support Beatrice by reuniting her with her daughter Penny, who has recently died at the grand age of eighty-nine. Penny is now awake and aware, and Beatrice is perfectly addressable too.

"Let's invite them both to a space chosen from their life on earth," suggests Inessa, and I choose Beatrice and Ernest's peaceful garden with the cherry trees. I find pictures for Inessa, showing blossoms sprinkling the grass.

We imagine a restful scene: deckchairs and a tea table on the patio, dappled light. With angelic support, we invite the two souls, and they arrive, full of questions.

To my consternation, neither recognises the other. Beatrice sees an elderly stranger in Penny. In her turn, Penny sees a young woman from a long-faded photograph whom she cannot recognise as her mother.

Recognition comes first through a deeper stratum—an older life—then awakens forward into the present names.

Inessa describes how they recognise one another not as Penny and Beatrice, but as brothers, from long ago. In that life they appear to have been artisans—young journeymen—happy and active, fulfilled in their work. This insight helps to orient them to their present soul identities, allowing their affection for one another to flow freely.

Now Penny and Beatrice have a small connection, which may grow with time into a source of support for each other. It's a satisfying conclusion to our endeavours.

Forgiveness

I'm curious to know whether Beatrice could feel my interventions, when I worked with her during all those weeks, encouraging her to step out of her cocoon. "Oh yes," says Inessa, "she could see and hear you, but she thought it was the voice and face of an angel at the window. That's how she saw you."

So, Beatrice finally concluded that angels are real, I think.

From Beatrice comes a sensation I struggle to name. "She's learning to reflect and forgive," says Inessa. "She's forgiving herself as well as others. While she's seeing all the ways she went wrong, she can also see all the ways she was able to express love. She's learning that love is not an ideal given to us, but a work we choose—again and again."

I'm relieved that Beatrice is on track, now, to digest her experiences and make her way forward. A turbulent life that led to a period of entrapment has ended, and a new phase of Beatrice's existence has begun. It's time to leave her, so finally I wave goodbye in my imagination. Looking back, I see Beatrice and Penny sitting together, enjoying the cherry blossoms sifting down, quietly held by mutual memory.

Ernest

Emotions are Living Beings

Inessa finds Ernest in turmoil. "He seems quite hostile," she observes, "yet beneath—only fear."

She describes him trapped in a translucent sphere that is cast from his own emotions. Its surface ripples with the violence of his struggle. Inside, he beats frantically at the walls while fragmented memories of his life flash before him. His cries echo back distorted.

Inessa explains to Ernest that he is only seeing his own feelings, projected outward. "There's no need for fear," she adds. "Unresolved emotions can appear outside us, after death. Rage, fear—they might look fierce, but you're just witnessing them, that's all."

Something stirs in Ernest's mind. A recollection—dim but dear.

Rollo Blount, laughing in Ceylonese sunlight: "What if emotions are living things, like animals... If you were quick enough, perhaps you might catch one by the tail!"

Ernest smiles faintly, and the phrase *reaches* him. He begins to listen.

Inessa explains that during life he generated many strong emotions, feelings he never faced or transformed. Unacknowledged, they followed him here as forms—his 'wild beasts'. His alarm towards them blocks the soul-purification process.

Now Inessa looks into Ernest's soul and sees the trauma there. Outwardly, Ernest had been a model professional; inwardly, his sensitive and artistic nature suffered from the constraints of his father's strict ideals. Eric's death triggered an emotional landslide; Rollo's death triggered a second. In Ceylon, tender brotherly love had blurred with the physical in Ernest's mind, breeding shame he hid behind respectability. The split between outer and inner self became the seed of illness.

"I can see," says Inessa, "that he lived for others' expectations. Hiding his true nature cost him dearly."

By the end of his navy life, ending in the loss of Rollo, his soul collapsed. He rebuilt himself entirely, on his return home—and did so in ways that earned Arthur's praise but did not give Ernest himself inner nourishment or self-expression.

"I can see that hiding his true nature behind an orthodox exterior caused trauma in Ernest's soul—and eventually, it made him ill," concludes Inessa.

*Author's impression of Ernest battling with
strong emotions in the afterlife.
Media: Collage, pastels and pencil.*

Bursting the Bubble

How can we help my poor grandfather?

Inessa speaks to Ernest, addressing him with clarity and care. Her mission is to help him realise that the chaos he's trapped in is not a punishment but a construction—one he has unwittingly made for himself.

"It's a repeating pattern," she explains to me. "In his earthly life, he hid from truth about himself; here in the soul-realm, he's doing the same. He's built this bubble to protect himself—but it has also become his prison."

Ernest listens. At last, he is absorbing her words.

"You can melt that bubble away if you want to," Inessa tells him. "It's yours. You made it. Just step through the wall. There is light all around you."

Inside the bubble, Ernest's emotions swirl and shiver. But now, beyond these emotions, Inessa can sense the beginning of hope. Rollo's remembered voice has opened something in him. That moment of eccentric and amusing chat, shared with Rollo so long ago, has become a lifebelt that buoys Ernest up in his turbulent sea, and keeps him afloat.

Working with concentration, Inessa begins to cleanse the dark emotional residue that clings to Ernest's soul. She draws out the lingering shadows of illness and the imprint of years of heavy medication. She encourages harmony within him, and invites calming and healing influences towards his soul.

Then she offers him a gift—quietness.

"I've created a lake of pure, still water," she says. "Walk into it—it is the essence of quietness. Let it restore you."

Ernest peers through the translucent wall of his bubble. His memories stab at him: his hearing loss; his failure to understand Beatrice; his lack of effective nurturing towards Penny. Waves of remorse rise and fall within him, contracting his inner being, coiling heavily around his soul's heart.

I don't dare, he seems to whisper.

Now I step forward because childhood memories have come into my mind of walks with Ernest. I recall a pretty route through a quiet wood along the shores of a small lake. The pine scents mingled with the smell of damp earth, and our hands held ice creams. We chatted about nothing, watching the water sparkle. I cheekily shouted "Boo!" into Ernest's hearing aid. "Naughty," he laughed, wagging his finger.

I bring that memory vividly to mind and send it to him.

"Shall we go there now?" I ask.

"He remembers you," says Inessa. "He knows your soul well. Has he been in your reading group?"

"Yes," I answer. "He listens often when I read to the dead."

"You have a good connection," Inessa says warmly. "Try leading him to the lake."

I imagine the two of us walking side by side. Ernest is smiling. The light filters through the trees. The memory of belonging—the sense of love—begins to settle and comfort Ernest.

Suddenly, the bubble shimmers, stills—and vanishes.

It's just a shell, Ernest thinks in wonder. *A shell of my own making. I was never truly trapped.*

Hope lifts in his chest. He turns towards the lake, towards the sunlit shore. *So strange to feel warmth again,* he thinks. *So strange to feel peace.*

The lake stretches wide and still, its surface sparkling. I stand beside him.

"Try it out," I say. "Step in, it has a beautiful stillness to it."

Ernest hesitates—then steps into the water. As once before in his earthly life, when he listened to the music of Satie, his soul sighs at this baptism. Silence surrounds him. Gentle ripples play across him. He stands, engulfed, relaxed, contented.

Now blissfulness radiates from him in waves. I feel it, like sunlight breaking across a cold landscape. Pain, guilt, and fear begin to wash away. For a long time, he simply floats.

"We'll leave him here for now," says Inessa. "Let the water do its work."

Ernest rests, and in this resting, his soul begins the quiet work of salvation.

Tears Falling

When next we visit, Ernest sits beside the lake, his soul freshly bathed. Here he contemplates his life—the highs and lows pass before him. Some of the images bring lightness and joy; others draw tears from his soul's eyes.

As his tears fall, he wrings his hands, trying to wash away his past mistakes—a familiar gesture from earth.

It is a hard passage. He sees, equally, the good he did, and the suffering he caused. Both experiences stream through him. It is as if he reaches out his hands and grasps nettles with one, and calendula flowers with the other—pain and comfort received together.

"Let's send courage, clarity, and compassion to him; it will help him steady," suggests Inessa.

I once feared for souls in the purification realm, imagining their burden. Yet I now understand that souls *long* for this learning. They welcome the chance to see clearly, to grow.

Ernest will too. He will have the opportunity to make amends and reclaim the warmth that always lived within him.

"He's a good soul," says Inessa, "possessing great charm and goodness. He loved deeply, though in a flawed and faltering way."

"Will he be able to reconstruct his inner, true self from his fractured soul pieces?" I wonder.

"Yes, there's a good chance," replies Inessa. "In this life, Ernest was tested beyond his limits, but he has learned a great deal from his trials and he'll be stronger as a result."

Some souls crack under the pressure of the life they must live on earth, and Ernest's is one of them. His suffering was a blend of karmic consequences and the external forces of war and disease. His life crushed him, and in turn, he unintentionally caused pain to those he loved most.

I reflect on Ernest, of whom I was fond. His legacies are mixed, but in my heart, he has left warm memories.

Every life is complex. Each path runs through sunlight and shade. I believe Ernest will find his way, no matter how long it takes to come home to the spirit.

Author's Note: Rollo Blount

Rollo Blount is a fictitious character, but he is grounded in a real young man for whom Ernest felt a deep, formative affection. I have a photograph of this unknown figure—handsome, poised, dressed in tropical naval uniform around 1919.

When I showed the image to Inessa, she immediately perceived a special soul-connection between the two young men: easy companionship, cafe evenings, and the youthful bravado of experimenting with alcohol and drugs. For Ernest, the love he felt was intense and confusing, and he struggled to make sense of it for the rest of his life. Inessa also sensed that the real young man died in an accident in Ceylon, though the details remain hidden.

It is touching that this photograph was preserved among the family images, even though only Ernest would have known its meaning. It found its way to me in the suitcase and became the germ of the story thread in this chapter: Ernest's longing for a male soul-love, which echoes his deep grief at the loss of his elder brother, Eric.

In the afterlife section for this chapter, I suggest that it is the soul-memory of Rollo that softens Ernest's fear and offers the 'golden thread' that leads him towards healing. This is, like Rollo himself, a fictional device—but I believe it conveys something emotionally and spiritually truthful from Ernest's perspective. Rollo represented openness, warmth, and possibility: qualities that helped Ernest access a more honest emotional life.

This is the only point in the book's afterlife work where I have used such a construction. I chose it because, during our visit, Ernest's shift from fear to trust was unusually swift. It was almost as if he had been listening from within his bubble, pondering our perceptions of the young man in the photograph, and then found courage to step forward.

When Ernest walked out of the bubble, he walked into a new phase of his development. I like to think that Rollo had a hand in that.

Turning the Page

Beatrice and Ernest's marriage was karmically significant but emotionally unfulfilling. Though they entered it with love and hope, each expecting life to work itself out, they found themselves travelling parallel paths, never quite managing to connect. Ernest's inner conflicts, largely invisible to others, caused behaviour that deeply wounded Beatrice. In turn, Beatrice's quiet suffering only reinforced Ernest's sense of failure. Neither had the tools to meet the other's needs.

Yet, despite their difficulties, they remained together, and were devoted to their daughter, Penny. As they grew older, the harsh experiences they endured seemed to refine them. They never found harmony in life, but, as we've seen, they were able—once beyond the threshold of death—to begin the work of self-reflection and spiritual growth.

Penny inherited the imprint of her parents' troubled relationship. Her self-confidence was impacted and her own fulfilment was uneven. She and her husband discovered Rudolf Steiner's Spiritual Science, and its insights fed into the next generation, at the same time nourishing deep needs within Penny's own soul. But after her marriage ended, Penny's emotional life dimmed. She remained gentle and loving at heart but her mental wellbeing declined in later years.

Beatrice and Ernest's limitations were not born in a vacuum. Their patterns—their strengths and blind spots—were shaped by their parents, whose stories we will encounter soon. These older generations passed on temperaments and tendencies that ran like seams through the family line. Much that unfolded in Beatrice and Ernest's marriage echoes the unresolved dramas of Arthur and Lily, Emmie and Thomas.

Children often either repeat or reject their parents' patterns— sometimes both. Beatrice and Ernest sought to avoid their parents' mistakes by marrying for love, by trusting their own heart-based choices. They dreamed of a modern union, free of the compromises they had witnessed, one that was nourishing and rewarding to both partners. But neither could fully escape the shadows of their upbringing. Beatrice inherited Emmie's pattern of endurance. Ernest absorbed Arthur's moral rigidity and anxious social striving to 'do the right thing'.

Their story is, in the sense of our detective story, the 'scene of the crime'. It becomes a hinge-point in the family line—the karmic wound through which understanding first enters. From the suffering of Ernest and Beatrice, a new awareness flowed into the family stream—an awakening that enabled others to live differently. Like a pearl formed through pressure, their hardship also contained a light that waited quietly to be recognised. The moment of the slap—echoing through Penny's memory to her final days—marks this turning, the instant when a shaft of understanding first pierced the darkness.

And so, the time has come to meet someone who quietly broke the mould—Beatrice's younger sister, Marion. She observed, learned, and took a different path. In many ways, Marion lived ahead of her time. Later, we'll also meet Dulcie, Ernest's younger sister, another surprising moderniser. Both women came from the same start in life as their siblings. Yet something in them resisted the grooves of family repetition.

Why? Because we inherit more than the influence of our parents. Alongside the psychological legacy of upbringing lies a deeper inheritance: the spiritual-soul qualities we bring with us from our previous lives. These too shape us—and they are not bound by blood or convention. They are the real source of our individuality.

In the chapters to come, we'll go further still—back to the generations who shaped Arthur and Emmie themselves. We will see the deeper roots of certain patterns, both emotional and moral: how Arthur, for instance, blindly repeated his father's dominance over his wife, yet quietly rebelled against that same father's professional expectations. Arthur was a modern man in some ways, but not in his personal life. These older stories are the strata beneath Beatrice and Ernest's marriage—the buried but living legacies that echo across time.

Now, let us turn the page—and meet Marion.

6:

A PROMISE BEYOND

THE THRESHOLD

MARION GWYNDAF 1899–1977
My Great-Aunt, sister to Beatrice

In the waiting room before birth,
the soul stood before the Three Destinies.

"I shall spin for you duty, sacrifice, and challenge," said the First.
That sounds serious, thought the soul, anxiously.

"And I shall weave for you steadfastness, vigilance, and devotion,"
said the Second.
That sounds awfully sober, thought the soul, despondently.

Then the Third bent her kindly eye upon the soul.
"Poor dear," she said. "Given all that my sisters have bestowed, I
shall bequeath you a sense of humour."

Thank goodness, thought the soul—and with that, she was born,
carrying a bottomless bag of laughter and amusement
for all to share.

Astral Knitting, Lorenzo Ebrio (2019)

1906: A Dolls' Tea Party

Marion kicks the embroidered kneeler and stares for the hundredth time at the high windows of St James, where sunlight pours in. She wants to be back home, where she and her sister Beatrice are in the middle of planning a dolls' tea party. It will be complete with little cakes—baked by the girls with help from Lizzie the maid—and all the dolls will wear their best hats. Beatrice has written out tiny visiting cards, onto which Marion has carefully painted roses.

*Marion, 1922, at her sister's wedding in
Birmingham Botanical Gardens, Edgbaston.
Marion looks out at us, with sadness tinging her
pleasure at her sister's happy day.*

Emmie, Marion's mother, frowns at Marion's kicking legs, and Marion sighs and steels herself to be patient.

The vicar gives a long sermon today about being faithful to one's promises.

"If a man vows a vow to the Lord, or swears an oath to bind himself by a pledge, he shall not break his word. He shall do according to all that proceeds out of his mouth," recites the Reverend Hamish Campbell in his lilting accent, which makes everything sound a bit poetic.

He fixes the congregation with a stern gaze, and explains that oaths and promises are sacrosanct, especially those made to God. Marion wonders whether a promise she made to her mother counts as sacrosanct—the one about only having two desserts at Myrtle Turner's birthday party. Marion broke it, of course, and felt sick.

"Serves you right," said Beatrice. Older sisters can be sanctimonious sometimes.

That word, uttered in a cross voice by Daddy to Mummy one evening, was new to Marion.

It sent her sidling off, away from the sharp voices and compressed lips of her parents, to seek illumination in her Children's Dictionary.

Sanctimonious: a person who thinks they are better than others.

Ha! That could be Beatrice, Marion giggled to herself. A younger sister must always keep a sharp eye on the elder.

At last, the congregation are let out into the fresh air of Edgbaston, where the pretty church gardens bloom with heather and Canterbury Bells. After a polite word with the vicar, they stroll through the park before heading home to an excellent Sunday lunch of pork with apple sauce, then sponge pudding with custard—Marion's favourite. The girls are set up for an afternoon of quiet play, permitted by Mummy on Sundays, so long as they behave nicely in church. The family are not religious, but Emmie feels it is imperative to be seen meeting one's societal obligations. A Sunday service is one of those duties she observes.

The dolls' tea party is a great success. The small cakes are iced in pink, and are devoured by the guests (although only the human ones). Mummy, visiting the nursery, compliments the girls on their social graces, Lizzie takes a cake for later and puts it in her apron pocket, and even Daddy eats a Garibaldi. *What a wonderful afternoon,* thinks Marion happily, though a small part of her is still chewing at the question of promises. Something about the vicar's message—its weight, its insistence—lingers within her, like the recognition of an old tune.

1926: The Flying Pustule

Marion shrieks in horror, dropping her corselet on the floor. Her mother, Emmie, comes running. "Oh Mother, what is it, what is it?"

moans Marion, pointing fearfully to a large pink shining pustule on her stomach. Emmie bends down to take a closer look. It appears to be… can it be… she touches it with a delicate finger and without warning it shoots free of Marion's body, veers sideways to ricochet off the dressing table, and drops onto the carpet. They both scream.

It is a gleaming pink glass bead.

Afterwards, Marion dines out on the story. "My dears, you should have seen our faces," she chortles. "I thought I'd acquired some awful disease, but Mother knew better."

Earlier that day, Marion is sauntering across the public hall of Lloyds Bank, where she works. She's wearing her new dusky-pink day dress. At her neck swings a chic necklace of glass beads. She's feeling very à la mode. Her pen and marvellous new 'spiral-bound' shorthand pad—an English invention!—are clasped in her hand, and she's on her way to a board meeting.

"Morning, my beauty," calls the cheeky young bank clerk, Ned Beddows, and he wiggles his fingers at her through the counter glass.

Marion swings around to smile, and—oh no! Her beads catch on the clever spiral-bound pad. Marion yanks, in irritation. The weak necklace string snaps and the heavy glass beads cascade to the floor. Chaos ensues as a crowd of clerks rushes to help repatriate the beads to their owner. Somehow, in the melée, one bead sneaks down Marion's blouse and worms its way into her corselet where the pressure from that garment presses the bead into her stomach. She has an irritation there all afternoon, and worries she's got a flea bite from a visit to the flicks the night before. But no, it is the flying pustule, as she now dubs it.

Laughter all round greets this tale. Marion is famed for her stories, told against herself, and with great good humour. She is the family's comedienne.

At twenty-six years of age, Marion's an independent, professional girl. She's a secretary at Lloyds Bank in Birmingham. She's popular, efficient, pretty, and funny. Her shorthand is excellent, her typing speed is high. Her manager thinks she'll go far—if she doesn't get married. He regularly loses his freshly trained typists to marriage. It can be rather trying.

But Marion shows no signs of planning a wedding. She's focused absolutely on her career, living at home with her parents, and saving, one day, to purchase a little house. She's had chances at romance— boys like her. She's a flapper, flirtatious and glamorous, with a wardrobe of fashionable dresses and a flair for all the latest dance steps. But somehow, none of the young men are fooled. Beneath her polish, they sense a different girl—serious, observant, and quietly distant from romance. This inner girl doesn't feel passion will be her destiny, nor marriage to be her soul's desire.

At her sister Beatrice's wedding, Marion had felt the grip of sadness and envy inside herself. *Why should it not, one day, be my turn?* she'd wondered, as she held tightly to her bouquet of flowers and concentrated on walking elegantly in her high heeled shoes.

She's watched Beatrice's married life since then, comparing it to her own. What would her life be like if she met a handsome suitor and took him as her husband? Lately, something in her instinctively retreats from the thought of the closeness, the lack of freedom, the intimacy. It is as if an oddly potent shadow is cast by the word 'marriage'. Where is this shadow from? She is not sure; yet there it is, casting doubt on any romantic speculations.

As well, to Marion the physical aspect of marriage is a rather uninteresting subject, amounting to little more than her non-existent curiosity about what's under the bonnet of a car. While she's an engaging and playful girl, she never lets anything get out of hand with the boys. A flapper she might be, but party girls can also draw their own boundaries if they're sensible.

1936: A House of Her Own

Marion signs on the dotted line. The house is hers! A new little semi, just a mile from Beatrice and Ernest. It's perfect—a long garden plot, a sunny lounge with French windows, and a pleasant kitchen overlooking the garden.

Her promotion to personal assistant made this possible. Two months ago, Mr Pinkerton had called her into his office. She'd sat down, braced for some sort of reprimand, and then been stunned by his offer.

"We've been watching your progress, Miss Gwyndaf," he said, adjusting his glasses. "Your skills are excellent. We'd like to offer you the position of PA to the Deputy Manager."

Goodness me!

With only the briefest of pauses, Marion had replied, "Yes, please," her cheeks glowing. She's not personally ambitious, but she believes in doing her best. Challenges are there to be met, and Marion is happiest when she rises to them.

Now she stands in her garden, surveying the bare plot with the excitement of a chef assessing a pile of promising ingredients. She already has plans: two apple trees and two cherry trees for the lawn, trellises for climbing roses, and borders filled with colour and fragrance. She plants something for each family member—orange nasturtiums for Penny, a white clematis for Beatrice.

"And this is for you, Father," she says, patting the soil around a magnolia sapling. Thomas Gwyndaf is not fond of flowers, yet Marion feels all souls need their beauty and comfort.

It soothes her, this quiet act of honouring. Of keeping everyone close, without needing to explain it.

She adds in a bay tree for her friend Dulcie. Dulcie Mallory, Ernest's younger sister, is something like a bay plant in Marion's eyes— unshowy, tender, yet precious and with an essence all her own.

Dulcie is unmarried, like herself, and a great asset to Marion's single-girl life. Ever since Dulcie had that disappointing relationship with 'the rotter Charles', as Marion terms him—the boy Dulcie had met at Ernest's wedding—the two women have got on like a house on fire. They gallivant off on outings and meet regularly for tête-à-têtes over coffee. Why, they've had outrageously fun times together, and now there's the added mischievousness of Dulcie's new friend Vera to spice up the menu in the unmarried girls' club.

In Marion's new garden, the breeze stirs the leaves, carrying a faint scent of blossom. For just a moment, she feels a subtle warmth at her back, and a sensation like a hand brushing her shoulder. She glances behind her—no one. A small laugh escapes her.

"Silly me," she murmurs, brushing her hands on her skirt. "There's my angel passing by again, as Mother would say."

Although Marion believes in no such things.

Right to left: Beatrice, Penny, Marion. Location unknown. c. 1937.

On Saturday mornings, Marion often walks over to Beatrice's house to cook lunch, and in the afternoons sometimes she babysits. Together, she and Penny make jam tarts and rock cakes. Penny begs Marion to teach her the Charleston again, and they collapse into laughter at the odd leg movements. Family is central to Marion. Career might come first on paper, but it's the moments with her loved ones that fill her heart with pleasure.

When Dulcie and Vera come to tea, she leads them proudly around the garden. "Do look at the roses," she says, or: "You must see how the asters are blooming!"

But when they admire her work, she demurs, saying modestly, "Oh no, it's nothing now. If only you'd come last week, it was much better then…"

Marion is a creator of beauty, like her sister Beatrice. The sisters share this gift, as well as the graceful hospitality that offers it freely to others. They are alike in that way—though Marion has always been the more outgoing of the two girls.

With her new independence under development, Marion sets her face to the single life with philosophical contentment.

1938: New Faces

The year 1938 brings plenty of interest.

Hardly has it begun when Dulcie meets a young man—a plumber. At first, Marion thinks Jimmy Ruggles is a Jack-the-lad, on the make for what he can get. But very soon she reassesses this pleasant man. Yes, perhaps he's keen to better himself and sees Dulcie as a means for that, but he also shows every sign of being kind and attentive. And Dulcie herself has more than one agenda—escape being high on her list of hopes. Marion sympathises with Dulcie's desire to gain independence from the parental household, and Jimmy could perhaps be her ticket to freedom.

On top of that, there's the naughty Irene, who appeared on the scene last year and is now a regular and rather exciting presence in the social calendar.

Irene is Vera's friend—and clearly more than a friend. A variety hall entertainer turned beauty consultant, Irene is charismatic. Marion watches the two women and sees in them an interesting alternative to conventional life. This couple are both vulnerable—due to societal prejudices—and extraordinary—because they boldly follow their hearts. Irene herself is every inch a card, and Marion likes her for it.

Her heart still aches for the tragedy that overtook poor Ernest two years ago, measles robbing him of most of his hearing. Shocking, that something like that could happen out of the blue. Marion helped Beatrice during the worst of it by having Penny to stay at her house. It was precious, those days of being an honorary mother, but oh, how Marion wished that the reason had been a happier one. While she feasted on the pleasure of her relationship with her niece, Beatrice nursed Ernest diligently, and later suffered his pain vicariously as he struggled to come to terms with his impairment.

Everyone admires the way Ernest has pulled through the worst of it, and this year he's begun to step back into his old life with a renewed vigour. *A brave man*, thinks Marion, *even though a difficult one*. She knows there are tensions in the marriage. She's ever aware of her supporting role—sister, aunt, protector. Her own prospects of marriage shine more and more dimly as time goes by, and the odd shadow that flickers over her thoughts whenever she considers relationships—well, that shadow grows longer with each passing year.

She's begun to understand its origins, too. She only has to look at the chilly interactions between her own parents, and the autocratic landscape that is the world of Ernest's parents—Arthur and Lily—to see that the single life has advantages. Perhaps, reflects Marion, Irene and Vera are, in their own quiet way, the most successful couple she has met so far.

1940–1945: The Strangest Tale

"An ARP Ambulance Driver!" Dulcie gasps, when Marion tells her the news. "Isn't that terribly dangerous?"

"Oh, it's dangerous all right," exclaims Marion, flicking ash deftly from her cigarette into the cafe ashtray, "but what a dash we girls can cut in those natty little uniforms and jaunty hats! And working in the ARP gives a girl contacts, my dear—contacts for all sorts of desirable goods!" She winks, opening her handbag and showing Dulcie a fat pack of butter and some juicy-looking sausages.

"Oh, Marion, you wicked girl, you're a black marketeer!" cries Dulcie in mock-dismay, and Marion chuckles delightedly.

"I know, so wayward. Marvellous, isn't it? Just say the word, Dulcie, and knicker elastic shall be yours!"

In joining the Civil Defence Ambulance Service—one of the ARP divisions tasked with first aid and evacuation—Marion is, indeed, attracted to the public's perception of its glamour. But inside, she feels a serious conviction that she must undertake this war work, and a worry that she may not be brave enough to face its attendant danger.

The snazzy uniform of an ARP driver that tempts Marion towards volunteering—from a government poster appeal.
Unknown (artist), ARP (Air Raid Precautions) (publisher/sponsor),
Charles and Read Ltd (printer), Her Majesty's Stationery Office (publisher/sponsor).
Public domain, via Wikimedia Commons.

The training is gruelling—wounds, collapse risks, crushed bodies, ambulance repairs on the fly. A far cry from shorthand and typing, but Marion puts her best foot forward.

One evening, before dusk, Marion is in the depot yard polishing the windscreen of the ambulance. Suddenly the field telephone crackles with a warning, given in clipped tones:

"Enemy aircraft have crossed the coast. Midlands sectors are advised to expect activity."

That means Birmingham. It always means Birmingham.

As soon as darkness settles over the city, the air raid sirens begin wailing. On and on they scream, and then the bombs start falling.

"Incendiary raid on a row of back-to-backs in Saltley, girls—survivors reported—let's go!" yells Muriel, the supervisor. Marion and crew barrel into the ambulance and they set off.

The scene is one of absolute chaos as they approach the area of bombing. The night air is thick with smoke and the sharp stench of explosives catches in the throat. The bombs whistle and boom, and fire gobbles the houses like a ravenous dragon. Somewhere, a baby screams, dogs bark, and sirens in far-off districts continue to wail their warning, distant and haunting.

Incendiaries are triggering—delayed fuses igniting the small magnesium and thermite bombs. They aren't meant to destroy buildings by direct hit, but to cause fires, pure and simple—fires that rip through crowded city streets, taking lives with them.

Rubble blocks Marion from driving any closer, so she leaps out with the other crew members, and they hurry forward to crouch low behind a partially collapsed wall. From here they assess the situation.

It looks concerning. Flames lick around the terraced houses. Smoke pours from the glassless windows, some of the roofs are ablaze. A warden is dragging a fire hose towards the building. Another is frantically shovelling sand onto an unexploded incendiary bomb lodged in a cellar grille. Sparks are flying. The distant sirens fade, leaving only the roar of explosions and collapsing walls.

A shout goes up—"Two kiddies and their gran in Number 17! Front room. We need stretchers!"

Without waiting, Marion grabs a stretcher. The others—Edna, Betty, Muriel—are right behind her. The ARP women's arms are up to shield their faces, sleeves already singed and filthy. Noses are filled with dust and soot, eyes sting from the heat, breath comes in short pants, scorching air sears the lungs. Hell and bedlam, fire and brimstone. Into the building they plunge, heading for the front room.

It's pitch dark, except for the glow of firelight through cracks. There in a heap on the floor is an elderly woman with her arms around two children. She's unconscious. One boy cradles a trembling puppy—fur streaked with ash, its eyes huge and unblinking. The floor creaks ominously underfoot. The smell of burning tar paper and scorched clothing is nauseating, but the three survivors are essentially unharmed.

Marion kneels, talking steadily all the while—calm, quiet, practical. She doesn't let her voice shake. She hears herself say things like "It's all right, my dearies, no need to worry. We're here to get you out. Soon be safe, now."

The ARP women carefully lift the unconscious woman onto the stretcher. "Go!" cries Muriel, as Marion and Edna, choking and coughing, lift the still figure. Muriel scoops up the little boy and puppy. Betty lifts the other child. Now they're all stumbling out.

A fresh explosion shakes the ground and there's a whump as masonry falls just nearby. Dust rains from the ceiling. Someone swears. Then they're out, and hurrying towards the ambulance. Behind them, No. 17 catches fire, and the roof starts to fall in.

Back at the ambulance, the crew tends to the survivors. Marion's hands have started to tremble, and she's craving a cup of tea.

"Everyone all right here?" asks the warden, running over. "Can I get you ladies anything?"

Marion regards him sardonically. "I'll have a nice gin and tonic, please," she says, and grins. It breaks the tension, and they all laugh.

"I must say," Marion confides mournfully to Betty later, "when I joined up for the sake of the uniform, I didn't realise it would get ruined quite so regularly!"

"Oh Marion, you are absurd," chuckles Betty, and pokes Marion in the ribs.

Not all nights are as bad as that.

One night in 1941, Marion is called to drive a bombing raid survivor to hospital. When she picks him up, he's carrying a large object draped in a blanket. "What on earth is that?" asks Marion, intrigued.

The man lifts the blanket, and there, in the cage, is a grey parrot, a cockatiel, and two budgerigars. "I rescue them from bombed out 'ouses, Miss," he explains. "Birds are me life. I've always kept 'em, and I care what 'appens to 'em."

Marion is touched to her core. *This man risks his life regularly for these birds*, she thinks. How much there is to admire about people, in these awful times.

But the story that Marion loves the best, the one she tells to everyone, is the rescue of the red-haired man.

One grimy dawn, in the aftermath of a bombing raid, Marion is cautiously combing shattered buildings for the injured. Poking her head carefully into a gaping doorway, she spies, partially buried under rubble, a head of bright red hair lying terribly still in the dark interior. She gasps.

"Quick, come quick," she yells. "Victim here, partially buried."

Edna and Betty come running. Marion is already picking her way through the debris. She nears the man and reaches towards his head, ready to check for signs of life. Her hand brushes the head of hair and—it moves! Across the floor it races. "Oh girls, catch it!" cries Marion, as the guinea pig makes its dash for freedom. Edna grabs, Betty leaps, and they have it! It's a perfect rescue.

The story makes the local paper and there's a picture of the three girls holding up the guinea pig, with the headline: "Daring rescue! Fur flies as our brave girls save a life!"

The guinea pig is later claimed by a little boy called Benny, after it has spent two days being spoiled by the ambulance crew at the depot.

Marion and Dulcie laugh as they sit in The Parade Tea Rooms in Sutton Coldfield. "Dulcie, you would not believe the things I see!" exclaims Marion. The stuffy air of the restaurant is thick with the smells of toasted 'Government Cheddar', scorched toast, and that unmistakable tang of Camp coffee essence.

"How's your treacle tart?" asks Dulcie, eyeing her own plate of bloater paste sandwiches.

"Quite nice really," says Marion. "Anyway, It's the closest thing to indulgence you can get in these places!" The noise of cutlery clatters around them, cups and saucers chink. Marion pulls her chair closer to the table.

"But I want to tell you something, Dulcie. It's the strangest tale. Really quite spooky. And it's about the raid that killed Jimmy's mother."

Dulcie sits up straight. "Oh my goodness. Well—tell me," she says.

Marion had been posted to Kingstanding Ambulance Depot one night, because they were very short-staffed. As the crew sat drinking tea, alert for an air raid warning, they fell to talking. The subject turned to the terrible raid on the Carlton Cinema back in October 1940.

"So much has happened since then," Marion yawned, stirring sugar into her tea. "We were all so horrified by it, weren't we? Little did we know what else was to come!"

A tired-looking woman called Gladys cleared her throat. "I was there, you know," she said quietly. The others became still. Heads turned, cups of tea were placed carefully on the table.

"I was on duty that night," began Gladys. "After the raid had finished, an ambulance crew went in to rescue the injured and dead. I was working on another street, but towards the end of my shift, I went to the cinema to see if there was anyone left who needed help. What I saw was inexplicable. There were people there, lots of people, sitting in rows in the cinema seats. They were completely still. Their eyes were open. They were looking up at the cinema screen, but it was shattered and torn. Those eyes never blinked." Gladys swallowed and continued.

"I thought to myself, all indignant-like: *Who's left these people here? Why aren't they at the hospital?* And I went up to them, to speak to them. But, when I got closer, I realised they were dead. All dead, just sitting and staring at the screen." Gladys shivered. "I can't understand it. It made my blood run cold, I can tell you."

The crew looked at one another. It sounded wrong, ghostly, like a vision from another sphere of existence.

"Sometimes we see things we can't explain," said another woman, pressing Gladys's hand. "We'll probably never know the truth of it, but it sounds like something you'd be best off forgetting."

In the cafe, Dulcie regards Marion with questioning eyes. "My word, that's extraordinary! Do you think what Gladys saw was real, or could she have imagined it?" she asks.

"I don't know, Dulcie," replies Marion, thoughtfully. "It's just the oddest story. I think I'd faint if it happened to me!"

"Should I tell Jimmy, do you think?" wonders Dulcie.

"It's up to you, Dulcie, but it's not like either of you can do anything. I just thought it was a strange coincidence, to hear about that night and poor Polly Ruggles' air raid."

"Mmm," agrees Dulcie. In the end, she doesn't tell Jimmy when she writes to him, but the strangeness of the tale stays with her for many years.

Of course, the most marvellous event of the war, as far as Marion is concerned, is the marriage of Dulcie to Jimmy in July 1941. How Jimmy's fortunes had changed within the family after that disaster of the leaking hot-water cylinder at the Mallory home in Erdington! Summoned to this opportunistic emergency by the enterprising Dulcie, Jimmy had quickly proved his worth as a plumber. In the critical eyes of Arthur Mallory, the mishap marked a turning point in Jimmy's standing as Dulcie's beau—and from there, the rest was history. Marion, watching from the sidelines, saw in their rather unlikely match the subtle workings of fate and... something else?

Because sometimes, Marion wonders whether Dulcie might not have punctured the walls of the hot-water cylinder herself, just to seal the deal on her future marriage.

1946: The Decision

Five years have passed since Marion's father, Thomas, died. His loss left her mother, Emmie, unanchored. After much soul-searching, Marion makes a life-changing decision: she invites Emmie to move into her house. The arrangement is bittersweet. Emmie's gratitude is immediate and heartfelt, but for Marion, who values her independence, it comes at a cost.

For the first time in her life, Marion has met someone who makes her truly happy. Leslie is twelve years her senior, a manager of accounts at Barclays Bank, and their bond is rooted in shared values and professional understanding. What begins as a warm companionship evolves into a deep soul friendship for Marion. For Leslie, however, it's more. When Emmie moves in, the dynamic shifts. Marion's sense of duty eclipses her personal hopes, and the tender wings of this late-blooming love are clipped. Leslie, ever the gentleman, never voices his disappointment. Yet his affection for Marion endures, unfulfilled, until his death.

Today is a sunny day in 1946, and the family has gathered for a special outing. Petrol is still rationed, but Ernest has secured a small allowance through his firm, Graham James Engineering, under *Special Circumstances*, to collect Penny from boarding school for the summer holidays. Marion waits at the base of the grand front steps of Linden College, soaking up the cheerful bustle of students. She's already anticipating the treat ahead: a lunch stop in Llandudno to indulge Penny's love of sausages and mash at the George Hotel.

The sight of Penny bounding down the stairs brings joy to Marion's heart. Her niece's excitement is infectious, and Marion gathers her into a warm, perfect auntie-hug.

On the car journey, Penny chatters on about her school life, which Marion is relieved to see suits her so well. Penny is a cricket umpire now, no less, and has won a medal for her ballroom dancing. "Well done darling," says Marion, meaning it from her heart. Marion had supported Beatrice's determined campaign to send Penny to this Welsh boarding school, agreeing that it was the best way to shield the child from the stormy atmosphere at home. It has been a good decision.

Beatrice and Ernest's marriage is strained and thin. Marion suspects the situation is unlikely to improve. She no longer envies her sister's married life. Instead, she offers quiet support where she can, knowing full well that Ernest's unpredictable temper and Beatrice's stoic endurance are an unbreakable stalemate.

As the car speeds towards Llandudno, Marion reflects on her own choices. She's grateful on the whole to have sidestepped the risks of marriage. Her career has become her anchor, her source of pride. Next month, she'll move into her very own office as personal assistant to the managing director of the bank.

*Clockwise from top: Ernest, Marion, Beatrice.
Sutton Coldfield, Birmingham c. 1949.
An interesting composition with the two sisters
creating a wall behind which Ernest is perched,
small and distant.*

"I'll have my own room!" she enthuses to Beatrice and Ella one evening. "I think I'll be the very first female PA to achieve it in Birmingham!"

They listen, impressed but bemused. Marion's world of offices and promotions is so alien to them that they can scarcely imagine it. And yet, as Marion looks at what she's achieved, and her own bright future, she feels a quiet satisfaction for a life well-lived, even if the underlying sacrifices create a small shadow in the sunlight.

1952: Looking Back

Sitting at her desk in her tranquil semi, Marion sighs deeply and pulls another sheet of paper from the drawer. Ernest's poetry, for all its brilliance, is a chore. Each draft brings another tweak, another rework. "You'll have to type the whole thing again," Ernest is fond of saying. The constant revisions test Marion's patience. As she types the final word, Emmie appears with a cup of tea and a biscuit as a gesture of support. Marion smiles gratefully, removes the top copy from the typewriter, and checks the twin carbons beneath. Neat, clean, perfect. Surely *this* draft will satisfy Ernest?

Later, at a coffee morning with her girlfriends, Marion rolls her eyes. "If I've typed his verses once I've typed them twenty times. My typewriter will catch fire one day!" she exclaims, drawing laughter from the table. Her stories about Ernest always entertain. Her friends laugh, but Marion knows there's a starker reality behind her tales.

That terrible incident with the slap is burned into Marion's memory, even though it happened a decade ago. While it was the first of such incidents, she suspects it has not been the last.

She was furious with Ernest that day in 1942. After the slap, and his rapid exit, she pursued him at speed, running out onto the gravel driveway where she grabbed his shoulder.

"Don't you know *what you've done*?" she shouted, her voice shaking with rage. "You've violated a *sacred oath* in hitting your wife. You're supposed to protect and cherish her, not—this!"

At first her words seemed to find their mark. Ernest looked thoughtful, then furtive, and finally dismissive. "What business is it of yours?" he snapped, slouching off with his hands in his pockets. Marion looked after him.

What business is it of mine, indeed? she wondered, unsure of her ground in this domestic dispute.

Back in the house, she discovered Beatrice with her tea party guests fluttering around her, abandoned teacups scattered forlornly across the occasional tables. Marion wished with all her heart to make things right, but it wasn't her conflict to resolve. Whatever bound Beatrice and Ernest together, it was beyond her understanding, and the responsibility lay with them to work it through. She could only hope it would lead somewhere better—for both of them. But the cost already seemed too high.

1958–1960: An Unconventional Woman

When Emmie passes away in October, Marion is at first a little unsettled by the new freedom she has. She looks around at her house, her life, her small society of friends, and thinks: *Well, I can do anything I like now.*

The question is though, what does she actually want to do?

She's due to retire soon, and spends some quiet weeks pondering how best to shape the years ahead. Leslie recommends walking—he's a stalwart of his local rambling society—and he makes Marion a cheerful gift: a thermos flask and a pink Tupperware sandwich box, all the rage that season. Marion laughs aloud, reminded of an escapade years ago with Dulcie and Vera, when the three of them took a mystery train excursion to a mud-filled destination. Dulcie had been the only sensible girl in their trio, turning up in sturdy shoes with hot tea and a packed lunch. She'd shared her provisions gallantly with her two empty-handed companions.

Taking Leslie's lead, Marion joins several local groups, including the Women's Institute and a gardening society, where she is quickly made treasurer. She begins staying with friends by the seaside, tries out new recipes, visits museums, and attends interesting local history talks. Her diary fills quickly, but her focus remains firmly on her family. She babysits for Penny's children, sees Leslie often, and takes pleasure in small, thoughtful routines.

It astonishes her, really—how happy she is, despite never doing any of the things she once assumed she would: marriage, children, domesticity. Perhaps she *is* a modern woman, after all. Unconventional. A woman who's quietly broken the mould.

1960: The Promise

Marion gazes at Beatrice's pale face, her throat tightening as she takes the frail hand extended towards her. Beatrice's voice is faint, but her request is clear. Marion steadies her own voice and promises, as asked, to watch over Penny after Beatrice is gone.

"But it mightn't be for years yet," Marion adds, her tone encouraging.

Beatrice smiles wanly, then closes her eyes. Unexpectedly, she murmurs: "Mother is here." So quietly that Marion thinks she's imagined it. There's a slight movement of air in the room, warm and soft, and then it passes. As once before in her life, Marion glances over her shoulder to find there is nothing there, yet the merest hint of her mother's perfume hangs in the air like an almost forgotten memory.

For a moment, Marion stays still, her hand still clasping Beatrice's, her thoughts drifting back to another promise, made long ago.

It is winter 1912, and she and Beatrice are still girls, cocooned in the imaginative worlds of their favourite books. Beatrice devours *Anne of Green Gables* five times, utterly captivated by Anne Shirley's tender, spirited nature. Marion, meanwhile, is immersed in *Little Women*. She has lost her heart to the passionate and fiercely independent Jo March, who strides through the book with a true and creative heart while honouring family loyalty above all.

"I want to be like her," Marion confides to Beatrice one afternoon. "Except I'd have to stop short of selling my hair to support Mother." The two of them burst into giggles, their breath fogging the frosty glass of the window beside them.

Suddenly, Beatrice's eyes light up with a romantic idea. "Marion," she says, leaning closer, "let's swear an oath of love and devotion to each other, like Anne and Diana in my book. It would be so special."

Marion catches the spark in her sister's notion and feels a kindling in her own heart. "It's like the promise the March sisters make to one another," she says, eagerly. "A vow to always stand by each other, no matter what."

*Author's impression of Marion and Beatrice
discussing their promise.
Media: Acrylic, crayon, chalks.*

The idea takes hold; they cannot resist. Throwing coats over their dresses, they run out into the crunching snow of the garden, to the back of the lawn where stands the spare, ancient oak tree. Its bare limbs twist into the sky, its presence lending solemnity to their actions.

Standing beneath its boughs, they clasp hands as their breath rises in clouds around them. Together they recite the vow: "I will never leave you alone. I solemnly vow to love and support you for my whole life, so help me God."

It is momentous. For a minute, they stand in silence, the weight of their words sinking into the stillness. Marion feels the promise settle within her, and Beatrice, too, seems struck by the magnitude of what they have said. But as they begin to shiver in the biting wind, the solemnity gives way to laughter, and they run back inside to the cosy warmth of the living room. The oath is done. It cannot be undone. They are bound together forever.

Over time, though, the memory slides away from Beatrice as she is swept forward into the whirlwind of growing up. For Marion, however, the promise sinks deep into her soul, and takes up residence there in a little promise-shaped space that it finds. *You have promised never to leave Beatrice alone,* it whispers. And Marion hears it—clearly, unmistakably—as if the vow lives in the very air around her.

1977: The Fall

When Beatrice dies, Marion extends her caring attention towards Ernest, and watches faithfully over Penny's life. Jimmy and Dulcie move to the Cotswolds, leaving a gap in the family network, so Marion secures for Ernest a housekeeper, who orders his widower's life with a patient and motherly hand.

Family visits to Marion's home are frequent, and her scrumptious teas are legendary. Sticky meringues, decadent chocolate cake, and other treats line her table. Her failed attempts, she jokes, are served to the wild birds. "They're too heavy to fly!" she teases. But everyone knows her baking is superb.

Lately, however, Marion has felt uncharacteristically tired and light-headed. Occasionally, she senses an odd figure lingering at the edge of her vision. At night, she dreams vividly of her mother, Emmie, who always appears walking towards her, hand outstretched. "Where am I meant to go?" Marion asks, but her mother doesn't reply.

Marion loves her quiet retirement, filled with her garden, her friends, her cat, and most of all, her family.

One evening, she tucks herself into bed early, the cat curled by her side. She feels cosy and content, but as she drifts towards sleep, something startles her awake. She gasps—there's the figure she's been sensing, standing at the foot of her bed. Then she recognises her mother. Emmie's hair frames her face like a nimbus, her gaze tranquil and kind. Marion barely breathes as a voice speaks softly in her mind: *You are going to cross the threshold, Marion dear. Very soon, you'll come to be with me. I am here, loving and supporting you. Come when you're ready—I'll be waiting.* And then Emmie is gone.

Marion blinks at the empty space where her mother stood. Did she imagine it? No—her heart knows it was real. More than this, she recognises the truth of the message that has come to her.

Rising, she makes herself a cup of tea and sits at the living room table. She breathes in the familiar scent of wood polish. The pop of the gas fire mingles peacefully with the ticking of the grandfather clock. Emmie's flower paintings line the walls, their delicate blooms glowing in the lamplight. Around her, Marion feels the presence of her family in the cherished objects they've left behind: Beatrice's embroidered linens, her father's gleaming gateleg table, her grandmother Matilda's escritoire filled with Leslie's letters and Penny's childhood drawings.

She ponders what to do. *Should I go to the doctor? Tell someone? But no—there's nothing solid, after all…*

"But if it *is* my time, then I shall leave without fuss, and without fear," she says firmly to the cat, Smudgie, who purrs in front of the fire. She is Marion, an independent girl, brave to her core. *It's been a good life*, she thinks, stroking the pink blanket that once comforted Emmie. *And now, perhaps, it has been lived.*

The next morning, she begins quietly setting her affairs in order. A few busy days follow, but Marion soon retreats to her sanctuary—the garden. The August sun bathes the roses in golden light, their intoxicating perfume filling the air. She moves from plant to plant, caressing petals and leaves, savouring every detail. *This has been my perfect creation*, she muses, her heart swelling with love. *This, and my family. Perhaps I've been like Jo March after all.*

Three days later, a neighbour finds her dead on the kitchen floor. "A brain haemorrhage," the doctor explains to Penny. "She would have fallen unconscious immediately. She didn't suffer."

Marion's absence leaves a large gap in Penny's life. But Penny takes comfort in the knowledge that her beloved aunt continues to exist across the threshold. She carries Marion's love securely in her heart, hoping they will meet again one day. Until then, life goes on—infused with the buoyant memories Marion leaves behind, and something deeper still: a lingering devotion, like the scent of roses from the garden Marion so lovingly tended.

Afterlife Encounters
Marion: visited 2025

A Rare Soul

"I wasn't expecting this!" Inessa exclaims, her attention fixed on Marion's soul in the post-mortem realm. "She is a rare soul indeed!"

I had not been able to connect with Marion, which led me to think she might have already moved beyond the soul-realm into the higher spirit-realm. But this, Inessa discovers, is not the case. She finds that Marion remains in the soul-realm, though she is remarkably close to its edge, her essence already infused with the purity of the spiritual world.

"Interesting—tell me more!" I request.

With the meticulousness characteristic of her physicist background, Inessa delves deeper into this surprising encounter, seeking to understand what she is perceiving.

"She's in the soul-realm," Inessa clarifies. "After her death, she ascended with dramatic speed and reached almost to its outer boundary. She was knocking on the door of the spirit-realm within days of her passing. That is very unusual."

It is a phenomenon neither of us has encountered before. Normally, it takes a soul some time to process and absorb its life lessons— perhaps, on average, about a third of the time spent on earth, when measured from an earthly perspective. Marion's journey, however, has been unusually swift and smooth, as if her soul carried no heavy burdens from her life. Yet I wonder what has held her here, just shy of the spiritual world?

Inessa begins to perceive an image of Marion's journey—a hot air balloon rising gracefully—until it encounters an unexpected barrier. This 'ceiling', Inessa explains, is an emotional force: a profound regret that anchors Marion in the soul-realm.

For the first time, Marion has seen what her earthly life lacked. She feels deeply the absence of tender, intimate relationships, and she grieves for the companionship she might have found in Leslie, or the love she could have experienced as a mother. The loneliness of her incarnation now presents itself as a sharp and sorrowful truth.

Yet this regret is tempered by a higher understanding. Marion's soul recognises the necessity of her choices: independence, selfless loyalty to family, and unwavering pursuit of virtue and duty. Her uncompromising view of love meant she sought a perfect partner and, finding none, chose a solitary path. It was a life lived in alignment with her destiny, though not without sacrifices.

Marion's purity of soul, which allowed her to ascend so rapidly, appears to be a hallmark of her past incarnations. Inessa senses that Marion's previous lives were deeply spiritual, and that these experiences shaped the unusual integrity and wholeness of her being.

Marion's developed spirituality, explains Inessa, is also evident in her androgynous inner nature—an integration of qualities that enabled her to thrive in the male-dominated world of banking long before such roles were common for women. Her graceful femininity belied an inner strength, rooted in her spiritual past.

Despite her lack of explicit spiritual beliefs in this most recent life, Marion carried an innate connection to the spiritual world. Inessa perceives that she sometimes received spiritual inklings and that, in her final weeks, she experienced a quiet vision of her mother foretelling her death.

Deep Layers

It is clear, however, that Marion's journey was not without complexity. Inessa observes a karmic thread from a distant incarnation, where Marion—then a father—had sworn an oath of loving loyalty to protect his daughter, a soul now recognised as Beatrice. Though this vow was fulfilled in that life, its deep imprint carried forward, shaping Marion's relationship with Beatrice in their most recent lives. This time around, they were sisters. The protective dynamic Marion had formerly felt as a father was therefore less vividly experienced but still subtly present, a quiet gesture linking two lives.

Inessa pauses as she senses a deeper layer to Marion's karmic connection with Beatrice.

"Yes, there is something more here," she says.

What she perceives is a powerful undercurrent—an unforeseen complication—that sharpened Marion's bond to her sister, even though the original vow of protection from their previous incarnation had already been met. That complicating factor was Ernest.

Ernest's karmic history inclined him towards exerting his will over those around him, a tendency that shaped his relationship with Beatrice. When Beatrice chose him as her partner, her innate longing for creative self-expression came into conflict with Ernest's need for dominance. His inner struggles cast a shadow over their marriage, impacting Beatrice's physical and spiritual well-being. These challenges drew Marion into a deeper bond with her sister, compelling Marion to assume the role of protector once again—a choice that came at a cost.

Marion's soul had not foreseen the extent of this burden in her current incarnation. Yet, with unwavering loyalty, she embraced it, setting aside her own concerns to support Beatrice in ways neither of them had expected.

Even after both had passed away, Marion stayed beside her sister, remaining steadfast while Beatrice lingered in her cocoon. Only after Beatrice's release could Marion begin to shed the weight of these karmic ties and move forward, approaching the spirit-realm. At last, the long-ago vow beneath the ancient oak was fulfilled.

"Marion's moving now," Inessa notes, "but very slowly. The release is gradual, aided by the recent work to free Beatrice. As Beatrice awakens, the path opens for Marion to continue her ascent."

*Author's impression of Marion and Beatrice
in the soul world. Once Beatrice is freed,
Marion reaches towards her to offer help.
Media: Acrylic paint, crayon, chalks.*

The Family Gathering

Marion is now poised at the threshold of the spirit-realm. Inessa suggests connecting her consciously to the souls of Beatrice and Penny, both currently in the soul-realm.

We use a photograph showing a moment when Marion, Beatrice, and Penny sat together in a sunlit garden. We invite their souls to gather around this image, drawing on the shared memory to foster their connection.

Penny arrives swiftly, with her guiding angel accompanying her. Beatrice and Marion approach more hesitantly, their angels helping them forwards. The reunion is tinged with initial confusion—why, what and who questions arising in the souls of all three women—but it takes just a short period for recognition to dawn, and a tentative connection to form.

"This will take more time," Inessa observes, "but the groundwork is there. They will work together on their soul-ties, so we can leave them in the garden, with their angelic helpers."

As for Marion's future, Inessa foresees a path of spiritual study and renewal. Her next incarnation will awaken the dormant spirituality within, drawing Marion towards aesthetic wholesomeness and a life of quiet dedication in the cool landscapes of Scandinavia. This new life will carry the echoes of Marion's loyalty, devotion, and clarity, though it may also be tinged with a poignant loneliness.

Reflecting on Marion's story, I am struck by the depth and beauty of her soul. Her outward cheer and humour masked a being of profound selflessness and spiritual potential. Marion's journey reminds me of the hidden greatness in lives lived with quiet and often solitary fortitude, and of the eternal growth that awaits every soul.

Turning the Page

Marion's life ends with grace, courage, and integrity. She leaves behind no children of her own, yet her legacy is woven through the lives of those she supported and loved—especially those of her sister Beatrice, and her niece Penny. Hers was a soul that chose service over self, and loyalty over ease.

In life she read the signs of her inheritance—the imprint of a troubled parental marriage—and understood that the surest way to avoid repeating it was to live differently.

To break the mould and to help those around her, she would have to be the unconventional woman.

Her gift of giving completely to others lifted her life out of the ordinary and onto another plane, one of sacrificial love, but her spirited and comedic personality ensured she was very far from presenting herself as a saint.

Marion's story feels unusually light in its telling, and it stands in poignant contrast to the forces that shaped her brother-in-law, Ernest.

To understand the torments in Ernest's soul, we must now look back—further back—into a couple who placed appearances, ambition, and compliance above happiness and personal fulfilment. It is here that we find a source of the pattern which dominated Ernest's life—here in the stories of Arthur and Lily.

We will find that Arthur was a man shaped adversely by his father's will. In marrying Lily, he chose a woman of deeply loving character who might have been able to provide some balance for him. But Lily's ability to temper Arthur's faults was diminished by a world where a woman's obedience and a woman's silence were not only expected, but also mistaken for virtues.

7:

AUTHORITY AND SURRENDER

ARTHUR MALLORY 1868–1959 & LILY PLUM 1870–1943
My Great-Grandparents,
parents to Eric, Ernest, and Dulcie

"If one revels in a challenge,
simply choose an unsuitable man and marry him."

Lucy Almond to Jemima Porter, in *The Chiming Hour,*
Lorenzo Ebrio (2016)

Arthur c. 1893, aged about twenty-five
—around the time he married Lily.

Lily c. 1893: a lively, stylish girl.

1891: Lily: Songs of the Music Halls

Travers Cooper, sitting at the grand piano, rattles out the tune of *The Man Who Broke the Bank at Monte Carlo.* His friends cluster around him, singing along. It's a favourite of their set, and as the tune winds into the chorus, the young ladies and gentlemen grab one another and gallop up and down the large drawing room carpet.

As I walk along the Bois de Boulogne with an independent air,

they sing, the room echoing with their laughter. By the time they reach the punchline—

...the man who broke the bank at Monte Ca-a-a-r-lo—

they are collapsing onto the sofas, tears rolling down their cheeks. The parents of the youngsters look on indulgently, smiling at the antics of their offspring.

Lily loves this sort of evening: music, company, laughter. What could be more delightful? As she regains her breath, she folds her hands in her lap and watches Connie Wenlock launch into: *The Boy I Love Is Up in the Gallery* with extravagant eye-rolls and theatrical flourishes. Travers is showing off again, adding fancy chords and runs up and down the piano. Meanwhile her best friend Monica Fitzwarren is whispering with a young man she doesn't recognise.

She glances across at the stranger. He's neat, dapper, with a handsome moustache and twinkling eyes. He has a way of sticking his hands in his pockets and rocking to and fro on his heels. *A little bit self-satisfied*, thinks Lily, but she is intrigued because Monica and he are clearly talking about her. Monica steps over to where Lily is sitting, young man in tow.

"This is my neighbour, Mr Arthur Mallory," explains Monica, indicating the beaming young man, who bows over Lily's hand. "And this is Miss Lily Plum," adds Monica, smiling at Lily.

Arthur compliments Lily on her pretty voice. "You sing beautifully, and do you also play the piano, Miss Plum?" enquires Arthur. He has no ear for music but he considers it most desirable that young ladies can shine their talents within the local cultural scene.

"Oh yes, Mr Mallory," exclaims Lily, brightening. "Mostly salon pieces, you know—Chaminade, a little Sullivan. I've been learning *The Skaters' Waltz*."

Arthur nods. "I like a waltz myself, Miss Plum. And I fancy that you, too, are light on your feet, judging by your charming performance to the music hall song just now?"

Lily laughs and dimples. She leads the way to a sofa and pats the seat next to her. She and Arthur settle on the velvet cushions, watched from across the room by Lily's parents Mary and John Plum. The conversation drifts onto light social topics. Lily is full of playful stories about the neighbours—the Fauve girls who claim their poodles can juggle tennis balls, and Mr and Mrs Harrison who planted out seed potatoes which grew into dahlias before their very eyes! Arthur laughs aloud, watching Lily's green eyes gleam and her pretty neck turn this way and that. *What a girl*, he thinks, and he smooths his moustaches thoughtfully. Plum by name and plum by nature. His fingers itch to pluck her off the tree.

1892: Arthur: The Art Gallery

Now the courtship begins. Genteel walks, tea in the Plums' parlour, conversation and card games. For propriety's sake, and Arthur is very keen on propriety, Lily's mother, Mary, is always in attendance. At these soirées, Lily plays the piano, sings, and reads poems aloud. *Delicious*, thinks Arthur—she's lively, playful, altogether perfect— exactly the sort of prize a man should choose when he's on the rise. Arthur is thoroughly enamoured. And where else can he find playfulness? The Mallorys are a sober lot. But the Plums are merry, and fond of fun.

As winter turns to spring, Arthur invites Lily and her mother for a row on the local park boating lake. Arthur climbs neatly into the boat and helps the two ladies step aboard. The day is warm. He throws aside his jacket, rolls up his sleeves, and heaves manfully on the oars. His eyes assess Lily as he shows off his prowess. It stands to reason that Lily approves. She surely will like his directness, his confidence, his decisiveness. Arthur's strokes are strong and even. His steering is sure, and they slip smoothly around the other boats, despite the crowded waters.

Conversation turns to the subject of electroplating. "Your father's moved into electroplating cutlery, I believe, Miss Plum?" asks Arthur. "His works are on Smethwick Street?" He begins to swing the boat round the curve of the lake. "That's quite near my pa's old electroplating workshop. He was apprenticed there years ago," he continues, pulling steadily. "I should think he'd be interested in looking around Mr Plum's works one day. You could arrange that, I imagine?"

"Why yes, Mr Mallory," replies Lily, feeling flattered by Arthur's interest in her family. "Papa would be happy to arrange that. But surely," she adds, "your family have a background in fine gold and silversmithing? Don't they resent the intrusion of these modern industries into their traditional craft?"

"Pa worked for quite a while as an electroplater," responds Arthur. "Grandpa Mallory thought it best that one son understood the new industry, and that son was my old pa."

Now he's puffing a little, exerting himself against the wash of a passing boat crammed with eight raucous youngsters. "In my view, there's no shame in being modern," he exclaims. "The future is in speed and economy of effort, Miss Plum. If one can achieve finishes that look as good as the real thing, and for a lot less outlay... well... that's the trick, isn't it?"

Lily raises an eyebrow. "You are a pragmatist, then, Mr Mallory?"

"I'm whatever I need to be, Miss Plum," responds Arthur, with a wink.

A month later finds Lily, Arthur, and Mary Plum in a perambulation of the Birmingham Art Gallery's collections. They stand in front of *The Blind Girl* by John Everett Millais and consider its merits.

Lily clasps her gloved hands. "Oh, what a beautiful painting!" she cries. "Mama, just look at the colours! See that tiny tortoiseshell butterfly on the little blind girl's shawl... and the double rainbow! But how sad that the blind girl can't see those natural wonders, don't you think, Mr Mallory?"

Arthur sniffs disapprovingly. It looks maudlin to him, and the colours seem lurid, exaggerated. And if this girl is meant to be a vagrant, as the picture label claims, why is she so well-fed and neatly dressed? *It's a painting for women,* he thinks, a little disparagingly.

What he says aloud is more decorous: "It's lifelike—I'll give you that, Miss Plum—but I find these Pre-Raphaelite fellows altogether too sentimental for my taste," he judges.

In truth, there is still—decades after the fact—racy gossip circulating at Arthur's club about painterly love triangles and bohemian behaviour among the Pre-Raphaelites, but he holds back from mentioning anything so crass.

Changing the subject, he exclaims, enthusiastically: "What about a turn in the landscape gallery? I saw in the paper that they've acquired some charming oils of the Lake District. I might recognise some of the views. You know I walked around Windermere just last summer? Shall we...?" And he's off at a pace, with the two ladies straggling after him.

Mrs Plum would really like a cup of tea. Her feet ache. Chaperoning her daughter is vital, but it's hot in the gallery and there's a strong smell of polish from the wood floors that's making her head swim. She coughs delicately. "Let us go to the restaurant, Lily dear, and take tea," she offers, faintly, fanning herself with a gallery pamphlet. Lily is immediately alert to her mother's flushed face, and appeals to Arthur to find the refreshments room. Arthur dons the mantle of leadership at once. Straightening his cuffs, he leads the way through the crowds with an important air about him until the safe harbour of a cafe table is secured and Mrs Plum is furnished with a hot cup of tea.

Afterwards, pacing through the gallery towards the exit, the three visitors come unexpectedly upon a monumental and brightly coloured watercolour. It's called *The Star of Bethlehem*. On one side are Mary and Joseph, with the baby Jesus. Before them stand three ornately-dressed Magi. In the centre hovers an angel, with his toes pointing straight down to the earth like a ballet dancer en pointe. He holds a shining star in his hands. The whole effect is stupendous, and oddly overwhelming. Lily halts and stares. The detail is extraordinary. The faces of the people are rapt and transported.

"It's very big," says Arthur, casting an eye over the painting. "And it's by another one of those Pre-Raphaelite fellows. Makes me feel like I'm in church! Whatever did the gallery want such a thing in their collections for?" His mouth turns up at the corners. "And look, the artist has made Mary look like a crab apple!"

Lily laughs, because it is true—the face of poor Mary looks pinched and peaky, like an old crab apple left too long upon the bough. And yet, there is a real beauty and tenderness in the way Mary is holding the baby Jesus. Something in the painting—in this sweet gesture of motherhood—arrests Lily as she gazes at it.

Love, says the painting. *A mother's love will be the centre of your life.*

Lily gasps. Did she imagine it? Yes, she must have done. Pictures don't speak, do they? She dismisses the impression, lets the call of the artwork pass on by; she cannot, yet, hear it.

"It's certainly impressive, Mr Mallory," she says, weakly, "and... there is something quite profound about it, don't you think?"

Arthur considers the work with his head on one side. Profound? Hmm, it doesn't do much for him. But wait... it's odd, there seems to be some sort of invitation coming towards him from the painting. *Look at me*, it appears to be saying—*Listen.*

Arthur clears his throat. What nonsense. Pictures don't give orders! "I prefer straightforward landscapes Miss Plum," he says briskly, and steers them towards the door.

Lily c. 1895 in fashionable evening gown with rose bud trim.

Arthur and Lily do not speak of the painting again. In fact, the memory of the actual watercolour fades away. But something subtle seems to settle within each of them, like the trace of a poem once heard and long forgotten; it comes to rest inside their souls, quiet as a mouse. Though neither Lily nor Arthur can quite name it, that moment standing before *The Star of Bethlehem* has left its mark.

1898: Lily: Diamonds Galore

Time moves quickly after the gallery visit. A year later, in 1893, Arthur and Lily marry, and Lily steps into a new life with all the optimism and energy she has always carried. But marriage brings with it more than music and romance. There are new rhythms to learn—households to run, expectations to meet. The world begins to narrow its gaze upon her. And though Lily still laughs brightly at parties and charms visitors with her lively wit, something more thoughtful begins to take hold beneath the surface.

Five years on, and she is the mother now, of two boys, Eric and Ernest. Arthur's relentless appetite for tidiness and control keeps her running from pillar to post, always striving to appease him. Nothing out of place is permitted. It is tiring, although the rewards are certainly there in the form of generous gifts from husband to wife.

For her troubles, Lily receives a diamond bracelet at the birth of her firstborn. Cold, sparkling, heavy—it lies in its box, gleaming with satisfaction.

Arthur's chest puffs out two inches. A son—an heir! It's perfect. The beautiful, dark-haired babe is gentle, well-behaved and loving, swift to learn, attentive and grave. Lily is transported with love and pleasure; Arthur, with pride in accomplishment. It is as if he himself has given birth.

"My son," he says to everyone who will listen. "Clever, such a clever boy. He'll follow in my footsteps, you'll see."

With the arrival of a second son, Arthur's pride brims over. Lily receives a diamond necklace to go with her bracelet. But as her days are full of nappies and bottles, she has no occasion on which to wear these gifts.

She finds Arthur disappointingly domineering. She had taken him for a man of action, decisive, a leader of men—but more and more, he shows himself as overbearing, even insensitive. His father, John, is similarly bossy towards his quiet wife, Mary Ann, but Lily is no Mary Ann, she tells herself. She is not timid. She is lively and popular. And yet, it is exhausting, pitting her will against Arthur's.

Just the other day, there was a tussle about Eric's schooling.

"He can begin his lessons this year," insists Arthur. "He can't start too soon if he's to be a credit to me!"

"But he's only four, Arthur," protests Lily, "and he's such a sensitive boy. We don't want to push him. I've read that it's bad for the child's temperament to pressurise him."

Arthur snorts. "Nonsense, my Lily. Neville Hepplewhite's son has just started tutoring children. I'll arrange for him to come over three days a week from next month. Our boy must have the best chance we can give him."

And it is decided—without any more discussion being entertained.

Lily fumes, her mouth sullen. How can Arthur overlook her views so completely? He used to be more considerate—didn't he? She ponders this. Perhaps it was all in the eye of the beholder—and she, in her eagerness, had looked too lightly, beheld too little. She had glimpsed a handsome, confident, promising young man who had swept her down the aisle without a backward glance. Had she missed his less desirable traits in the rush?

Yes—perhaps she had mistaken the wolf's smile for warmth; perhaps she had wandered too trustingly into his keeping.

Lily shakes herself. Nonsense. She is Lily Plum, beloved of all her friends. She can take care of herself.

1905: Lily: Sweet and Wondrous

The years pass in a steady rhythm of small boys, domestic duties, and the ongoing push-and-pull between husband and wife. Lily, ever determined to hold her own, finds herself giving way more often than she'd like, though she never quite surrenders her spark. Arthur's ambitions grow, as does his certainty, and the household moves forward under the force of his will.

Nowadays he has advanced from mechanical draughtsman at Graham James Engineering Works to the position of production manager. He marches onwards, fast-tracked by Graham James himself to ever more responsible roles. His workers like him. Towards them, Arthur is always polite and encouraging, Lily has observed. How odd that he cannot do the same for his family.

After a long quiet spell, Lily is with child again. The pregnancy is blessedly uneventful, and leads in due course to the night of the birth.

"A little girl!" cries Arthur, with some satisfaction, when the doctor comes to tell him the good news at the end of Lily's labours. After such a long pause in the birthing department, the arrival of a new baby— even a girl—is welcome. "We shall call her Mary Ann, after my own mother!" declares Arthur, as he strides into Lily's bedroom.

"We shall do no such thing!" exclaims Lily, firmly, her face darkening. "She is to be Mireille." Lily tastes the pretty French name on her tongue. "It means something like *to be wondered at*." Arthur frowns. Lily continues: "And her second name is Dulcie, meaning sweet. Mireille Dulcie. My sweet, wondrous girl." Looking defiant, she finishes: "You have had your way with the boys' names, and I shall have my way with the girls'."

Arthur looks stormy, but the nurse shoos him out, chastising him for upsetting his wife.

Lily lies in bed cuddling little Mireille and considering her husband. His determination to have his own way must come from that unimaginative and rigidly traditional father of his, John Mallory, whom Lily has never much liked. Arthur's mother is a quiet, self-effacing woman. Lily cannot really object to her; she is almost undetectable these days. Mary Ann's achievement in bearing four sons and nurturing them to the full bloom of adulthood—*rather like a row of prize marrows* thinks Lily—seems to have worn her to a thread. As her sons expanded, so Mary Ann contracted, until she is now just a wisp of a woman.

I shall never be like that, vows Lily.

Lily's parents visit later, and back their daughter's choice of names. They don't want a granddaughter named after poor, downtrodden Mary Ann. They wish for pretty, romantic names. Arthur can see that a row threatens, and, uncharacteristically, he gives in. *It's not a son, after all*, he thinks. *Very well, Mireille Dulcie it shall be.*

"But we shall call her Dulcie," he adds, peevishly. "Mireille is a ridiculous name to saddle a girl with!"

*Baby Dulcie 1905—she gazes out at us from her cot,
as if weighing the life ahead with thoughtful wariness.*

1908–1913: Lily: Attrition

Dulcie grows into a ringleted, dimpled toddler—the delight of her two brothers, who tease her gently and treat her like a doll. They dress her up, push her along on a tricycle, and teach her long words.

"Thonorous"… "Thagacious"… "Thcrumptious"… lisps three-year-old Dulcie, smiling gap-toothed at her wonderful brothers, who have taught her the terms for comic effect. She has no idea what the words mean, but the grown-ups laugh every time she says them in her high little voice.

Arthur in early middle age—dapper,
presenting a careful image to the world.

Over time, Dulcie's role as the family pet fades. In its place grows something sadder—a sense that she is unimportant, unnoticed, and unheard.

The boys' education is paramount in Arthur's eyes. Eric must go to Grammar School; Ernest, too, although Ernest is a dreamer and needs to be pushed. Arthur does the pushing, to the detriment of Ernest's mental wellbeing.

"Don't be so hard on the boy, Arthur," placates Lily for the umpteenth time, as Arthur growls about Ernest's class marks. "He's artistic, poetic—you know how clever he is at writing comic verse. Think how our friends relish it!" she hears herself wheedle.

"He can't make a living at that, Lily. Don't indulge him. It's down to you that he's distracting himself with such silliness," Arthur replies, repressively.

Lily bites back a retort. She loves her children and wants to encourage their talents, not force them into moulds of Arthur's choosing. But she cannot fight Arthur effectively; his is the breadwinner's voice, the one that counts. She has come to believe this, the way the world believes such things. A woman's place is to stand behind her husband and support him in every way.

Once, she had hoped to stretch herself further. Just last year, Monica invited her to join The Rosamund Society. Lily perused the proffered leaflet eagerly.

We are a group of women who aim to cultivate beauty, harmony, and healing in the lives of children through art, poetry, music, and nature, promised the opening paragraph.

The leaflet went on to describe artistic projects for children based on the Kindergarten movement in which Lily is deeply interested. Visits to hospitals and orphanages were mentioned, and—best of all— monthly meetings at the homes of society members: tea, discussions, performances, and artistic lectures would all be on the menu. Lily's eyes lit up with pleasure. A new circle of friends, and a way to develop herself outside of her role as wife and mother. But when she mentioned it to Arthur over supper, his response was discouraging.

"But Arthur," Lily protested, "I would so love to help the poor sick children, and I'd enjoy the chance to meet new friends." She thought for a moment, then tried: "It might bring us new connections socially as well." But her arguments made no impact on Arthur.

"You don't need more children to care for, my dear girl," Arthur said, firmly. "I can't think you want to be running around with bohemian types, either. One never knows what sort of women are in these arty societies."

He folded his newspaper crisply and brushed a crumb of pastry from his sleeve. "No, my Lily, I'll ask Mr Eldridge's wife to invite you to join the Ladies' County Club. It's highly respectable, and the club premises are at least as nice as my own club!"

He smiled—not unkindly, but with the air of one who has settled a matter beyond appeal—and rose from the table.

And that was that.

Lily, with drooping spirits, duly joined the Ladies' County Club as directed. Actually, she found it pleasant enough but not… special, like her own choice of club had been. Lily kept the leaflet, though, tucking it into the flyleaf of a book of romantic poetry. A small, secret reminder of a wider world she hadn't entirely given up on.

Now she looks on as Arthur, fuelled by aspiration, enrols Ernest into Mr Herbert Wilson's cramming school (*Results Guaranteed*) during the summer holidays—a place for boys who are deemed to be falling short—marks not quite good enough, concentration a little poor. Here she sees Ernest's nervous temperament become more and more apparent. He wakes at night grinding his teeth; headaches cloud his temples. Still he strives to meet his father's ambitions, because he wants to please, and he aches to live up to Eric's fine example. Eric has no need of a crammer. He's a natural scholar—bright and able, with a good mind for numbers and words alike.

"Try to be more like Eric, young Ernest," exhorts Arthur, to Ernest's shame, and Lily's chagrin.

Dulcie, on the other hand, slips beneath the radar of Arthur's critical gaze. Girls don't need such testing study, he reasons. So Dulcie has a home tutor in her early years, then moves on to the local Girls' High School, where she acquits herself well and without fuss.

She is a watchful child. She learns from her mother's silences. She begins to understand, without anyone saying it aloud, that, like Lily, she must be dutiful. She must agree with her father, avoid standing out, and conceal any interests that might invite mockery or disapproval.

One day, Lily brings home from the shops a frivolous, lacey French-style dress for Dulcie. It was an impulse purchase after a talk about Parisian Fashions at the County Club. When Arthur sees it, he frowns. "Oh no, my Lily, it looks rather common, don't you think?" he decides. "We can't have Dulcie looking like a shop girl, can we? Standards, dear girl, standards," and he picks up his letters with a gesture of finality.

Lily's protests seem to float away from her mouth before she can utter the words. But when Arthur has left for his club, she lays the frothy dress out on the bed and runs her hand over it. Then, quickly, she calls Dulcie in and places it over her head, does up the buttons, smooths the frilly skirts and sleeves. Together they regard Dulcie in the mirror. A vision of dainty prettiness, like a ruffled poppy, looks back. Dulcie and Lily both sigh with satisfaction. In the drawing room they sit admiring the dress, and secretly enjoying cocoa from the best china cups. When the clock strikes nine, Lily whisks the dress off and hides it away. It remains a secret between her and Dulcie.

By 1913, Dulcie is a self-effacing eight-year-old, quietly stepping back behind every other member of the family. Lily stands just in front of her in the pecking order, feeling as faded as a rose petal left too long in the sun.

That year, on Lily's birthday, the children give her their handmade cards and Ernest modestly offers her a sweet poem entitled *A Mother's Love Is For Always*. But she waits in vain for some small token from Arthur—a card, a present, a posy of flowers. None comes. Arthur is at his club, or out on business, or simply preoccupied with other matters. Her birthday—which had entered his mind, it is true— somehow never found its way out again, as action.

The day drifts past, unmarked. Disappointment sharpens in Lily's breast like a cold breeze on an autumnal evening. She sees in Arthur's forgetfulness a quiet proof of her diminished place, and inwardly she yields to it.

That night, after the children are asleep, Lily takes a glass of sherry into the music room. Quietly, by the light of a candle, she sits at the piano and begins to play Chopin's sighing Prelude in E minor. Its bitter-sweet cadences stream fluently from her fingertips, the melancholy beat carrying her sad acceptance that she is no longer the apple of Arthur's eye.

Tomorrow, she knows, Arthur will bluster and moan—why did she not remind him? His diary is so full—and presents will follow, pressed upon her with apologies and charm. But it will never be quite the same again, for now she can glimpse her increasingly peripheral status in Arthur's life.

She plays the Prelude over and again; then, drawing back the curtains and blowing out the candle, she sips her sherry and gazes out at the dark garden. The moon is up. Her reflection looks back at her. The dark world encloses her.

And so, Lily begins to vanish, like the moon sinking towards the horizon until it slips from sight. As she fades, Dulcie, who was never very visible to begin with, vanishes too.

1914–1924: Arthur: Death and a Wedding

The onset of war takes them all differently. Arthur is all excitement, Lily all dismay; Eric is for king and country, Ernest quakes in his boots. Dulcie, just nine, has no opinion at all. Now Eric is going off to train for the Royal Army Medical Corps. His father is proud, but Lily is fearful for his safety. *Still, the Medical Corps, won't he be all right in that?* she thinks.

The postcards home come in batches. A dollop of Eric's news, then long silences. After a few months, the messages slow, then stop altogether.

One dreadful Saturday morning, a telegram arrives. Its news is horrific. Eric is dead, wasted away from a foul disease. He is never coming home again. Lily trembles. She gasps, stares at the paper, lays it on the kitchen table, and stares again, unseeing. Something inside her gives way. Arthur, assuming the knock on the door was the postman, clatters downstairs for his letters. He spots the telegram; Lily's face is distorted with shock. Without thinking, he reads the dread message aloud. Lily cries out, as if struck, clutching her hands to her heart. Racking sobs escape her.

Ernest and Dulcie come running. Ernest, too, breaks down. His beloved older brother... never more to be seen. It is too awful.

Dulcie stands frozen, beholding her mother as Lily crumples to the ground.

Arthur walks around in a daze. His heir, his firstborn, vanquished by death. *And such an utterly wasteful death, too,* thinks Arthur. He'd nourished ambitions of grandeur for his boy, out there on the fields of battle, but now Eric's life has been fruitlessly spilt into the barren earth of Egypt. Not a drop of him is left.

Lily's parents come to stay. They try to comfort their daughter. Meanwhile Arthur shuts himself up in his study and will see no one, not even his wife. Lily, distraught, struggles on, and eventually the grief subsides a little, so that she can breathe again. It becomes a part of her. She never totally accepts that Eric is gone. She keeps his room just as it was—clothes washed and pressed, books dusted, sheets aired. She knows it's illogical, but it's the only way she can cope.

Arthur begins to have illogical thoughts as well. He begins to blame Lily for Eric's death. He knows it makes no sense, but the thought wriggles in and won't leave.

Didn't you encourage the lad to enlist? says a little voice inside. No! He presses the voice down. It was Lily. It had to be Lily. The irrational idea curls around his mind like a putrid worm, feeding on his guilt.

At last, he puts the grief into a box inside himself, and partitions his life into present and future. He becomes, in a sense, a man without a past. He makes himself busy turning the wheels of industry and he excels at it. He takes Graham James' works from success to success and vanquishes all rivals. Screwing machines, boiler mountings, steam and water fittings, and fire appliances all flourish beneath Arthur's ambitious and able attention. He travels the length and breadth of the country in pursuit of excellence, using his Birmingham–London season ticket with the brisk regularity that will mark his next forty years. "Mr Mallory's got guts and go," say his workers, and they agree they're lucky to have him as their boss.

Arthur's a well-liked, charismatic man. On the shop floor, he's always ready with a word of greeting to each employee. He murmurs an enquiry about wives, children—well, you have to like someone who remembers your baby's name—and is generous with advice. He pockets complaints and comes back the next day with a solution. He's fair in a dispute, judicious in his decisions. And he always gives praise where it's due. Yes, Arthur earns his popularity by charm and attentiveness. But at home, his patience deserts him. His family bears the brunt of his suppressed feelings, which manifest as drive and expectation, demands and anxieties.

Ernest, who had been occupied with war work during the years of conflict, now volunteers for service in the Navy. He acquits himself very well and Arthur feels a small flame of pride in his second son.

Ernest's stepped up all right, he thinks to himself. Service in the Royal Navy Volunteer Reserve, a posting to Ceylon—how Arthur envies that! —and praise from his Rear Admiral, no less. Definitely something to boast about at Arthur's club!

Lily is pink with pleasure as she reads Ernest's letters, which become brighter and chattier as his service time wears on. Suddenly, though, his parents hear that Ernest has resigned and is travelling home. *Probably missing his lovely fiancée, Beatrice,* thinks Arthur. There's a beautiful girl, now, and wealthy, too. Well-connected—a useful alliance.

1922: the wedding of Ernest and Beatrice:
Lily sits, Arthur lurks behind her.

When Ernest arrives home, Arthur is gleeful to have his son and heir back in harness. But to Lily, something in Ernest has changed; a new melancholy and nervousness shadows his formerly gentle disposition. Ernest says he's all right, but Lily doesn't quite believe him. It must be the change in climate and the prospect of a new job, she guesses. And marriage. Is he ready for it? She's a little doubtful. Ernest is emotionally young for his age, raw, delicate. Lily tries to nourish him with motherly attention, praise and encouragement. She showers love upon her daughter-in-law to be, and in truth Beatrice is an adorable, tender girl. She and Lily get on very well.

The wedding is held on a glorious day at the Birmingham Botanical Gardens in Edgbaston. All the family gather, turning up in their finest. Lily is relieved to see that she has come out well on the official photograph, looking chic and youthful, while Arthur looks distinctly shifty. Her father-in-law John sits belligerently, with Mary Ann wilting apologetically at his side. Dulcie, as bridesmaid, looks uncomfortable but well-turned out. And hadn't she been seen chatting nineteen to the dozen with that nice-looking young chap to the far right? Charles someone...

The Gwyndaf family are full of flowers, wedged in hats and hands. There's Emmie, mother of the bride, looking rather grand, with her peaky husband Thomas standing behind her. The handsome Arthur Peat, Emmie's brother, stands nonchalantly to one side with his amusing wife Florence—*what a jolly couple they were!* thinks Lily, wishing she had taken their address.

Yes, the photo's better than she'd hoped, and so it goes into a frame on the front-room wall. Arthur is annoyed at his likeness, but he cannot object to the photograph—it depicts Ernest's wedding, after all.

Now Arthur has become works manager, there is no governing his sense of self-satisfaction, especially following the award of the MBE. When the notice arrived from the Palace, Arthur practically popped with excitement.

18th May 1918... Sir,

read the invitation,

I am directed by the Home Secretary, on behalf of the Prime Minister, to inform you that, in view of the service you have rendered on work connected with the War, it is proposed to submit your name to the King for appointment as Member of the Order of the British Empire.

Although Arthur had patented several innovations, it was the invention of one special valve that had won him this accolade. The device had been tricky to get right, requiring months of precise designs and trials, but it had all been worthwhile. That clever little valve revolutionized the deployment of ordnance and contributed to successes in the naval campaign.

Arthur still recalls the day of the ceremony vividly. The Palace, the kneeling, the King, the pin fastened to his breast, the Royal warrant in his shaking hand... he'd never felt so alive. He could barely breathe for the glory of it.

*Lily in middle age, showing a thoughtful
and kind face, slightly inward-looking.*

Later, at the celebratory dinner, he'd allowed himself a rare moment of reflection. "Who'd have thought an electroplate worker's son could come this far?" he'd marvelled, champagne glass held high as he toasted himself. Lily had squeezed his hand. "Rightly so, dear Arthur," she had said softly, with a pride that surprised even herself. "Rightly so."

These days young Ernest is freshly employed as assistant company secretary at Graham James. "Not so long ago, he was always buried in poetry books. And now? Model of hard work," approves Arthur. The boy's a little edgy, of course, but then, the job is new to him. He'll soon settle. Beatrice's father, Thomas Gwyndaf, is now appointed as a capable company secretary at the works. It's handy, all this home-grown talent.

Keep it in the family, advises Arthur.

1925–1935: Lily: The Austin Seven

The cracks in the marriage of Ernest and Beatrice don't take long to appear. Lily watches in dismay as Ernest's attitude towards his wife takes on sinister overtones of Arthur's domineering behaviour. Lily sees it too clearly: Ernest is repeating the same patterns. And Beatrice—dear Beatrice—is in the role she herself has held. Ernest brushes aside Beatrice's opinions, casts doubt on her choices, and seeks to control her actions. *Oh no,* thinks Lily, *this is Arthur all over again.*

Like Arthur, Ernest is generous towards those he commands, a mix of appeasement and influence. Yet he is a kind, gentle, good-hearted boy, Lily knows. So what has gone wrong? She tries to talk to Ernest, to subtly convey her sympathy to Beatrice, but it is all to no avail. Beatrice and Ernest are locked in a struggle, and only time will tell how it will end. Arthur remains blithely oblivious to the couple's troubles, assuming that the costly clothes and jewellery worn by Beatrice are proof of a successful partnership. It is, after all, his own modus operandi.

How like my own marriage is that of my son! reflects Lily. The opulent and extravagant presents from Arthur, though unpredictable in timing, are fitted to Arthur's good moods. Sometimes gifts also arise from Lily's usefulness, and occasionally from a capitulation she has made.

A fox fur cape arrives after Lily makes some excellent business contacts for Arthur through the Ladies' County Club; blue Italian leather shoes and handbag are her reward for Arthur's election to president of his gentleman's club; and a set of golf clubs marks her turning a blind eye to his dalliance with Mrs Jane Summers. *Well, at least I'm doing rather well out of life,* Lily thinks wryly.

Arthur's romantic liaisons, at one time a terrible blight to her happiness, are now part of the wallpaper of her life. They are meaningless flirtations, she understands, never passing beyond giggling private luncheons, footsie under the table and a trip or two to the races. Arthur, in his way, is genuinely fond of Lily, sincerely admires her style, her social grace, her passionate nature and musical abilities. The flirtations are partly about escape. Other women know nothing about Arthur's dark clandestine life: his grief at Eric's loss, his own shameful feelings of culpability, and the blame that he lays at Lily's door—unfairly, as Arthur well knows in his heart.

Then again, Arthur cannot make do with just one woman. His ego will not stand it. His dalliances offer him more adulation than one woman alone can provide, more ladies to hang off his words, more laughter to bubble up in response to his witticisms.

When Arthur comes home, he is quite attentive to Lily these days, although his kisses taste of something sour: is it guilt? Lily doesn't know about the putrid worm in her husband's soul, the one that says: *Lily is to blame.* Of course, Arthur tells himself it's nonsense—Eric's death was fate, a tragedy, no one's fault. But deep down, the worm whispers otherwise: *Lily should have saved him.* Arthur, without tools to understand his own emotions, is in thrall to his turbulent thoughts and cannot escape their grip.

The years tick along, and for Lily they are intensely social years. Despite the Ladies' County Club being a poor second to her own choice of charitable society, she finds it a satisfying arena for friendship and the conspicuous display of marital presents. Before a luncheon—with an after-dinner speaker, naturally—Lily loads on her diamonds and her most elegant apparel, then sweeps out to show all and sundry the successful life she leads as Mrs Arthur Mallory.

Most are taken in, and so they should be. Arthur is the epitome of good looks, suave charm and thoughtfulness when in social circles, and Lily often feels envious glances resting upon her at dinner dances.

"Such a kind man," gushes Mrs Fairweather, taking down Arthur's recommendation for foods to alleviate her husband's stomach ulcers.

"What a prince you have, there!" exclaims Mrs Chartwell, as she accepts Arthur's offer to secure her a case of fine wine for her daughter's wedding.

Yes, Lily is lucky. She knows it. Her jewellery twinkles in the lamplight, her teeth gleam in a determined smile, and her large diamond wedding ring flashes upon her finger. It is all there, for the other ladies to admire.

The apex of success comes on Lily's sixtieth birthday. The club members throw her a luncheon party, at which Arthur has provided champagne as a surprise. The event is merry, the drinks flowing freely amidst canapés and a multi-course meal. Beatrice and Dulcie, invited guests at the function, watch Lily with interest as she manoeuvres her way around the room, displaying an external appearance of confidence that has little to do with the Lily they know in home life.

They hug to themselves a little secret, too, a special present that, to their surprise, Arthur has purchased for his wife.

When Lily returns home, slightly squiffy from her birthday luncheon, Arthur insists she be blindfolded. Dulcie leads her into the courtyard. Whispers, chuckles—then the blindfold whips away.

A car. Gleaming, beribboned. It's an Austin Seven.

What have I done to merit this? wonders Lily.

"Reward for years of good behaviour, Mother," murmurs Dulcie, sotto voce, with an unusual note of dryness in her voice.

"A mark of my deep regard for you, my dear wife," says Arthur, sticking his hands in his pockets and rocking on his heels. Suddenly Lily remembers the first time she ever saw him, at the Coopers' soirée. Would she have married him, had she known how life would turn out? She dares not ask herself the question.

Tears spring to Lily's eyes. Arthur, ever ready with a solution, flourishes a handkerchief. Lily's moods are a puzzle to him—women are a mysterious landscape—but he believes he understands. "Are you anxious about learning to drive?" he asks kindly. "I've booked lessons for you. Come now, my dear soul, there's no need for all this fuss."

He's very pleased with himself. This present is just the thing to show the world how successful he is in marriage, business, and family life. At the Sutton Coldfield showroom, he'd insisted on every refinement: "Leather upholstery and polished mahogany dash, if you please—none of that painted metal business. Maroon body, grey piping on the seats, proper carpet, not rubber mats. Chic and smart, just like my Lily."

At the end of his instructions, he'd patted the shoulder of the dazed car salesman, murmuring: "Thank you, dear fellow, for indulging a foolish husband's desire to please his wife."

The story, courtesy of the salesman's brother—a fitter at Graham James—soon swept through the engineering works, accompanied by twinkling smiles and nods of approval for 'the boss'.

Lily dabs at her eyes and smiles tremulously at her husband. "No, Arthur, it's just... it's so splendid. I can't find the words," she sniffs, sliding into the driver's seat. Here is freedom indeed. Her hands close on the smooth leather-covered steering wheel. She breathes in the scent of independence.

With a yip, Barney the terrier bounds in beside her and waits for the off. And that is how they travel henceforth, on their adventures.

To Arthur, standing in the warm sunlight of that June afternoon, the world feels right. With such a wife at his side, he looks a fine fellow, and now she has a car too. She'll be the envy of her friends, which is always desirable. All is well: Lily is happy, his marriage is good, his children are healthy, his work is successful. The little worm of guilt and blame is quiet for the moment, which is a kindness to everyone, all things considered.

*Lily with her first car, her terrier beside her
—a glimpse of longed-for freedom.*

1936–1942: Arthur and Lily: Something Is Up with Dulcie

The blooming of contentment between Beatrice and Ernest, with the arrival of their baby girl, is very welcome to Lily's tired motherly concerns. Little Penny, now past the toddler stage, charms Arthur into thinking that girls are grand after all. She chuckles and chatters to him, while he softens to treacle. He pays a photographer to produce an album of his granddaughter, to great success and Beatrice's delight. Leafing through the book with Penny, Arthur is gentle, teasing. "Look out, there's your giggle, trying to run out between the pages," he'll say, watching as Penny squeals with laughter. Lily is astonished—Arthur was never this playful with Dulcie or the boys

Clearly in this relationship there's a little finger waiting to wind Arthur around it, and it'll do Arthur the world of good in Lily's opinion.

*Penny smiles winningly for her
grandfather's photo album.*

But something is up with Dulcie. On a recent holiday to the Lake District, Dulcie kept to her room for hours, writing letters, or so she said. Lily then watched her walking briskly to the post box in all weathers to send out her efforts by the afternoon mail. In return, she received a great many letters of response. *A love affair?* wonders Lily. Dulcie is so silent about her own business that no hint may be gleaned from the limited conversations between mother and daughter. So far, Dulcie's main friendships have certainly been with women, especially Marion and that nice pair of girls, Vera and Irene. Lily believes them to be a couple, though it is never spoken of. They're pleasant women, good for Dulcie. They build up her confidence and take her out and about to cafes and concerts.

Perhaps it is at one of these outings that Dulcie has met a beau—so who might the secret man be? Dulcie blooms beneath Lily's gaze. A glow flushes her cheeks, she has her hair done in a new, pretty style, and she buys some dimity dresses and a smart coat. She begins to take an interest in learning to cook, purchases a beginner's cookery book and rustles up a very passable shepherd's pie, then lamb chops with potatoes, and finally a showy soufflé. Lily is most intrigued, until one day, the mystery resolves itself into Jimmy Ruggles.

*Lily standing with Dulcie—their touching gesture of support
and shared happiness conveys rare tenderness
in the Mallory family.*

"A plumber?" says Arthur, knocking his pipe on the fire-grate and groping to find a mechanism that would extract Dulcie from this unsuitable match. "He's ten years your junior, too. His family deals in offal, for goodness sake. Not our type, surely." He sighs, suddenly weary. "Is this really what you want, Dulcie?"

Dulcie colours, fiddles with her handbag, and then blurts out: "He's a plumbing and sanitation engineer. Jimmy is my choice, Father. He's a good man. He loves me and I am very fond of him. His family are nice people, genuine people. They like me. I am perfectly happy with Jimmy and I shall walk out with him, whatever you say."

Good girl, thinks Lily, and intervenes to praise the handsome young man, who visited recently to 'meet the parents'. She had found Jimmy a most likeable fellow.

Jimmy Ruggles is ebullient, amiable, attentive, kind. Lily cannot think of better characteristics for her shy Dulcie, who has been so overlooked in life until now. Lily knows that Dulcie had a little pash for that Charles fellow whom she'd met at Ernest's wedding, but it had gone nowhere. Now here's the ideal candidate—someone not too threatening, not too grand, a man who clearly adores Dulcie and won't press her for excitement or glamorous escapades.

Dulcie pads quietly out of the front door, off to meet her Jimmy, and Lily wishes the best of endings to this welcome liaison. Arthur looks bemused, then annoyed, but is soon immersed in the evening paper, pressed upon him by his wife as a handy diversion.

Lily, though unable to reshape her own life by moderating her husband's extremes, has yet become adept at exerting tenderness to help Dulcie carve a gentler groove in life.

A few weeks later, there's a plumbing crisis at the Mallory home and— oh happy chance—Jimmy is summoned, toolbox in hand, to put everything right. There's no fuss—just efficient plumbing. Arthur is impressed despite himself, and a thaw in his frostiness towards the young man sets in, from that day on.

In 1941, Dulcie and Jimmy marry at last, in a snatched weekend when Jimmy is on leave from the Royal Army Ordnance Corps. It's a modest occasion, but the vows made by each party seem heartfelt to Lily's ears. Arthur is back to being all smiles. He's been converted wholeheartedly to the idea of Jimmy, thanks to the young man's efficient and economical overhaul of the ancient plumbing at the family home.

At the wedding, Marion, Beatrice's sister, is maid of honour. She and Dulcie are close friends, something Lily has been very glad of, for Dulcie's sake. Marion is outgoing, amusing, confident, giving Dulcie's social life the lift it needs. Today Marion looks poised and classy, in a leaf-green silk dress and—*are those real silk stockings or the clever new rayon?* wonders Lily.

Irene and Vera serve as witnesses. Arthur, surveying the scene, allows his gaze to pass over them. *Beautiful girl, Vera,* he thinks appreciatively. She's got up in some sort of flowing, flowery gown— very feminine—while Irene, her ex-male-impersonator friend, is dressed in a mannish tailored suit with a formal hairdo. These days

Irene is respectably employed as a beauty advisor for the upmarket store *Marshall & Snelgrove*—and her skills are evident today in Dulcie's polished bridal shine.

Arthur recalls that Dulcie first met Vera at the engineering works. They soon became bosom pals, and the whole family welcomed Vera as a regular guest at their house in Apple Tree Road. After a few months, Irene appeared in the picture. Eccentric but entertaining, she was happily absorbed, too, as Vera's 'friend'—no questions asked. Arthur wonders whether Lily and Dulcie quite grasp the true nature of Irene and Vera's companionship. For himself, the raciness of his daughter having two 'devoted lady friends' is rather diverting, and after all, he supposes it's harmless enough. Irene's a good sport and ever ready to amuse. Her *Burlington Bertie* routine always brings the house down, even though it's such an old number.

With the start of the war, Jimmy enlisted. He can't share much about his service, but suffice to say he makes it sound like he's having a ball. Lily suspects it's a lot more complicated than that, but she nods along to his stories and jokes, as it soothes Dulcie's worries. Today he and Dulcie look very happy together, so much so that Lily's heart catches within her. She prays that Jimmy will come back safely. *Dulcie needs this steady young man in her life,* she says to a vague notion of angelic support, *so please protect him and bring him home to us again…*

To herself, she cannot help adding: *Not like Eric…* which she hopes the divine realm doesn't hear.

Meanwhile Ernest has become an air raid warden. Too deaf to serve in the forces, after his terrible tussle with measles—*poor boy, it's too harsh,* thinks Lily—Ernest nevertheless is determined to be of use. He turns out to be an excellent warden—just the right mix of methodical, meticulous, polite, and reliable. "You don't need to be exciting to be a good air raid warden," he's fond of saying, and he's quite right. He's brave as well, going into bombed-out buildings and helping injured people—Arthur and Lily both feel pride in Ernest's war efforts, as does his wife Beatrice.

But the mood within the family changes after the slap. Marion, Beatrice's sister, lets it slip. Ernest's behaviour is increasingly irascible at home, she says. Tantrums, shouting, and harsh words are becoming a regular outlet for the boiling pot of his emotions. It is unacceptable, wrong, says Marion. Can Arthur not talk to him, can Lily not stop him?

Lily is appalled and distressed. Guiltily, part of her wonders whether Ernest's wild moods could be a mirror of her own repressed temper and hidden stormy emotions.

For his part, Arthur's disgust knows no bounds.

Despite his faults, Arthur would never raise a hand to a lady. Lily knows this and is grateful for such mercy. She steels herself for a row, as Arthur corners Ernest about his behaviour. But Ernest storms out of the room, yelling that it is no one's business but his own.

Minutes later, Lily finds Arthur staring at the door Ernest slammed behind him.

He turns to her. There is a strange mix of emotion in his eyes: bewilderment, disappointment, grief—and, beneath them all, anger. Here is something Arthur cannot fix with a clever invention. Here is something deep and unfathomable, a part of his life he cannot bear to examine. Lily catches a flicker behind his eyes—fear is there as well, she realises, though Arthur would never call it by its name.

"That boy's crazy," says Arthur, coolly. "How has this happened? One son dead, the other mad. Dulcie with no children and no prospects either. I've done my part, providing for the family." Now the inner voice takes over—the burrowing worm Arthur cannot stop. And it has something new to say. "You were the mother," it reproaches through Arthur's lips. "Why didn't you do better?"

This accusation—half-formed and unforgivable—slithers from the locked box of feelings deep inside him. Its escape into the world horrifies Arthur because he knows that its words are untrue, gratuitously cruel, and unjust.

But in his mind, the accusation is a defence against guilt. The blame cannot be his, or he would collapse. It must belong to another. It must belong to Lily. Lily is to blame.

Lily blanches, then flushes. Her hands start to shake with the distress of the unfair words. A detached part of her mind watches Arthur's face as it registers a kind of unanchored shock. She perceives he is possessed with a trauma he is unable to understand. Yet she cannot prevent her voice rising as she replies. "How can you say that, Arthur? Ernest's always been nervous—things go into him too deeply. He can't cope with difficulty like you can. And Eric's death is nobody's fault. And Dulcie—well, Dulcie's a dear, and she might have a family yet. We just don't know." She twists her hands, willing her tongue to silence as Arthur's brows knit. But she burns with unsaid truths.

She wants to say: *Look in the mirror, Arthur, and you'll see who's really to blame.*

But she doesn't dare.

Harumph, Arthur growls, and stalks away. There is a defeated set to his shoulders, though, Lily can see, and she cannot help but feel a touch of sympathy.

Later, Lily goes out into the garden, where the roses are all bloom and brilliance. She deadheads the faded blossoms with trembling fingers, reflecting how each flower must die before the bush can bloom again.

1943: Lily: Crab Apple Mary

Lily's distress at hearing she has both a serious heart problem and a skin cancer comes on top of her resentment at those mean allegations Arthur hurled at her a few months ago, and her worries about Ernest's volatility. How can Arthur think she is to blame for all the family ills? The idea is clearly ridiculous, illogical. She can see that he doesn't really believe it, that he's deceiving himself because he lacks the courage to face his own demons.

Well, let him tell himself lies, she thinks, crossly. *I'm too tired to argue.*

She moves restlessly in her bed, throwing off the sheets, then tucking them back up as she runs hot and cold with a fever.

These days, Lily feels as though she has lost both her sons. Dear Eric, sucked into the machinery of war, and now Ernest, damaged by the strains of existence. Dulcie is the high spot in her life—the marriage to Jimmy will prove a great asset for her daughter, so long as Jimmy comes home. Perhaps they will have children, although Dulcie is of an age where that might be harder.

Has my life been a failure? Are all my children's lives failures? asks Lily, of the blank wall that stares back at her in her quiet bedroom. *What is a woman without children? What is a marriage without love and trust?* Such deep questions, directed to a wall, are a waste of time, she realises, but she does not really believe in divine presences, despite an occasional flirtation with the idea.

Arthur comes in. He looks pained at Lily's gaunt appearance. He has no idea what to do in a sick room. He stands awkwardly, then unbuttons and rebuttons his jacket, smooths his hair, blows his nose, and carefully refolds his handkerchief before placing it back in his pocket. He sidles around the bed, pats Lily's hand vaguely, offers her some water, and sidles out.

Lily watches with half-closed eyes, and witnesses the sight of her commanding husband floundering—diminishing.

Arthur drives to and fro: home, work, home, work. Always he comes in to see how she is. He is sure Lily will get well soon. She must get well, or how will he manage his life going forward? He feels a guilt at his own cruel words towards his wife, but he cannot take them back, and he doesn't know how to mend what they broke.

Arthur has not absorbed the gravity of Lily's condition. The doctor comes and goes with medications, a nurse visits to give Lily care, but it's hospital treatment or death, she is told. What should she do? Should she try to stay alive, or should she let go? Lily ponders.

She has pondered big questions many times before—the what-ifs have filled her waking hours far too frequently. What if she had not married Arthur, or he had been a less driven personality? What if Eric had come back from the war, or Ernest had been more resilient, happier?

If she took the medical treatments and survived a while longer, could she make a difference? She shrinks from the operations and the unpleasant drugs. She doesn't believe that her presence on earth will help anyone, or make a real difference. No, she will go, she decides. She's had time enough on this earth, and now she can sleep. Through her own efforts, she has already softened the path of those who follow after—she has a dim understanding of this, as her breathing steadies. Her warm heart has brought more tenderness into the Mallory line than had ever been there before.

She closes her eyes, decision made. Eventually there may be some pain, a period of suffering, but she hopes it will be short and merciful. Her mouth curves into a small smile as she contemplates seeing Eric again. Surely he is there, waiting for her? Surely she can find him again?

Then an odd thing happens. Floating towards her comes something large, bright, colourful. It looks familiar. There are figures, exotic costumes, an angel standing en pointe with a star in his hands. Why, yes—Lily recognises the painting that she saw—oh, so long ago—when she and Arthur were courting. *The Star of Bethlehem.* She remembers thinking, foolishly, that the picture had once spoken to her. How could it have? But now it is speaking again. The Virgin Mary turns her crab apple face to Lily and smiles.

Love. A mother's love will be the centre of your life, says the Virgin, kindly. *Now go and fulfil your destiny. Find your boy and heal him.*

The vision fades, and Lily's breathing becomes slow and steady as she falls into a pleasant slumber. The angel with the star lingers, though, right at the edge of her dream, guiding her onward with infinite compassion.

1958: Arthur: Star of Bethlehem

At eighty-nine, Arthur is old now, though still bright and determined. He looks in the mirror and mourns his vanished youth. Where did the time go? He no longer cuts a dash. *I look like a woodpigeon—round tummy and skinny legs*, he thinks.

It's been many years since Lily passed away. At first loneliness gripped him, but later on, work became his consolation, in similar fashion to that darkest of times after Eric's death. He stayed on long after retirement age as a consultant to Ernest's managing directorship, but now he wonders whether he crowded Ernest a bit. Perhaps he had been too eager to push his own ideas forward. Well, it's in the past now.

Arthur lives a quiet life these days. He's come to prefer the company of vegetables and gnomes to the ladies with whom he used to flirt so smoothly. While his gnomes stand sentinel over his crops, Arthur nurtures onions, cabbages, and marrows to prize-winning size. It gives him satisfaction. In an odd sense, the marrows remind him of his mother, but why, he cannot tell.

Dulcie and Jimmy took him in just a couple of years ago. He wasn't managing well on his own. His housekeeper had left to work in a factory. He hadn't got around to replacing her, when one day he fell and broke his hip. No chance of coping with that on his own. So he'd moved in with Dulcie and Jimmy. It was very good of them to offer. He's grateful for the company most of all, as well as the care. And the food. It turns out that Jimmy is a cook, cordon bleu no less. Meals are a treat. Dulcie had no need to learn how to make a soufflé after all.

Arthur often reflects on how wrong he'd been about Jimmy. A plumber hadn't seemed a fitting match for his daughter, but Jimmy had proved himself time and again—a steady, cheerful presence in the family.

As his ninetieth birthday approaches, Arthur finds himself looking back more often. He wonders if he was too hard on Ernest, too exacting in his hopes. Ernest's nervous condition, the doctors said, was due to some illness, but Arthur wonders now whether he contributed to his son's struggles—with his clipped words, his constant disapproval.

Lily tried to temper me, he thinks, his heart tinged with regret. He hadn't listened though, hadn't thought she was right. Couldn't face the fact that she was right.

And Lily is another regret. He feels he was often unkind to her, holding her accountable for troubles that were never hers to own. And perhaps he could have been a bit more demonstrative. He sees how Dulcie and Jimmy are with one another. *Lovey dovey*—all holding hands, cuddles and sweet smiles. He'd have felt a proper Charlie doing that, with Lily. But Lily would have liked it. He realises that now.

He misses her, that lively girl prancing around on the rug in the Cooper's house, singing music hall songs and laughing fit to bust. What happened to her? Oh, he happened to her, Arthur realises. He sees, dimly, that he trampled Lily underfoot in his rush for social success...

As he sits quietly, a distant memory comes back to him. Something about crab apples. A star. The baby Jesus. What is it? Ah yes, that Pre-

Raphaelite painting, so pretentious in its size. But the colours, now... they were handsome. Lily had loved it, hadn't she? And the angel. Rather nice. The picture was called *The Star of Bethlehem*, wasn't it? Perhaps he'll ask Jimmy to take him to see it again one day, at the Birmingham Art Gallery. Then he hears something—a voice, or maybe just a thought. The angel in the painting turns its beautiful head, smiles, and beckons to Arthur.

*Arthur at his ninetieth birthday party
—mellowed by the passing years.*

Come, Arthur, time to learn what life is really about, it seems to say. *Time to learn...*

And another, more austere sitting room complete with armchair and books seems briefly to emerge behind it.

Woozily, Arthur blinks, then sits bolt upright. *What a funny dream,* he thinks. *An angel giving me lessons, of all things. Well, I never.*

From the kitchen comes a cheerful clatter, and Jimmy's voice rings out. "Tea and cake coming up!" Arthur smiles, settling deeper into his chair. The fire crackles in the grate, as its warmth seeps into his bones. Life, he reflects, has been a good journey in some ways, and a demanding one in others. He places his book on the side table, folds his hands over his tummy, and falls to gazing into the flames, as the evening newspaper rattles through the letterbox and the kettle sings on the kitchen hob.

Afterlife Encounters
Arthur: visited 2024

A Comfortable Spirit

When we find Arthur, I am pleasantly surprised. I'd expected to meet my great-grandfather stranded in a no man's land of confusion, a man of the material world lost without a map. But no—he's here, quite at ease, in what looks, to my inner eye, like a gentleman's study: deep armchair, quiet fireplace, polished wood, and shelves of regimented books.

"Yes, I can see something very similar," confirms Inessa. "Arthur's created this space in the spirit-realm to reflect his nature—his orderliness, his love of learning. It's both real and symbolic, shaped by who he is."

I learn that Arthur is a soul with great intellectual strength and discipline. Developing his intelligence to such an impressive degree, however, carries a price. Like a weightlifter who trains only one set of muscles, Arthur developed his cerebral power at the expense of his emotional centre—his heart. So, while his brightness of mind lent him the capacity to forge through the soul-realm, it was a long haul.

The lack of developed heart qualities meant that Arthur's soul needed to work extra hard to navigate the afterlife—he had so much ground to make up in terms of emotional warmth towards his family. While on earth, he caused real difficulties for those he loved—Lily and Ernest in particular. He therefore spent a long time experiencing the consequences of his actions and omissions.

Dying at the age of ninety-one, he might have expected a sojourn of perhaps thirty earth-equivalent years in the soul-realm. But his passage took far longer—sixty-four years in all—a sign of how much inner effort was required, and of how firmly he had remained attached to earthly values.

"I can see it wasn't easy for him," considers Inessa, as she studies him. "To begin with, he was in complete confusion. He had no notions of spiritual concepts and felt himself plunged in darkness after death. He thrashed about inwardly, searching for guidance."

As a man of action, though, Arthur quickly grasped that he had a job to do, and so he simply decided to move forward and see what would happen. "At first he believed in nothing—not what he saw, not what he heard. Angels, other souls, the panoramic life-review: it all seemed unreal to him. And yet, gradually, he came to understand the truth of these experiences and to embrace them with a good heart. There's real vigour in his soul," Inessa concludes.

Through sheer determination and power of will, he made his way.

But Arthur wasn't always this man. His soul carries older echoes—strong roots from a much earlier life... "Let's look further back," Inessa suggests. A long-ago image arises for her...

The Spartan Life

"How interesting," exclaims Inessa, "I can see the origins of Arthur's inner rigour. He had a life long ago, set in a Spartan-like society. I see hints of a young man, very upright in bearing, vigorous, living a military style of life full of healthful, well-regulated exercise. In this life, physical vitality and discipline were central."

This being's soul brought echoes of its ancient, highly-regulated life into its new incarnation as Arthur. The deposits of restraint and energy lay beneath the many new strata that Arthur developed for himself—mental brilliance, worldly ambition, pragmatism, and shrewdness.

In the guise of Arthur, he incarnated not only with determination but also with talent and drive. In his business life he became a successful man. His pride in his achievements—his engineering, his war work, his MBE—still radiates from him even now.

But as a man, he was unbending. His focus was narrow: he lived entirely within the boundaries of convention, with no room for divergent opinions or 'bohemian eccentricities'. Rules, regulations, and structure were his touchstones—habits that made his soul something like a soldier's, even in the civilian world. "He liked to be in control," Inessa adds. "But there's a rigidity here—a lack of warmth, of fluidity in his feeling life."

Reflections

I am intrigued to hear that Arthur is active in something we, on earth, might simply describe as a kind of spiritual school.

"Yes," Inessa says. "He was startled to come upon it at first, and yet he expected it too—he somehow had an inkling that he would have the chance to study after death. And once he found himself there, he applied himself with real intensity. He works hard and learns voraciously. I must say," she laughs, "the force of his mental energy is impressive. He must have been hard to live with!"

Arthur is in a genuinely positive state, well-positioned in his current path. He can recognise this himself. There is a quiet satisfaction emanating from Arthur as we survey him. He's reviewing his learning from the comfort of his armchair, and what he sees contents him.

"He's learned a lot, I can see, and there's a measure of humility in that learning," says Inessa. "He's realised that he's been hard on those around him. And he's learning to call hardness by its name."

I nod. "It seems he suppressed those around him to a wounding degree."

"Yes indeed, and he can recognise now that he ignored his children's inner needs through attending to his own egotistical desires," agrees Inessa. "He can see that what he thought was love was often, in reality, domineering behaviour, and the impacts of that were destructive."

It must be a hard lesson to absorb.

His wife and children bore the brunt of his exacting nature. Ernest felt this most keenly. He could never break free of Arthur's influence, and in the end this harmed both him and Beatrice.

Dulcie, by contrast, found the courage to resist Arthur's exalted expectations when she made her bid for freedom and married the charming Jimmy. The success of her marriage allowed Dulcie to affirm her right to choose her own path, which bore good fruit both in her earthly life and onwards into her after-death existence.

"Arthur was too demanding," Inessa reflects. "One could not live up to his expectations as a child of his. This is something Arthur will need to address in his next incarnation. It's part of his soul's journey towards balance—developing that warmth, kindness, and understanding he lacked in this life."

Concerning Lily, Inessa sees deep flaws in Arthur's attitudes. "He could not admit his own hand in shaping Ernest's volatility, nor could he properly accept Eric's death. He began to lay false blame on Lily and would make harsh accusations towards her," she explains.

"His affairs—emotionally insignificant to him—served mainly as escape routes from his own shame and his inability to form true emotional intimacy. He needed approval from women who did not know of his failures as a father and husband."

For Lily, this brought deep sorrow and disappointment. She remained loyal, but her early vitality ebbed away, and she gradually confined herself to the role of the dutiful wife society expected her to be.

In his afterlife, Arthur has had to process all this, and accept his role in creating such difficulties for his former family.

I can see that his soul journey is far from complete, yet his progress is unmistakable. The rigidity that so defined Arthur is beginning to soften. He grows in both self-knowledge and humility, qualities that will serve him well in lives to come.

Afterlife Encounters
Lily: visited 2025

A Mother's Love

Lily is not with Arthur. Nor is she alongside Ernest, or Eric. Where, then, is she?

When Inessa looks for my great-grandmother, she finds her at the far edges of the soul-realm—a long way, both in space and time, from those she once loved. Given that Lily died in 1943, she could easily have been in the spirit-realm by now. So, what has kept her tied to the soul-realm?

"What I'm seeing is quite unusual," says Inessa. "Lily was earthbound for forty-five years or so, then by her own efforts she moved herself forward to the soul-realm. That's a remarkable feat and shows a purity of soul. What is the story behind that?"

On further investigation, a moving tale emerges.

Lily was a deeply loving mother, concerned for the two children she knew she was leaving behind.

Staying close to her two children, from the other side of death, was her solution. Although she desperately wished to leave to find Eric, her heart drew her to the side of both Ernest and Dulcie.

In a way, she felt that she had lost Ernest, during her earthly life, to illness and personality change. "Love seemed to leave Ernest, as he grew up. His capacity to love properly departed. That left him bereft of the warmth of soul that he originally had," explains Inessa. Lily set herself to help Ernest from beyond the threshold, sending him her maternal love in hope of softening the emotional collapse she had witnessed.

As the years went on, Ernest needed more help, while Dulcie needed less. And still Lily searched for Eric, but she could never locate her boy.

Eventually Ernest and Dulcie passed away. At last Lily freed herself from her earthbound state and entered the soul-realm to work upon herself. "She only managed this because she was so loving, so devoted to her children," adds Inessa. "Those qualities gave her soul additional power."

Over the following three decades, Lily reflected, reviewed, and processed her life experiences.

She saw how her emotions, rather than her intellect, had always guided her—making her warm and likeable, though also moody, choleric, and sometimes strong-willed.

"Yes, Lily's life was very heart-centred," explains Inessa. "She was vulnerable to Arthur's criticisms, blaming herself for Dulcie's childlessness, and Eric's loss, although intellectually she knew this to be illogical. She was astute enough, though, to recognise her own choleric failings in Ernest, and to feel some real responsibility for that."

Lily was strongly persuaded by the mores of her time— women were foils to men, expected to follow their leadership. They should be mothers and wives—feminine, pretty, well-presented, and artistic.

"She was musical, and had a soft spot for pretty dresses, parties and dancing," explains Inessa. "She read, but only light material— romantic novels, glossy magazines—enough to sparkle in social conversations without ever threatening to turn serious. Though these pursuits can make her sound a little superficial, that's misleading. She had an innate purity of soul and a simplicity of outlook."

Lily was outwardly sociable, yet inwardly she suffered from poor self-esteem and an uncertain sense of self. "It was as if she inhabited her body only partially," adds Inessa. "She slid sideways into her 'Lily' persona without any real certainty."

This left her relatively undeveloped as a personality, and the profound shock of losing Eric made everything worse.

"There is an interesting contradiction in Lily's sociability coupled with her poor self-confidence," ponders Inessa. "I think she used her social life to heal her inner sadness after Eric's death. I can see how Lily strove to present a successful face to society, but she never recovered from Eric's loss."

Lily preserved Eric's room as it had been in life, placed photographs of him all over the house, and travelled with those photos whenever she left home. In her heart, she thought that he might one day return—a magical resurrection, an enactment of her abiding love. She never stopped trying to connect with him, and after her death she strove towards the same. But as we now know, Eric's state at death was so extreme that it would have been challenging for Lily to find and rescue him without calling on divine help. And for this, she certainly lacked the spiritual knowledge.

Social life was also Lily's salve for the wounds of her marriage. Although she loved Arthur—and he loved her in his way—the marriage was one-sided. Arthur placed himself first and overlooked Lily continually. In the family pyramid he put himself at the apex; then came Eric, Ernest, Lily, and finally Dulcie. In Arthur's eyes, both women occupied the base of that pyramid.

Arthur's love, bound to obedience and order, could offer no real stability. For Lily, this eroded her confidence.

She used display—the visible tokens of success—to show society how successful her marriage was. Lily herself was not materialistic, but a display of good things was essential to maintain 'face' and status in her social groups. Perceived failures—her lost boy Eric, her wounded Ernest, her childless Dulcie—had to be transformed into successes through conspicuous ownership of good things. The car was the top of the tree, as far as possessions were concerned.

"She loved that car, too, I can assure you!" laughs Inessa. "It gave her independence and freedom from Arthur, and she adored that aspect of his gift to her. It made up for quite a lot."

Apple Tree Road

"I'm sensing something else," confirms Inessa. "It looks like Lily is still in the family home, the house where she lived when Eric died. Once she made her way forward, into the soul-realm, she decided to position herself here, symbolically. She sits in the front room, working upon herself, and waiting for Eric to come home. Her devotion is very touching."

I'm eager to discover whether the house still exists. I have an old photograph of it, ivy-covered, genteelly walled and gated. The house is bathed in sunshine. Lily rests an arm on the sill as she leans out of the first-floor bedroom window, while Dulcie stands awkwardly by the gate in a light cotton frock.

Apple Tree Road: Dulcie stands at the gate while Lily
leans out of the upstairs window on a sunny day in summer.

I find the house on Google Maps. There it stands, minus the ivy and the pretty front wall and gate. It looks denuded, reduced. And here Lily waits—perhaps for eternity—until Eric comes home. The clock ticks. Sunlight slants through the curtains. The sofa sighs as she sits down once more after pacing to the window. *Is he coming yet?* she might ask. And then she waits, as she always has.

A Doorway to England

"She is stuck, poor soul, and I think we can certainly help her," says Inessa compassionately.

She investigates the possibility of linking Eric and Lily. Would this be permissible and supportive? she asks, of the divine world. "Yes, it's a good thing to do, I believe, so let's concentrate on bringing them together if we can," she adds.

Now we view a photograph of young Eric with his mother, Lily. "Where do you see Eric now?" Inessa asks me. "How do you think he is doing?" I reply that Eric appears to me to be better, sitting up in bed but still in hospital, still looking longingly out of the window of his room towards England.

"Yes, my impression is very similar," confirms Inessa. "But there is something stopping Eric from getting up out of bed and passing through the door of the hospital room to walk 'home'. What could that be?" After a moment, she laughs.

"Well, there is no door!" she exclaims. "So we shall need to put one in!"

Eric is much improved, stronger and able to stand. Inessa describes how, at one time, he was so unable to hold himself within his own boundaries of soul that the divine world needed symbolically to apply bandages all over his soul to keep it together. I imagine a bandaged man, like in a comic strip, sitting in bed drinking tea through a straw and holding his cup with a muffled hand. Inessa chuckles. "Yes, it was something like that," she says.

As he no longer needs the symbolic bandages, these can be removed. But he still carries the pain of his heavily wounded soldier-self—he remains filled with fear, anger, and anxiety. These emotions, too, can be cleansed. Inviting help from the divine world, Inessa and I work to strengthen Eric and clear the attachments that hold him back. Inessa describes the bandages falling away and burning to dust, and I sense that the dark cloud surrounding Eric dissipates. Now he is more alert.

At Inessa's invitation, his guiding angel moves to the window and presses gently against the glass. At first, nothing happens—then, the frame begins to shift and swell. The window stretches, transforms— until it becomes a door. Light floods through.

And there is England, waiting for Eric to step forward. He stands, wavers, then stumbles towards the door—in a moment he's there!

He goes straight home to Apple Tree Road.

Reunion

Lily and Eric stand together in the same room, but they cannot yet see one another. Eric's awareness is blurry, unfocused. Lily is still looking the other way, but she seems now to sense that something has changed. A light shiver touches her as the two guiding angels awaken Lily and Eric to one another's presence.

Author's impression: Eric curls onto the sofa,
Lily watching over him—at last they are together.
Media: Acrylic paint, crayon, pencil, collage.

Suddenly, in my mind, there is a whoosh: Lily can see Eric! She swoops upon him, joy and relief radiating from her. She clings to him, enveloping him in her arms. "I knew it," she exults, "I knew you would come home one day!"

Now Eric's eyes widen, and his mouth falls open. "Mother," he croaks, "Mother!" and he falls into her arms.

"It is beautiful," confirms Inessa, with deep satisfaction. "A beautiful reunion. Eric now sits on the sofa with Lily at his side."

Inessa explains that Lily is saying: "We have lots of time, now, dear Eric, my beloved son, you can tell me all about it. You can tell me everything that happened..."

And Eric is saying: "Someone to take care of me…my mother…she will love me and make me well again."

"Yes, Lily will help him," affirms Inessa. "It's her gift to offer this love. I believe she will help him a great deal."

Reflections

Many accounts of near-death experiences describe groups of relatives waiting to greet the soul as it departs the body. But my experience of research into the lives of the dead suggests a more varied picture. Souls do not always remain linked after death to those they once loved in life. At times they travel together. At other times, they live apart, following paths shaped by their own spiritual qualities and choices.

In Lily's story, we encounter both possibilities. Her purity of heart and capacity for love bind her closely to her children, even after death. But she remains apart from her husband, Arthur—an absence that speaks for itself.

Lily's marriage was difficult. Her relationships with her children, too, were imperfect. She lived within a generational imprint of dysfunction: one that passed from her father-in-law, John Mallory, to her husband Arthur, and from Arthur to their children. In that milieu, she became increasingly overshadowed by Arthur's dominance, which dimmed her inner development. She blamed herself. She felt she had failed to stand firm. There was a dissonance—between truth and fiction—in Lily's choosing a life of outward success and wealth in place of true partnership. Yet socially her life was seen as enviable, and artistically—in her music and dancing—she found her own joy.

Where Lily shone most fully was in motherhood. Tested and challenged, she held fast to her self-defined role as a mother of *three* children, when she might well have let Eric go.

The loss of Eric came to define her in two significant ways. First, in enduring and gradually softening her grief, she became more emotionally aware—more conscious of the deeper challenges in her marriage, even if she could not overcome them. Second, and most importantly, her devotion to her children deepened into a soul quality: a quiet steadfastness that allowed her to remain connected, even after death, to Dulcie and Ernest, and to hold unwaveringly to her belief in Eric's return.

That quiet fidelity casts, for me, the longest and most lovely shadow from her life on earth.

The Mallory Family and Their Chosen Friends

For a family so committed to propriety and conventional values, it is striking that the Mallorys embraced—with every appearance of warmth and ease—a lesbian couple in an era and setting where this would have been rare. From the early 1930s onwards, Irene and Vera were regular guests at family gatherings, holidays, and celebrations. It's not what I would have expected.

Their place as friends—almost a kind of *chosen* family—hints at something more generous in the Mallorys than might first appear from their struggles in marriage and parenting. A quiet emotional maturity runs through this part of their story: a capacity to rise above convention, and I find that heart-warming.

Penny remembered Irene and Vera with great fondness, recalling how their warmth and humour lightened occasions that might otherwise have been tense. She herself had several gay friends over the years, and looking back, perhaps she was always seeking that same leaven of merriment once offered by Irene and Vera.

Without making them into symbols, I feel grateful that Dulcie's openness to an unconventional friendship brought something gently expansive into the family. Through this friendship, the Mallorys revealed a capacity for warmth, free-thinking, and—perhaps above all—a quiet generosity of spirit. In their own way, such gestures carry a spiritual grace, hinting at deeper qualities that can raise up even the most outwardly conventional of lives.

Author's Note: Detective Work: Arthur's MBE: researched 2021

When I sift through the suitcase in 2021 and find the papers and medals associated with Arthur's MBE, I'm intrigued.

I ask my mother whether she knows the reason for the award, and she sorrowfully admits she has no idea. "I wish I knew," she says, wistfully. All we know is that the award was something to do with war work.

While searching for information on Graham James Engineering Works, I stumble over an online thread within a local history forum that has been discussing specific aspects of the firm's history. The company has long shut down and the discussion is old, but in a spirit of hope, I join the forum and put out an appeal on the webpage for information about my great-grandfather's MBE. As he was managing director during the First World War, my hunch is that the two are connected.

To my surprise, in a very short time, I receive a reply showing my great-grandfather's obituary. I learn that during the First World War, the government so valued Arthur's technical inventiveness in connection with naval weaponry that they recommended him for the MBE.

Suddenly, I receive the impression that Arthur is glowing with pleasure to have his achievement rediscovered. I tell Inessa, and she laughs and says: "Yes indeed, I can see that Arthur is beaming at you from the spirit-realm, because you have woven his story back into a full tapestry."

Penny is delighted to understand Arthur's wartime triumph. There is a feeling that this discovery draws the family generations closer: Arthur seeking some sort of contact with us, Penny cheering me on, and me discovering the solution to the riddle.

Turning the Page

Arthur and Lily's story reveals a couple driven by very different forces; one led by the head, the other by the heart. Arthur, all dominance and self-regard, was ruled by ego, ambition, and convention. Lily, all maternal devotion and repression, was shaped by her yearning for love, social acceptability, and womanly cultural norms.

In this environment, Ernest grew into a nervous man—eager for his father's approval, yet unable to meet Arthur's expectations. Ernest's artistic nature went unseen and unvalued. That he still achieved success in business is a tribute to his intelligence and thoroughness, as well as to the quiet support of Lily and Beatrice.

The habits of his parents—Arthur's controlling will, Lily's subdued resilience—were passed down to Ernest and cast long shadows over his marriage to Beatrice. The parental pattern repeated itself. Like father, like son. No one in the family could yet see clearly enough to break the chain. No one yet could save Ernest.

The loss of Eric in the First World War was a blow to them all, but perhaps most wounding for Ernest. It tipped the balance in a life already under pressure, and from that moment, new fault lines began to form—running outward into the lives of others.

So where did Arthur's powerful habits originate? What forces shaped him into this wilful, overbearing, yet undeniably successful and—in many people's eyes—charming man?

It is time now to meet Arthur's parents: John and Mary Ann Mallory. I turn to a marvellous old family portrait—Arthur with his three brothers and his parents, posed outside the family home in Sutton Coldfield (see the next chapter for a reproduction of this image).

Six pairs of eyes meet mine. Six people wait to be discovered. There are no family stories here to inherit—only census records, intuition, and the spiritual research Inessa and I have undertaken together.

I invite my ancestors to approach. Here are John and Mary Ann Mallory, my great-great-grandparents.

8:

A VICTORIAN BARGAIN

JOHN MALLORY 1840–1925 & MARY ANN SMITH 1840–1922
My Great-Great-Grandparents,
parents To Arthur

"A cloak of invisibility is easy to acquire if one works at it," said Miss Ellison to her blushingly shy pupil Amelia. "But why work at it? Be your own dear self, and then you will certainly be visible to those who matter."

The Kissing Gate, Lorenzo Ebrio (2024)

1856: John: Acid

The air in the electroplating room at Stowsmith and Sons is thick with heat and acrid fumes. Sixteen-year-old John stoops low over his work, polishing a nickel silver plate to a dull gleam. Around him, the clatter of tools and murmured voices form a constant backdrop.

John's fingers move with care, each motion deliberate. He's a cautious, methodical young man—well-suited to the precision that electroplating demands. His father, Thomas, who also works in the trade, recommended John to the master, Josiah Gaunt, who is more than pleased with the boy's steady hand. John is neither happy nor unhappy in his role. It's just what's expected—a move in his father's footsteps, as inevitable as autumn following summer.

John and Mary Ann in late middle age.
A highly respectable pair.

Not so John's brother Edwin, who's shaping up to be a feckless wastrel, in John's opinion. Edwin is as restless as a weasel in a sack, always in trouble, and never to be relied on. His eldest brother Tom, already climbing the goldsmithing ladder, thrives on ambition and nerve. Tom's craft is less polished than his self-promotion, in John's opinion, but he keeps this to himself.

In the far corner, Ben Bradshaw tends the glass carboys of sulfuric acid, heating and cooling them in steady rhythm. Suddenly there's a loud crack and then an explosion. A vessel has splintered, acid hissing across the floor. Around the corner of the studio comes John's friend Percy Timmins, blind to danger, arms laden with wooden crates. As he strides forwards—"No! Percy, no! Stop!" Ben shouts, panic-stricken.

John turns as Percy steps straight into the acid. Percy's shoe leather curls black; he staggers, falls and his leg slides into the corrosive fluid. Percy's scream rips through the room.

John doesn't think—he grabs Percy's arm, drags him clear, and upends a bucket of water over the burns. The acid hisses and fizzes, sending up a sharp, white vapour. Percy collapses, whimpering.

Josiah Gaunt rushes in, barking orders. "Well done, John," he says curtly, clapping John's shoulder. Percy is carried out on a pallet, and within days John hears the news he has dreaded: blood poisoning has claimed the life of his friend.

From that day, John's naturally methodical and cautious nature hardens into rigidity. Routine starts to rule him, superstition to govern his actions. Everything must be just so, orderly, tidy, safe. He lines up his tools in exact order, he checks and rechecks all that he does. Percy's face floats before his inner consciousness, contorted with pain. It becomes lodged in John's inner sight where it regards him sorrowfully. John presses down his feelings. They are not safe to entertain. He concentrates on his work. Order and control become his shield against disaster.

Three brothers c.1880s, Birmingham. Clockwise from top: Tom, John, and Edwin Mallory.
This photo appears to have been ripped from a larger shot, probably a wedding photograph. The looming form of the oldest brother dominates the two younger men, even down to the controlling hand Tom places on John's shoulder.

John's fellow apprentices withdraw from him. He's a dullard these days, and they pursue their friendly larks in the yard without him. His brother Tom barely notices the change, too wrapped up in his own success. Edwin snorts at John's dreariness. Lifeless and loveless, Edwin dubs him, and in a way, Edwin is correct.

But John doesn't care. He believes he can keep himself from harm in this way, if only he's careful enough. He doesn't yet know that life cannot be held at bay, no matter how tightly one controls one's world.

1858: John: A Whopper

"It's an opportunity that will only come once in our lives, Pa," insists the bumptious Tom, slapping the papers down on the dining room table in front of his father, old Thomas. Tom excitedly stabs his finger at the text. The legends *Invest in Gold* and *Your Passport to a Golden Future!* are printed large and bold at the head of the documents, below which lie some dense text, maps, and drawings.

"They've been striking gold near Victoria for years, but this is different—a whole new claim in Queensland!" declares Tom.

"Look here—" he reads aloud the text of the pamphlet: "Subscribers are invited to participate in this unparalleled Opportunity for British Enterprise and Reward. Fortunes are daily secured by the Industrious and the Bold."

He looks around the table, gauging the effect on his audience. "It's promising to yield the most incredible haul," he ploughs on, sticking a thumb in his waistcoat pocket self-importantly. "A prospector called Chapple's found gold at a place called Canoona. The Gladstone settlement authorities are looking for investors to expand operations. They're saying early subscribers will triple their stake within a year." Tom pauses for breath. "My pal Richard at the bank says they're pulling nuggets out like apples off a tree—it's money for old rope! No digging, no dirty hands, just profit!" he finishes.

John squints at the papers. There's a blurry engraving of a man clutching a strange, lumpy shape. A golden nugget, supposedly. The print's too smeared to tell, but the man has an odd likeness to a squirrel with a nut. Beneath, the caption reads: *Mr Stacey holds the Prodigious 'Welcome Nugget'. At 152 pounds it's the largest ever found! Pictured at Bakery Hill, near Victoria, scene of the Nugget's discovery, Mr Stacey asserts: "There's more to be had. Come and invest now!"*

"It's not a safe bet though, Tom," John says, doubtfully. "We know nothing about gold mining. What if there's no more to find?"

"But look at that nugget, brother! It's a whopper!" shouts young Edwin joining in the sales pitch. "And we know gold—Tom and I are goldsmiths, and Pa, so were you before you went to Stowsmith's place. We know gold's value. The family needs this investment, with Pa's health as it is. This could set us up to run our own jewellery business in Hockley—no more foremen, no more wages, just us. We'll be in clover by Christmas, as flash as rats with gold teeth! You'll see!"

Old Thomas coughs hard into his hand, his thin shoulders shaking. His fingers tremble as he reaches for his cup.

"No, Edwin, Tom, no," he quavers, his voice thin and breathless. "It's too uncertain. What if we lose our cash? I'll get my health back... you'll see."

Recently, old Thomas's health has been failing. His cough, the tremors in his hands, the fevers and sweats—they all gnaw at him. He's fifty-eight, not a young man any more. But the family's income is dwindling, and pressure is mounting.

Tom leans in. "I'll bet my bottom dollar we can make back our stake and more," he says. "It's a government scheme—safe as houses, surely?"

"I want no part of it," replies John, "And Pa, you shouldn't either."

Hettie, John's mother, slams her mending down on the kitchen table. Her face is mutinous. "Now look here, John," she starts, her voice sharp. "I've got to put food on the table and coal in the grate. I'll not have you and your father spoil our chances with your feeble talk." She stands and places her palms flat on the table, leaning in towards her resistant menfolk. "You're both so cautious you'd doubt the sun will rise in the morning," she scoffs. "We need this, and I'm all for it. That's the end of it." John knows his mother's worried about paying the bills. He can't blame her, and yet, this scheme is so risky...

John glances at his father, silent and weary in his chair. Pa doesn't speak, but quietly folds his hands in his lap. So that's it. The decision is taken, the fateful choice made. The family's savings are placed at the disposal of the Gladstone and Canoona Mining Company, and disposal is exactly what happens to them.

1859: John: Nothing to Say

The rasping of Thomas's breath fills the room, dry and ragged. In and out, in and out. Each breath sounds like his last. The reek of vinegar and carbolic acid cuts through the stuffy air, making John feel light-headed.

Another smell, remembered rather than present, floats into John's mind. The bitter almond smell of cyanide is ever present at work. Then there's the acids, the mercury, the metal dusts. Now he wonders: did the fumes from the electroplating rot Pa's lungs? There's poison enough at Stowsmith and Sons to fell any man over time. Perhaps he should leave the trade, set up as a goldsmith like Tom. No sense risking an early death like this.

Footsteps shuffle on the landing. Tom pokes his head in at the doorway, face tight with worry. "How's Pa?" he asks.

"As if you care!" John snaps, folding his arms stiffly. "It's your gold mining scheme that's done for him. I told you not to put all the money in, but you wouldn't listen."

"It was an absolute certainty," Tom protests. "Even the papers said so! Everyone swore it was copper-bottomed."

"Everyone except the ones who pulled out last month," John retorts. "Richard, Vernon, Edmund—they all got out in time. And we stayed in. Now our savings are gone. Every penny."

Tom flushes crimson, then storms downstairs to complain to their mother about the unfairness of John's accusations. He should be respected by his younger brother, he argues, loudly, rather than being reprimanded by him.

Edwin leans against the bedroom wall, mouth turned down, shoulders hunched. He watches Pa morosely. "It's a bad business, John," he says. "I'm sorry we didn't listen to the rumours that the scheme would fail, but there we are. We'll have to pull in our horns and manage somehow." He smooths down his waistcoat over his skinny stomach. "I'm with you on whose fault it is, though," he adds, conveniently forgetting his own sponsorship of Tom's madcap plans. "Tom always thinks he's right about everything, just because he's the oldest, and really he's as stupid with money as a drunk in a public house!"

John swallows his indignant retort as Thomas's breath shudders into a rattle. John's sense of dread and sorrow at the passing of his father threatens to catch him out for a moment, and a tear dews at his eye. But then his well-schooled emotions reassert their hold, and he thrusts down the pain into a place where it will not trouble him.

"It's the end, Edwin," John says, his voice calm. "He's going. Get Ma."

The family gather quietly around Thomas as he breathes his last. Tom's new leather shoes creak, as he steps to the bedside. Edwin, snuffling, wipes his eyes as he grasps Pa's pale hand. Ma sits on the bed and rests her hand on her husband's chest. One breath, two breaths, and then silence. No one speaks. There is nothing to say. The money is gone. Pa is gone. The future feels hollow.

John leans back in his chair, staring at the floor. *What now,* he thinks? How will they manage? How will they even pay for the funeral? There is no dignity in such a pauper's death. He won't ever gamble with his future, he promises himself. Not ever.

1865: Mary Ann: A Green Silk Bookmark

John has captured Mary Ann Smith, as neat as a button sewn to a shirt. He meant to do it, and timed it precisely to align with his twenty-fifth birthday. It was expected of him by society to find a bride by that age, and John always did what was expected. Marrying at twenty-five is respectable and proper. And Mary Ann is just the right sort of woman for him: quiet, demure, and amenable.

It is at the church that John and Mary Ann meet. Neither is especially religious, yet they attend, week after week, for appearance's sake— and because there's little else to do on a Sunday. Reverend Knighting's sermons are long and earnest, giving attendees plenty of time to think about business problems, family disputes, or upcoming social events. For those with the inclination, there is opportunity to flirt. A glance here, a smile there, a lift of an eyebrow, and many an alliance is made.

John spies Mary Ann in the congregation, and is at once attracted by her quiet demeanour. As he wages his campaign, John finds, to his surprise, that he is becoming quite fond of this young woman. He regularly goes to the Smiths' house after the Sunday church service, where he talks about his prospects and his hopes, while the Smiths listen politely. Hard graft has enabled John to make back a tidy little nest egg of his own. He considers himself now to be a proper, even exemplary young suitor for the daughter of the house.

Mary Ann's father, Toby, who is a market gardener, agrees that John will be a good match. The young electroplate worker looks to be going places. True, the Mallory family fell on hard times not so long ago, but for John that all seems to be in the past. John seems diligent and skilful, careful with money, and very respectable. He comes from an upstanding family of goldsmiths, and will keep Mary Ann in a comfortable manner. There is something a little unbending and conformist about John, mind you, but then nobody is perfect.

When John poses the big question, Mary Ann, blushing prettily, tries and fails to meet the determined eyes of her romancer.

"Will you accept my hand in marriage, Miss Smith?" John enquires, in his cool, formal fashion. He waits for an answer, feet together, coat neatly fastened, cravat precisely tied. It behoves him to present himself well, he feels—the outer man reflects the inner one. He lightly grasps Mary Ann's small hand, as he's poised to slip upon her finger the delicate gold engagement ring.

There's a long pause, into which falls the soft patter of rain on the window. Mary Ann catches a touch of melancholy in the soft sound. She looks up into John's face—and then immediately down again. She nods—just once.

There, it is settled. On goes the ring. John breathes out, Mary Ann breathes in, and John plants a dry kiss upon her cheek. It is their very first kiss. Inside John's chest, his heart beats steadily. Shouldn't there be some excitement? He considers himself in love, after all. But no, his heart remains calm and sensible. It will not discompose itself just for the sake of love. Emotions—feelings—aren't they a sign of weakness and vulnerability? They create chaos, pain; he wants none of them. He schools himself to remain aloof, yet attentive.

Mary Ann is shyly pleased. She regards the ring on her finger, slides her eyes across to her fiancé, and thinks: *He's going to look after me for the rest of my life.*

She finds comfort in that thought.

The wedding follows after a discreet interval. It is perfect—neither showy nor sparse. Mary Ann wears a modest cotton gown in white, with a narrow waist and wide skirt, lace at the neck and shoulders, pearl buttons. John thinks it's delightful. He had expressed a strong preference, during the engagement, for white weddings, given that "Our dear Queen herself wore a white gown to her wedding."

John went on to instruct Mary Ann about his views concerning adherence to convention and learning from one's betters. Mary Ann had listened quietly. With some courage, she had then ventured to disagree about white wedding dresses. White did not suit her, she had explained, and anyway it was so impractical. A deep forest green would be her own choice, with froths of creamy lace at the neck. She had proffered a slip of fabric for John's inspection—forest green silk, glowing richly in the dull light of the parlour. It could be worn serviceably for many years after the event, she had added, with some astuteness.

John felt pleased to have found such a practical girl, but the man's word should rule a household, and it was never too early to begin. He would not be castigated or directed by his wife, like his own father was. John made it clear that Mary Ann should revise her opinions, and, swallowing her disappointment, Mary Ann complied. She realised her fiancé was so ruled by convention that even the smallest divergence unsettled him. She had not imagined him to be quite so rigid.

The wedding dress is the first of many—indeed, of endless—capitulations that Mary Ann will make. For some women, this would be irksome or even unbearable, but for Mary Ann, it is not so hard. She has been raised to be an obedient daughter, a deferential parishioner at her local church, a suitable wife. At twenty-five she had feared she would be left on the shelf, as her friends had married around her. In her soul, she strikes a quiet bargain with fate—for this steady marriage, for food on the table, for a pleasant home and children, she will hold her peace when her opinions differ from those of her man. The bargain seems good enough to her.

She puts aside her swatch of green silk, in due course making it into a pretty, embroidered bookmark. Its smooth sheen slips between her fingers as she stitches it, the silk soft and cooling beneath her touch. It represents to her a symbol of remembrance. *This is what I have given up*, it says, *in return for a conventionally successful marriage.*

The bookmark remains with her for the rest of her life, slipped between the pages of her Bible or tucked into her prayer book. It reminds her of the choice she made—and of the blessings she tries to count.

1866–1871: Mary Ann: Better Than the Royal Family

At first, Mary Ann feels hopeful. Their little house in Aston is neglected, but John's brisk improvements make it feel fresh and promising. He engages a steady stream of workers to smarten things up, and soon the house is spruce. John is happiest when all around him is tidy and well-organised. He is disturbed when he sees Mary Ann leave her boots in the doorway, her gloves on the hall stand, or her hat on the dining room table. Not unkindly, he suggests these items be put in their allotted place: a shoe rack, a drawer, a hook.

"Yes, John," says Mary Ann, humbly. "Of course, John, you are right." And she trains herself to be tidier. It is no hardship. She wishes to please him, for it makes him comfortable and easy to live with. And she has only to ask, and John will buy her a new dress, buttons, or winter boots. Although she would like it very much if, just once, he would bring her a surprise. A small bunch of primroses would do.

Mary Ann falls pregnant almost immediately. John is buoyed up with the news. How proud he will be if Mary Ann has a boy. Every father should have a son to succeed him in his business, believes John.

In due course, the baby arrives, and it is a bouncing baby boy. "We shall call him John," announces John. Mary Ann had rather hoped to call the baby Adam, but of course she agrees with John. It makes him contented.

Babies create mess, and John is aghast at the paraphernalia—towels, baby clothes, perambulators—that clutter up his small house in Aston. After careful thought, and several nights of financial calculation, John decides that he can afford to rent a larger house. With his mother now set up as a baker-cum-shop keeper—Hettie's pastries are so successful that it's said she's put two inches on the waistlines of Aston—John no longer needs to support her. The whole household removes to new premises in Sutton Coldfield where the spacious rooms and pocket-handkerchief garden serve the family well. Baby John—soon nicknamed Jack—flourishes, and in short order is joined by baby Arthur, baby Alfred, and finally, baby Frank.

By this time, Mary Ann is exhausted, and hopes that the production of a fourth baby boy will be an end to her husband's ambitions. John is quite content to rest on his laurels. One son is good, two is marvellous, and further sons after that just gild the lily. He looks at the English royal family and thinks: *I'm a king in my own palace, with my four sons around me. Edward, the heir apparent himself, has fewer sons than I. How proud I am.*

He does not convey this thought to his wife, who droops beneath the weight of caring for her bevy of four boisterous boys. These days, John pays little direct attention to Mary Ann, although he continues to provide generously and carefully for her needs should she ask him to do so. He now works as a silversmith and goldsmith. This work is within the family tradition, and he follows in his forebears' footsteps without much thought as to whether such work suits him or not. John is a traditionalist, through and through, neither liking nor disliking his calling. He is good at what he does, due to his innate patience and meticulousness. Objects of beauty flow from his fingers each day, but he does not think much about them, nor devote any emotional energy to them. His energy is all for his sons, his home and his life of tidiness and order.

1882: John: Constriction

John loves his sons dearly, in his way. He works hard to provide the best for his family. He is out from dawn until dusk, and sometimes well beyond, believing that this is the only way for a father to behave. His role is to provide, and Mary Ann's role is to nurture and mother. There are no other roles possible in John's universe—nor in Mary Ann's either.

While John is absent at work, which is most of the time, his sons grow and develop into characters of their own. This challenges John's need to keep perfect control in his own kingdom.

First there is Jack. The lad is slow, it must be said. He cannot keep up at school, and is frequently found at his maternal grandfather's market garden. Blind to his oldest son's needs, John insists: "This is not the trade for you, Jack. Fiddling about with all these carrots and swedes in the garden—that's for poor men, not a boy from a goldsmithing family! I'll get you an apprenticeship before you're much older."

Mallory family, 1890s, Sutton Coldfield. My great-great-grandparents John and Mary Ann sit at the front, with their strapping sons Frank, Alfred, Arthur, and Jack behind.
There appears to be a genuine warmth to this family portrait, the two generations standing solidly together. Later events dissolve the intimate ties between Arthur, Alfred, and their parents, whilst Jack and Frank remain closer to their roots.

Jack looks alarmed and Mary Ann gently observes that her boy's concentration would be insufficient for such work. "Let Jack have a go at gardening with my Pa, John. It's a good job, reliable and honest," she tries.

But it is not until fourteen-year-old Arthur intervenes to stop John's plans for the goldsmithing apprenticeship, that Jack is saved. Bluntly,

Arthur states: "Father, he'll never manage goldsmithing—he'll ruin everything he touches!" John reluctantly admits the point, and at last Jack is allowed to pursue his passion for the soil.

Upon Arthur now rests his father's hopes. Perhaps Arthur will be the goldsmith? Emphatically not, says Arthur. He is captivated by engines and machinery. Upon the backs of all manner of household papers, he draws fantastical structures with cogs and wheels. John is bemused. Where did Arthur acquire this interest? Not altogether displeased, he yet cannot condone drawing as a hobby—boys should be making things, or studying, he declares. He redirects Arthur to mending the doorbell clapper, which has broken away from the bell. Mary Ann secretly slips Arthur drawing paper and a set of sharp pencils, advising him to keep them safe in a box beneath his bed.

Alfred haunts the stables up the road, polishing harnesses and saddles. His father cannot fathom the fascination, and admonishes him to knuckle down to his schoolwork—but Alfred pleases himself.

Frank, bumbling and gentle, follows wherever Alfred leads. His world, too, is full of horses, and he won't be diverted from it. John is left to scratch his head and wonder over the fact that not one of his four sons seems interested in following in the metalworking traditions of the family.

The boys are restive beneath John's constricting presence. He schools them to be tidy, orderly, meticulous. Unconsciously, he's visiting his own insecurities on his sons. Arthur is the only child who naturally falls in with John's practices. If anything, Arthur is even more military in his tidiness than his father. Arthur's three pairs of shoes are lined up under his bed with precision, his shirts are folded with knife-sharp creases, his trousers and jackets are hung in colour order and according to season. His three brothers, meanwhile, produce a terrible chaos all around them. They duck and dive to avoid their father's disapproval, but they attract it anyway. John is never intemperate, but he is unyielding.

What can Mary Ann do to help, to shield her sons? She tries to hint, to advise, to assert a mother's right to be consulted about her children's upbringing, but John does not hear a word from her. She is almost invisible by now, to her workaholic husband, and in truth, life is easier that way.

One day, Mary Ann opens her prayer book and regards the once-bright green silk bookmark with consternation. Without her noticing, it has faded and frayed, the embroidery unravelling slightly. It feels like so much else in her life. Mary Ann sighs. While she is not happy, neither is she very unhappy. She simply accepts. Of course, she longs for a kind word and the loving attention of her husband, but she has long since ceased to expect it. She fades, like her bookmark. She sits in the long shadow cast by the five men who surround her, and is almost lost to sight.

1886: Mary Ann: Gratitude

John and Mary Ann's strapping sons step forth into the world and forge their own paths. They are heedless of John's strictures about suitable career options.

"You must consider the family's status," admonishes John. "Think carefully about your futures. Choose wisely. Goldsmithing is a reliable trade. But if you must choose for yourselves, then don't be like my brother Edwin, who's flitted from one job to another with every change of weather!"

The boys roll their eyes and take no notice. They like their ebullient and risk-taking uncle Edwin, whose chequered career rolls onwards through goldsmithing, pork butchery, pawnbroking, bookselling, running a tobacconist shop, peddling bottled goods door-to-door, and, lately, selling insurance.

Jack establishes himself as a nurseryman. "I'm a smith of the botanical world, father," he jokes, in his slow way. "Never mind your goldsmithing. This is real work, in touch with the soil." John harumphs in disagreement, although secretly he is relieved to see his son finding a place in the world. But still. A son of his, toiling in the earth! He's glad his father, old Thomas, doesn't know.

From Jack comes a small kindness towards Mary Ann. Each week, he takes the short walk back to his parents' house carrying a bunch of flowers from his nursery beds. Roses, lilies, violets, primroses. The gesture brings tears to Mary Ann's tired eyes. "Now Ma," says Jack, gently. "There's plenty more where those came from. Dry your eyes and put those flowers in water!"

Alfred becomes a tackle maker for coaches. His skill in crafting the various metal fittings and fixtures mollifies John, who observes with approval the calibre of the rein guards, harness buckles, and lamp brackets that flow from Alfred's workshop. Frank toils alongside his older brother, making coach harnesses and leather trims for the carriages. Once they've saved enough money, they set up in business.

On their first day of trade, they swoop down on their parents to show off their letterhead:

Mallory and Mallory, the finest coach trimmers in Birmingham,

it boasts, beneath a crisp crest. John nods, silently proud.

It's Frank's idea to make their mother a present, every Christmas, of a new purse, crafted of the softest leather and fastened with a pretty brass clip. He has learned to appreciate his mother's special care of Jack, and her unceasing work to support the whole family. Mary Ann often looks at him, handsome Frank with his Italianate looks, and sees a likeness to her own father, Toby. Toby Smith is half Italian, darkly good-looking, and with a tenor voice that pleases any audience. Mary Ann is delighted to see Frank grow more and more like her dear old Pa, both in face and voice.

Arthur is the one who steps out of the tradition of craftsmanship completely. He becomes a mechanical draughtsman, rapidly ascending to an engineering job where he sprints up the ranks. Rigorous, diligent and clever, he seems to lead the family into places they've never stepped before. "All that drawing's stood me in good stead, Ma," he says, rocking on his heels, hands in pockets. "I'm thankful for those drawing pencils you gave me as a child!"

Mary Ann's life is full of a new sort of contentment and gratitude, as she enjoys her sons' little gestures of affection. John, absorbed with his goldsmithing, doesn't notice. Mary Ann is just family, just his wife. There's a remote sort of fondness, but nothing more.

Now the grandchildren start arriving. Jack's wife Millie presents a child a year until there are nine. Mary Ann feels some sympathy for her, but Millie is a happy and robust girl whose uncomplicated attitude to motherhood is, "Let them bring one another up, and we'll all thrive on Jack's home-grown vegetables!" Alfred, Arthur, and Frank have a more modest number of children—two, three and four respectively—and the family absorbs the riotous energy of so many youngsters.

Mary Ann watches them quietly, seeing traces of her own sons, and even herself, in their faces and gestures. Jack's oldest boy Cyril has his father's cheerful sturdiness, but young Winnie has inherited the green fingers. Arthur's boys Eric and Ernest are dreamers, promising to be artistic and sensitive. Eric, she notes, has inherited from her father those dark Latin looks.

In Frank and Flora's girl, Constance, she can see herself—a determined, steady, and calm girl with great patience to tolerate the awful escapades of her brothers Maurice, Wesley, and Stan. These small echoes warm her, giving her a sense that her family will carry on with its strengths intact.

John attempts to maintain order with limited success. Sometimes, in the rare quiet of the evening, he sits back in his chair and admits to himself that the noise and bustle are not altogether unpleasant.

How busy life has become! John and Mary Ann sink into the flow of it all, their world centred on their descendants.

1922: Mary Ann: Surprisingly Good

One winter's evening, Mary Ann sits alone in the living room, the fire flickering low. Jack's flowers stand fresh on the side table, their petals glowing in the dim light. The photograph of her four sons, with John and herself, sits on the mantelpiece, a treasured possession that expresses her achievement as a mother.

On the side table are more memories—smiling grandchildren, and a poignant picture of poor lost Eric, swallowed by the war. As well, there's a recent wedding photograph—the nuptials of Arthur's second son, Ernest to a pretty girl named Beatrice. She can see herself scrunched diffidently next to John, whose impatience with the photographic process is betrayed in his posture. That had been a fine occasion, though. The Birmingham Botanical Gardens in Edgbaston, no less. Beatrice's family are *Money*. Grandson Ernest has secured a prize there.

John and Mary Ann at the wedding of Beatrice and Ernest. They are beautifully and expensively dressed, but their body language speaks louder than words.

Mary Ann rises to her feet, hobbling from the pain in her hip—an accident some months ago when she had tripped and fallen down the stairs. Her right hip was broken. "Lucky it wasn't your head, Ma," commented Arthur, as he arranged for a daily nurse to come in and help his mother wash and dress. The hip did not mend, and now Mary Ann is an invalid, chafing against her new reliance on others.

Balancing with care, she steps across to the fireplace, and lifts the family photo towards her. How fine it is, how fine are her sons. She smiles and touches each boy's face with her fingertip.

Returning to her chair, Mary Ann's hands cradle the photograph, together with her old green silk bookmark. She remembers stitching it, each delicate leaf carefully traced in thread. It has been her talisman, her bargain with fate. *This I will give up, if I may have that instead.* She sighs with remembrance. It was a sacrifice to forego romance, but what wonderful things she has in its place! She thinks of the long years when she felt faded and faint in the world, yet she kept her quiet counsel and trusted that her family would flourish. Now, seeing her sons grown and thriving, she feels she has kept her side of the bargain.

She feels an odd sensation in her chest, as her heart flickers, jumps, and flickers again. She is so tired. She will just close her eyes for a spell, and then it will be time for bed.

John finds her the next morning. He hadn't missed her during the night, as he slept his sound sleep. A heart attack says the doctor. John looks upon his wife sadly. She has been a good wife, he realises—and he will miss her. A sob wells up in him, but he pushes it down. No weakness: he must be strong, for the boys. And so he lives on alone, until a stroke takes him, too, some years later.

In those last few years, he often thinks back to how he discovered Mary Ann still seated comfortably in her chair, with a faded bookmark resting gently in her hands, and the old photograph of the family in its silver frame lying upon her lap. There had been the faintest of smiles upon her face. It was, John ponders, as if she had been looking back at her life and finding it, after all, to be surprisingly good.

Afterlife Encounters
John and Mary Ann: visited 2025

Three Brothers

"There's a hook, a kind of tether," says Inessa, her gaze fixed on the ragged photograph of John and his two brothers. "It's hanging down from John, like a tail, and it's trailing back into the soul-realm. But, despite this tail, John himself has moved on into the spirit-realm."

I study the photograph—three brothers, stiff in their suits, yet something about the Image bristles with tension. "What's the tail composed of?" I ask.

Inessa frowns. "A disagreement—about money or property, perhaps. The eldest brother—Thomas—he's the source. I can sense how domineering he was, rather arrogant and entitled. He claimed things for himself at the expense of his brothers."

In this traditional type of family, it would not be uncommon for the oldest son to have expected to take charge—inheritance, business, everything. The younger sons were often left to fend for themselves.

"John still carries resentment," Inessa continues. "So does Edwin, the youngest. It's as though John is dragging a sack of old quarrels behind him. He's still holding on to it."

We turn to Edwin. According to census records, his life had been a patchwork of fleeting jobs as if he could never quite settle. "He was rootless," Inessa says. "Left without resources, always trying to find his path. But he never quite succeeded. He had to rely on his parents to support his children, and I can see that he had many children as well!"

The brothers emerge clearly in my mind now: John, the relentless workhorse; Thomas, brash and demanding; and Edwin, pleasant but unreliable, a dreamer drifting from one plan to the next. The photograph vibrates with their uneasy dynamic: a discomfort to John's back, a looming quality to Thomas's bulky body, an anxiety in Edwin's posture.

Four Sons

We examine next the family portrait: John and Mary Ann with their four sons. A softer energy surrounds this image. The six faces smile out at us. Mary Ann looks touchingly proud of her brood, and John looks every inch the patriarch.

"Neither John nor Mary Ann are stuck within their afterlife," Inessa assures me. "They're both moving steadily onward. Mary Ann's pace is slower, but that's just her nature—quiet, deliberate."

They aren't spiritually developed yet, nor are they drawn to deeper study like their son, Arthur.

"It's not yet their time," says Inessa. "But John carried strong moral values. He wanted to pass those on to his sons, though they all followed their own paths instead. He let that upset him, instead of being pleased that they all found their places in life."

John's disappointment gradually formed a rift between him and his children.

"He was emotionally distant," Inessa reflects. "His love was measured—real but tied to control. He loved Mary Ann and the boys in his way, but only when they behaved as he expected."

Premeditated duty rather than spontaneous warmth defined John's love. It was as if one had to offer something in return. I recall that my father once told me an interesting memory: Ernest, my grandfather, and John's grandchild, had a notion called 'reciprocity', which he would invoke when he wanted a favour in return for some generosity of his own. It seems to accord exactly with John Mallory's notions of love. *You give me this, and thereafter I give you that.* Something for something, never something for nothing.

I wonder whether this is where the idea originated, being passed down from John to Arthur, and Arthur to Ernest. "It's quite possible," agrees Inessa. "Such ideas do get passed on and it would be in keeping with the family character to hold such a view.

"John couldn't help being somewhat limited emotionally," Inessa adds. "That was his nature from the start—disciplined, and deeply conventional. Life events just drove him further into that groove."

In Mary Ann, he had chosen a compliant partner. "He loved her for a while, perhaps just a few months," Inessa tells me. "Then she became like a sister to him—familiar, dependable, but no longer cherished. There was no romance."

Poor Mary Ann. She had her early years to herself—as much freedom as a Victorian daughter could expect—but after marriage, she disappeared into duty. There were no surprises, no gifts, no tenderness.

"Yet," Inessa adds, "she didn't feel cheated. Mary Ann never expected romance. She accepted her role as mother and homemaker without complaint. In her mind, that was enough."

Inessa can see, within Mary Ann's soul, that when she married John, she made a silent bargain: if he provided for her, she'd ask for no more. And she kept that promise.

"She loved her husband and her sons," Inessa says. "But they didn't return that love as warmly as she hoped."

In the end, Mary Ann believed her life had been worthwhile. Her children had prospered, and that was enough for her. Now, in the spirit world, she turns her focus to developing her mind—slowly, steadily, just as she lived. Meanwhile, John wrestles with his stunted emotional life.

"How has he progressed this far, when love was such a weakness for him?" I ask.

Inessa smiles. "He worked hard. His diligence, his sense of duty—these things carried him through. But yes, he could have been kinder. More encouraging to his sons. Gentler with Mary Ann."

John wasn't a bad man—only tightly buttoned and profoundly Victorian in his outlook.

"Will they incarnate together again?" I ask.

Inessa pauses. "It looks as though Mary Ann will return as a man next time—to strengthen her will and develop her thinking. She relied too much on John to make decisions. Now it's her turn to stand firm. And John..." she hesitates, "he'll likely be a man again too. He needs to open his heart more fully in his next life, but as a man rather than as a woman."

"They seem to be doing very well," I observe. "Do they need assistance?"

Inessa ponders. After a pause, she judges that warm and loving thoughts will help John in particular, because he must begin to learn both to receive and to give love. "Send him warmth and positivity," she advises, "and a few spiritual ideas too. They will both benefit from an introduction to these."

Eclipse

Inessa perceives that, in later life, John's watchful control over his family was gradually dispersed by the winds of change. His position as head of the family unit was eclipsed by the rising planets of his sons' lives. Alfred and Arthur broke free from the family, distancing themselves due to circumstance rather than acrimony. They were happy in their own worlds, their former family becoming almost irrelevant to them.

Frank and Jack stayed closer to the parental home, although they, too, established their own lives, different from those of their parents. Times change, families transform, and nothing stays the same. John, their father, had to watch tradition slip away, and he could not prevent this shift. It was uncomfortable for him. For Mary Ann, there was no such difficulty. Ever regarded as low in the pecking order by her husband, she sat on the side lines and placidly observed the changes around her, without feeling any loss of authority or family-regard.

And so, the family unit wavered and dissolved. Inessa can see that, in a future life, they may gather again as friends or neighbours, but they will no longer be bound by blood ties. Their work as kin is done.

Quiet Lives

As we bid goodbye to John and Mary Ann, I reflect on their story.

John and Mary Ann have sprung to life with a tale that is poignantly rooted in its Victorian setting. In an earlier era, John's sons might have followed in their father's footsteps. But, living as they did on the cusp of the modern age, his four sons flew the parental nest and built their own futures based on other choices. Mary Ann, that sweet-natured and invisible woman, lived a life of apparent ordinariness, yet within its narrow confines it proved fulfilling for her soul.

John and Mary Ann were hard-working, with good hearts and moral outlooks. The quiet lives led by them have been followed by seemingly smooth and straightforward existences in the worlds of soul and spirit. Inner development is now their task. It seems that the diligence and simple devotion to duty shown by these two souls will foster their eventual spiritual progress, life after life.

As George Eliot wrote in *Middlemarch*: "...for the growing good of the world is partly dependent on unhistoric acts; and that things are not so ill with you and me as they might have been, is half owing to the number who lived faithfully a hidden life, and rest in unvisited tombs."

Turning the Page

The story of John and Mary Ann offers rich insight into the forces that shaped their son Arthur—forces that, in turn, impressed themselves upon Ernest's anxious and striving character.

Had John softened his didacticism, warmed his relationship with his sons, and allowed for a loosening of tradition... Had Mary Ann found the strength to hold her ground, to bring her own voice to bear on their household life... then perhaps the next generations would have been shaped by warmth rather than duty, by openness rather than rigidity.

Now, having traced the Mallory family as far back as I can, my attention turns to the formative influences upon Beatrice and Marion.

There have already been glimpses—scattered impressions—of Emmie and Thomas, the parents of these two very different sisters. In them, we find a new dynamic, markedly unlike that of Lily and Arthur. Emmie and Thomas occupy the same cultural era as Arthur and Lily—formed by similar social expectations—but their temperaments and family values steer them in diverse directions.

Where Arthur ruled and Lily yielded, here it is Emmie who leads with quiet determination, and Thomas who drifts—both charming and reckless. Emmie endures; Thomas tempts fate. The girls watch and learn; but from the same parental soil, they grow into sharply contrasting individuals.

It is time now to meet Emmie and Thomas Gwyndaf, and to walk beside them as their story unfolds. Mary Ann's precious silk bookmark slips between the chapters, as we turn the page and continue our journey of souls.

9:

A MARRIAGE OF CHARM AND CONSEQUENCE

THOMAS GWYNDAF 1867–1941 & EMMIE PEAT 1871–1958
My Great-Grandparents,
parents to Beatrice and Marion

She asked for love, he offered style.
The music played—just for a while.

The Sweetheart Waltz, Lorenzo Ebrio (2017)

1878: Emmie: Silly Moustaches

Emmie wriggles in her stiff dress, lifting her hand from the ornamental flower basket to scratch her wrist. She frowns at the painter, who's fussing with his easel yet again.

"Ah, madame, you 'ave so preetty a leetle girl," Monsieur Pierre chirrups to Emmie's Mama, Matilda, on their first meeting. "She could be a model at ze École. Le grand maître would adore 'er…" He smiles, clearly pleased with himself.

Matilda preens. She is visibly enthralled by the painter and his supposed training at the École des Beaux-Arts.

"He's *terribly* sought after, you know," she gushes to her friends at the assembly rooms.

"Terribly expensive, you mean," mutters her husband, John.

"Mademoiselle, pleeez to stand still," Monsieur Pierre directs now, in his exaggerated accent. "Et bien, smile, smile, not ze frown."

213

Oil painting of Emmie Peat c. 1878, Kidderminster. Emmie, looking both determined and serious, is depicted wearing an intricate royal blue outfit with white bonnet. It would have been a sign of status to have an oil painting over the mantelpiece.

Emmie frowns harder. Even at seven, she can smell a rat. Surely his accent is too rich, his clothes too flamboyant, his moustaches too silly? Shuffling her feet in boredom, she hears him mutter, "Drat the child," in a distinctly Midlands accent. Suppressing a smile, she turns to her Mama with a cunning look.

"How soon may I practice my piano pieces, Mama? I must be perfect for your party."

This month, she's learning the charming *Arabesque* by Burgmüller. Already accomplished at Schubert melodies, her speciality is Heller's flashy *Tarantella*, dramatic and fast. On Saturday, she'll perform it as part of her mother's salon concert in their dining room.

"Just a few close friends," Matilda insists, while posting a fat wedge of invitations.

Her music teacher, Miss Cordelia d'Aubray (a friend of the painter, perhaps?), has chosen these as Emmie's party pieces, along with some pretty English folk songs. Emmie laps up the attention these performances bring.

"She sings like a bird!" coo the ladies, stroking and cosseting her. "And her *Tarantella*—so full of feeling!"

Emmie looks down at her bonnet, her shoes, the basket of flowers, and sighs. It will be hours before she can touch the piano.

She consoles herself with the thought of her reward for standing through this ordeal—a new box of watercolours. She plans to try painting flowers, inspired by the exquisite pictures she saw with Grandpapa John at the Birmingham Art Gallery the other week. What a trip that had been—riding the train, marvelling at the paintings, and finishing with tea at a hotel on Corporation Street. Emmie and her Grandpapa, John Lunn, enjoy one another's company; their little adventures brighten both their lives.

When the portrait is finally done, it makes Emmie look neat and dainty, with a sweetly solemn face and the composure of a small duchess. Matilda hangs the portrait over the mantelpiece in pride of place.

"Oh yes, that's my little Emmie," she shrugs to admiring visitors, batting her hand as if to say, "We have so many paintings, we hardly know what to do with them."

An oil painting, no less—how they've gone up in the world! Yet of course, there is another oil painting in the family, that of her dearest father, John Lunn, lovingly presented to him by his friends and colleagues at his chapel. Never would Matilda have thought that she herself could afford such an item.

Her husband, John Peat, a gamekeeper's son, started as a humble painter and grainer. Now he heads a substantial painting and decorating business with seventeen employees and large premises on

Coventry Street. He's even on the Board of Governors for the Kidderminster Institute and chairman of the Kidderminster Trades Association!

They've truly arrived, and Matilda makes the most of it.

Soirées, card parties, balls and concerts—her diary is full. And they must be the right events, of course. As the daughter of Mr John Lunn, the engineering genius (as she likes to think of him), Matilda is ever mindful of their standing in Kidderminster society.

She and her husband are at the centre of a socially comfortable, culturally orthodox scene—nothing avant-garde, naturally. Tittle-tattle about her tastes would be unthinkable for the daughter of so august a man as John Lunn.

1893: July: Emmie: Rakish or Charming?

Gaslight flickers from chandeliers and sconces, reflected warmly in the mirrored walls. The floor is hidden by the sweep of the ladies' skirts, their satin slippers skimming the boards. Music fills the air as the small orchestra plays gallantly from their cramped corner—space is at a premium, with Kidderminster's glitterati crammed into the Town Hall.

The summer ball is in full swing. Emmie stands resplendent in a taffeta evening gown with lace trim. It is daringly décolleté, heavily beaded and embroidered, with short puff sleeves and a narrow waist. She'd begged her maid to pull her corset tighter—just a little tighter—as she was dressing. She can hardly breathe, but what a figure she cuts! Her friends Violetta Sanderson and Phyllis Bell hover at her side, both admiring and envious. Their dance cards dangle from satin ribbons, pencils poised as boys gravitate towards them requesting polkas, mazurkas, and galops.

Arthur, Emmie's brother, sidles up and peers short-sightedly at her dance card.

"Not full yet, Em? You're slipping," he teases.

"Oh, Arty, I've only been here ten minutes," she laughs. "Give me a chance!"

"Put me down for the waltz, then." Arthur wanders off with his friends to fetch glasses of champagne for the ladies.

Matilda and John mingle with the older guests, while the young people mill and flirt. A waltz strikes up, and Arthur and Emmie glide into the melée with a pleasing grace.

"I'm glad to see Arthur looking after his sister," John approves, in his old-fashioned way. "My Emmie's a treasure. We don't want any Tom, Dick, or Harry carrying her off just yet."

Though he loves both his children, John has adored Emmie from the moment she emerged, a little scrap of a baby with curly brown hair and a rosy pout. He can't buy her enough trinkets or indulge enough of her whims. Remarkably, Emmie remains unspoiled by the attention, being a kind and thoughtful child.

Her besetting sin is stubbornness. Everyone in the family knows that frown of determination when her heart is set on something. If Emmie wants a thing, Emmie will eventually get it.

Fate is about to offer her just such an opportunity.

There's a bustle in the corner of the ballroom, and laughter, as two couples collide. "So sorry," blurts Arthur, steadying Emmie with his arm, but she's not paying him a bit of attention. Her gaze is fixed on the young man whose thoughtless, flashy steering caused the problem.

He is striking, with finely cut features and a sharp, confident air that borders on something else—arrogance? His dark hair, swept rakishly off his brow, gleams under the gaslights. His steely eyes glitter. His tailored suit is perfectly cut to show his athletic build, while a gold signet ring glints on his little finger. He exudes the air of a man keen to shine profitably in any situation.

The young man's partner, Imogen Pevans, brushes herself down and expectantly waits to resume the waltz. But the gentleman's gaze is now as focused on Emmie as hers is bent upon him. With a boldness bordering on scandalous, he ignores Imogen and takes Emmie's hand instead. Poor Imogen stands open-mouthed until Arthur comes to the rescue. He smiles and chats lightly, to hide his intense disapproval, but inside he frowns. *Such a social gaffe is quite unpardonable*, he thinks.

Emmie and Thomas eye one another up assessingly.

"Why, hello, I'm Thomas. Thomas Gwyndaf," says the young man, his voice richly timbred. He takes Emmie's gloved hand and strokes it lightly with his thumb, his touch lingering just a little too long.

"Gwyndaf—what a pretty name," says Emmie, her cheeks warming, her hand straying to tuck a curl of hair behind her ear. "Is it Welsh?"

"Welsh as the misty hills," Thomas replies with a wide smile and an expressive sweep of the hand. "It means white river—a name full of Celtic mystery and magic." He raises his eyebrows as if to underline his mystical heritage.

Emmie is entranced. There's something about the way he stands, his head tilted just so, his deep, magnetic voice weaving around her like a spell. He looks every inch the romantic hero. Arthur tuts, as he steers Imogen back into the crush. *What tosh—implying he was born on the foothills of Snowdon!* Arthur thinks drily. *I'll bet he was born nowhere more exciting than Worcester!*

Thomas offers his arm, and he and Emmie stroll towards a pair of chairs at the edge of the ballroom for a tête-à-tête. His conversation is lively and intelligent but dry, more facts than wit. Emmie doesn't notice, however, excited as she is by his presence. She learns that his family are newly arrived in Kidderminster. His father has secured an excellent position as cashier of the Kidderminster Co-operative Society, while he himself has a post as accountant. The family lives on Bewdley Street in a handsome Victorian villa with a carriage house and a team of perfectly matched greys in the stables.

"Capital horses, Miss Peat," Thomas assures her, his eyes gleaming. "The best in Kidderminster. And there's nothing like a drive in the country on a fine morning, is there? Perhaps I might have the honour, some day…?" He leaves the invitation hanging.

Emmie's fingers tighten on her dance card, now full to capacity. She frowns, pencil poised. Surely some partners could be… dispensed with? A deft stroke of her pencil, a touch of ruthlessness—and three partners are consigned to oblivion. Thomas now has three dances available to him. It's a bold move, but she doesn't bat an eyelid, and he wastes no time in claiming his prizes.

When they waltz, Thomas's hand is firm and assured at her waist. He steers her through the swirling crowd with perfect control, sweeping her into the notoriously tricky Viennese waltz with breathtaking ease. Emmie is conscious of every eye in the room upon them.

"You've quite the talent for dancing, Mr Gwyndaf," she says, a little breathless as they spin to a halt.

"Only with the right partner, Miss Peat," he replies.

"I see you've found a new follower," Arthur remarks as he and Emmie ride home in the carriage later that night. Emmie doesn't respond. Her eyes are dreamy, and she sighs, smiling to herself. Arthur knows the signs. Emmie is in love.

But somehow, Arthur doesn't much like Thomas.

1893: October: Emmie: Courtship

The wind whips up the leaves; rain drifts in the air again. Thomas, meticulously avoiding splashes of mud on his polished boots, accompanies Emmie in a slow perambulation of Brinton Park. Arthur ambles behind, bored but resigned to his chaperone's lot.

The talk turns continuously on Thomas's doings in his new accountancy job. He holds forth about his many responsibilities—his keen eye for accounts, his vital role at the firm—and Emmie hangs on his words eagerly. Arthur rolls his eyes. Thomas is tiresome, a touch too confident, but Emmie's eyes linger on his lean, spare face. *Trouble brewing there*, thinks Arthur.

Tales of visits to London theatres follow. Thomas name-drops: Sir Edward Elgar, Henry Irving, Ellen Terry. They are all paraded before Emmie's adoring ears. "Thomas is so cultural," Emmie explains to Matilda later. "I'm going to learn some of his favourite music hall songs to tease him with." Later, the strains of *Boiled Beef and Carrots* and *Ta-ra-ra Boom-de-ay* drift from the sitting room, as Emmie practises her repertoire of catchy tunes.

Her father is not keen on this new amour of Emmie's. "Do you feel he's right for you, sweetheart?" John quizzes, but Emmie brushes the question away.

"He seems to be the kind of man who'll stop at nothing to get what he wants," comments Arthur, shaking his head.

"Like me then, brother, dear," laughs Emmie, and she plunges headlong into a courtship with Thomas.

1893: November: Thomas: High Stakes

Thomas pauses before a plate-glass frontage on Kidderminster High Street, studying his reflection. A smart young man looks back. *Tidy*, he thinks, straightening his stance.

Across the road, Emmie hurries towards him with Arthur in tow. Thomas plants a smile on his face, doffs his hat, and offers Emmie his arm. They stroll the High Street, discussing the Coal Strike headlines.

"The miners should be jailed," announces Thomas. "We can't have them holding the country to ransom. If they won't work, plenty will."

"But Thomas," says Emmie, hesitantly, "I read the conditions are dreadful—dangerous, with lives lost every week. Imagine the families' suffering."

Thomas nods indulgently. *Gentle girl,* he thinks. *Soft on such rascals.*

He changes tack. "Have you read about that elevated railway in Liverpool? Electric—first of its kind. Opened just last month. Quite the marvel of engineering."

Arthur chimes in. "We're going to see it. Father's arranging a visit."

"Oh yes, Mr Gwyndaf, I'm so excited!" cries Emmie, her cheeks flushed with eagerness. "Imagine floating above the city like a bird!"

Thomas feels a flicker of annoyance. Shouldn't he be the one offering such marvels? He forces a smile.

"I understand it's been sensationalised, Miss Peat. Not so special as the papers claim. In a strong wind it could rock like a nest in a tree. I'll stick to solid ground, thank you." A touch peevishly, he thrusts his hands into his pockets.

Emmie stiffens at Thomas's dampening tone, but he notices and quickly moves on.

"What about the Chicago World's Fair? They say the fairgrounds are ablaze with electric light."

"Oh, wouldn't that be a wonder in the home!" exclaims Emmie. "One could read and sew and play the piano into the wee small hours!"

Thomas smiles. She's easy to divert, thank heavens.

"Yes indeed—marvellous," he agrees smoothly, knowing he's safe from any Peat family trip to faraway Chicago.

He keeps himself alert: What pleases Emmie? What irritates her? How to charm without ruffling Arthur's feathers?

Thomas thinks well of himself—but he knows the stakes. The Peats are established; his family is not. He cannot afford a single misstep. So he is all poise and polish. This courtship is a game of high stakes, and Thomas means to win.

1894: Emmie: The Mikado

Some months later, Thomas appears, waving aloft tickets to *The Mikado*, at the Savoy Theatre in London. Emmie is ecstatic. She's heard about it, bought the sheet music, performed some of the songs at her mother's soirées. Now, she's going to be taken to see it, along with her parents. Thomas stands in the centre of the parlour, fanning out the tickets and explaining the details—train from Kidderminster, visit to the British Museum, tea at the Regal hotel and a rest in their rooms before the show, the theatre performance itself and finally supper afterwards.

The ladies are fluttering with excitement, and even John looks pleased. "Of course, it will be expensive," admits Thomas, smiling modestly, "but to give us all a family treat, well, it's so worthwhile."

The word family needles Arthur; this fellow wants to get his feet under the table. Naturally, Arthur himself is not invited to this extravagant 'family treat'.

The gods favour Thomas, and his plan succeeds brilliantly. Dressed to the nines, Emmie and her mother are thrilled by the whole adventure. The train journey is smooth and swift, the hotel luxurious, the tea sumptuous, the theatre box impressive, the show hilarious, and the supper delicious. They all hum the tunes of the light opera in their heads for many days afterwards.

But it is Emmie who is most affected by the performance. The entire spectacle of *The Mikado* envelops her, filling her with its vibrant colours, elegant costumes and exquisite, fantastical stage sets. A deep longing stirs in her soul for this land that seems so beautiful, so strange yet so familiar. She can feel her heart reaching out to the land beyond the stage, a place of shimmering beauty where her spirit seems destined to belong.

1895: February: Thomas: The Proposal

The logs shift in the grate, and the scent from a vase of early jonquils fills the room. Emmie settles into the deep cushions of the sofa, trying to look nonchalant. Before her stands Thomas. It's just the two of them for this moment, because everyone in the house knows what's afoot.

The lamplight catches the soft gleam of a sapphire at Emmie's neck, and her hair, set in soft curls, frames her face. She looks beautiful in a blue day dress that heightens the colour of her eyes. Her heart flutters with the thrill of the moment, though she tries not to show it.

Thomas clears his throat in a theatrical way, and straightens his stance, smoothing down his coat. He looks immaculate, as always. "My dear Miss Peat… my dear Emmie," he says, "my heart is full as I behold you. You are… extraordinary and perfect."

He steps closer, and Emmie breathes a little faster. "I can no longer imagine my life without you. Every moment we've spent together has only confirmed what I've known since the first time we danced. You are everything I will ever need." His words slip out, smooth, romantic. He takes her hand in his. Emmie's palms feel damp with nerves. She hopes Thomas won't notice.

He drops dramatically to one knee. "Emmie, let me be the one to fill your days with happiness, beauty, and adventure." He pauses to pat at his breast pocket. Emmie holds her breath. "Say you'll be my wife," he murmurs, producing a tiny box and snapping it open with a flourish. There lies a diamond ring, winking in the firelight as if it knows a secret.

Emmie blinks, then she raises her hand to her lips. The fire pops and hisses. Time stands still. Finally, she murmurs: "Yes, Thomas, I will be your wife." He slips the engagement ring on her finger, and her life is changed forever.

Success, thinks Thomas. He regards with pleasure and fondness the pretty and wealthy girl who has agreed to be his wife. She's from the cream of Kidderminster society, a well-established family. She will certainly open doors for him. He is satisfied.

Before the moment can settle, the door to the drawing room swings open, and Arthur enters. He takes in the scene before him: Thomas looking delighted, Emmie looking flushed, and the atmosphere warm with passions. "I see congratulations are in order," he says, eyeing the sparkling ring.

"Thank you, my dear fellow," responds Thomas, stroking his waistcoat as he absorbs all the congratulations for himself. "I am the happiest of men. Your sister has agreed to favour me with her hand in marriage. She will find me a most attentive and adoring husband."

Arthur's expression is inscrutable. "I'm sure she will," he says, and he walks out. A few moments later, a shriek signals that he has told his mother. In rushes Matilda, and everyone is swept up in the wake of her giddy delight.

1895: June: Thomas: Sweet Miss Emma

The June wedding is a grand affair, the talk of the season. Kidderminster society crackles with anticipation. John and Matilda spare no expense: a marquee, a large wedding reception, an archway of evergreens over the garden gate proclaiming in gilded letters:

Peace and Prosperity to the Bride and Groom.

Even John's workers have a party organised and paid for by their boss. They feast, drink, and raise their glasses with genuine warmth. "To sweet Miss Emma!" they cheer.

Thomas enjoys the air of provincial grandeur that hangs over the day. *It suits me,* he judges, surveying the scene. Everything tasteful, polished—a step up from church-hall weddings. He's nearly at the finish line; nerves hum beneath his polished façade. He adjusts his cravat. *A touch too tight? No, just right for the occasion. Stay steady, old chap.* The key is to maintain a look of effortless confidence, no matter how many eyes are on him.

He stands restively at the altar with Arthur, whom he has felt obliged to invite as best man. They tolerate each other for Emmie's sake, but there's no denying the tension. *Arthur's one of those judgemental types who'll never let a chap off his leash*, thinks Thomas. And: *Let's hope he keeps his sermonizing to a minimum today!*

There's some triumphant chords from the organ—and Emmie appears. She's dressed in a gown of beaded ivory silk. She looks radiant. The congregation let out a collective sigh. Emmie seems to float down the aisle on her father's arm and everyone can see her happiness.

Thomas cannot take his eyes off her. He swallows; for a moment he feels out of his depth. "She's flawless," he breathes. Pride mingles with something softer—admiration and even love. But underneath, there's just a touch of self-doubt: *Can I live up to all this expectation? And what if I can't?*

He pushes that thought down. *Not now*, he tells himself. No one can question his suitability, surely. Young, handsome, clever—he'll be sufficient for her, won't he?

The ball at the Assembly Rooms is a lively affair. In its glittering halls, the city's élite sip champagne and exchange pleasantries while the orchestra strikes up a Viennese waltz—the couple's speciality. Thomas guides Emmie onto the dance floor with a practised smile.

"Ready, dear girl?" he whispers.

All eyes rest on them, and the room hushes. Then—one, two, three; one, two, three—they begin, stylish and assured, their movements synchronized. They glide rather than step, and their styles are well-matched. "What a lovely couple," murmur the onlookers, smiling as the bride and groom sweep around the floor.

Never has anyone danced a more perfect Wedding Dance, thinks Thomas, with satisfaction, and he tightens his arm around Emmie's waist.

Never has anyone been happier, thinks Emmie, joyously.

Her going-away outfit—a slate-grey silk dress with petunia-trimmed black hat—draws admiring glances. They are not lost on Thomas. His belle of Kidderminster stands out from the crowd. She reflects well on him—it's a good beginning.

Their honeymoon in London is meticulously planned, as is Thomas's habit: Kew Gardens, the National Gallery, the best theatres. It's a blend of culture and leisure. But even before the train has gone halfway to London, Emmie is off on another flight of fancy.

"There's an exhibition of Japanese art at the Victoria and Albert Museum," she says, her eyes shining. "We *must* go! There'll be kimonos, woodblock prints, ceramics—oh, Thomas, it sounds wonderful!" She claps her hands with delight.

Thomas pats her arm, suppressing a sigh. "Of course, dear girl," he replies, smiling indulgently. He thinks: *Japanese art? Kimonos? Strange little vases? Well, if it keeps her happy...* He knows the secret to managing women: indulge their whims when it costs nothing and steer them gently when it does. This Japanese business will pass. All fancies do.

Besides, he persuades himself, settling back in the carriage, *it's harmless enough.* Harmlessness is what matters. And no one's the worse for a harmless distraction, least of all Emmie.

1899: Thomas: Poker and a Cuban Cigar

Thomas swallows his whisky and slaps his cards down on the table. A straight flush! He grins victoriously. The other men groan and toss their cards down in mock despair. "How do you do it, you young devil?" laughs Samuel Dobbs, his gambling pal. "Lady Luck's on your side tonight!"

Thomas has been on a winning streak this month. He's made up his losses and more besides. No fool, he quits while he's ahead, ignoring the protests from his fellow players. "One more game, Tom," pleads Samuel, but Thomas is adamant. No sense in pushing his luck.

Poker's a risky pastime, and Emmie knows nothing about his gambling. It's true—the stakes are low. Thomas is always cautious with money, but the thrill is addictive. Several nights a week he passes slyly from his workplace to the Grand Hotel and the Wellington Club for evenings of drinking and gambling.

Now he lights up a Cuban cigar, orders another drink, and leans back to admire the winking lights of the chandeliers, as they illuminate temptation and opulence in equal measure. While he adores his two little girls, and is fond of his wife, Thomas chafes at the ties of marriage. They're like chains! And after all he's a young man. There's blood in his veins, not water! He has to stretch his muscles from time to time.

He pulls out his pocket watch. Time to be off to the Gaiety Theatre. That delicious little actress, Moira Leopold, will be finishing her act soon. He'll go backstage as usual. A kiss, a touch, then the promise of more... It's harmless, he says to himself, so long as Emmie never finds out.

1900–1906: Thomas: The Widow's Coffers

Mrs Wishaw, the glamorous young widow recently arrived in Edgbaston, has become the talk of the town. Pretty, charming, and just bereaved enough to be irresistible, she knows how to work a room.

At a party some weeks ago, while Emmie sits comfortably on the sofa with the Kendals, Mrs Wishaw corners Thomas with her tragic tale.

"Dear Raymond," she sighs, "taken so young. Handsome, charming as a prince and just as reckless." She dabs at her eyes with a little handkerchief—"There are debts, Mr Gwyndaf. Losses. The estate is all gone." Her delectable bosom heaves with distress, her pouting lips quiver with a sob.

Thomas wants to be gallant. He inclines towards her as she asks if Mr Gwyndaf, being such a knowledgeable man of the world, might offer her some financial advice, some tips on investments? She flutters her eyelashes—blinkety-blink—and carefully surveys her effect on Thomas. His chest swells.

That first meeting leads to an innocent cup of coffee at the Imperial Hotel, then another. Under the guise of replenishing the widow's coffers, they flirt. It is the start of a liaison that continues for some months. Trips to the theatre, shared tipples, and discreet dinners.

Thomas showers Mrs Wishaw with gifts and whatever else she hints at. Meanwhile, he pats down Emmie's disgruntlement at his absences. Loving words and flowers pour towards her, but inside, Thomas is leading a double life of self-indulgence and duplicity.

Until one day, Thomas witnesses Mrs Wishaw's own duplicity. She is seen fluttering her eyelashes at another man. The gossip is that he's one of many. Thomas is indignant. He feels betrayed.

But really, can he blame her? Charm is a valuable commodity, and Mrs Wishaw has simply diversified her investments.

She becomes just one in a small trail of dalliances in which Thomas indulges. He is almost innocent in his enjoyment of these flirtations, with their whiff of sulphur. In hiding them from Emmie, he believes he solves the moral dilemma. What she doesn't know about cannot harm her, and after all, he looks after his family well enough.

He lets the distance between himself and Emmie grow. She's absorbed in the girls' upbringing. *She's happy at home,* he reasons. *And why should I not have a little fun?*

It's all part of being a man of the world.

Thomas's luck cannot last forever, though. Luck never does. Just one word of gossip, and the whole house of cards will come crashing down. But Thomas is ever confident. He never looks over his shoulder at the steam train hurtling towards him.

In the end, it is the work of a moment to bring about his downfall.

1906: Emmie: Tittle-Tattle

At first, marriage had delighted Emmie. There were trips to the theatre, drives in the park, dinner parties, and a whirl of morning visits. Emmie found herself thriving within her social milieu—always well-turned-out, always admired, her flair for fashion and décor made her advice much sought after. She peppered her home with oriental touches: a golden hair comb for her dressing table, a lacquered oriental-style letter rack for the hall, a vase painted with cherry blossoms. Thomas brought such gifts often, basking in her delight.

Emmie with baby Beatrice c 1897 Edgbaston, Birmingham.
There is a sweetness in Emmie's gaze towards her little girl
and Beatrice appears secure in her mother's adoration.

When she fell pregnant in the spring of 1896, Thomas fussed over her, excited by the idea of fatherhood. His delight was genuine when expectation became reality.

The baby was born on a cold December morning, a healthy little girl. They called her Beatrice. Thomas was enchanted by the experience of holding the baby. He was awkward at first, but soon became adept at cradling Beatrice, showing her off to the flocks of visitors who called. Emmie's world narrowed to this perfect little being. She gazed at her daughter's tiny hands, marvelling at how delicate they were, each nail a perfect half-moon. How happy her little world was!

Three years later, Marion arrived, as sweet-tempered as her sister. By now, Thomas had secured a promising position at Graham James Engineering Works in Birmingham as an accountant. He talked endlessly about his future prospects. "It's only a matter of time before they promote me, Emmie. Mr James himself finds I've a sharp eye for figures."

Emmie c. 1899-1904—her direct gaze and firm mouth hint at a later story of strength in adversity.

It was at about this time that Emmie noticed Thomas's attentions beginning to waver. Work seemed to be an increasing draw on his time, or so he claimed to Emmie. He was often home late, pleading business in town or a client dinner. Emmie believed him. Why should she not?

A few years prior to this, the family had moved to a large villa in Edgbaston, south Birmingham. Emmie made new friends amongst her neighbours, joined the social scene and spent pleasant hours watching the children play in the little summer house set amongst the rhododendrons.

But in 1906, all Emmie's quiet contentment is shattered when she hears the tittle-tattle.

It happens at a whist party one evening at the Hampshires' villa in Vesey Gardens. Emmie is studying her cards when a knowing voice drifts over from behind her. "I hear a certain accountancy gentleman from Graham James Engineering Works was seen at the theatre with that widow from Wylde Green. Not discreet at all, my dear. His poor wife's rather innocent, they say." There is a chorus of shushing, but not before Emmie catches several glances in her direction.

Her stomach drops. An accountancy gentleman? From Graham James? No—it can't be Thomas. Her hands go cold, her face hot. She places her cards carefully on the table, forcing a smile. "I'm afraid I must retire," she murmurs. "A sudden headache."

In the carriage home, her thoughts race. Thomas has been evasive lately—he stays out late, claiming work commitments. There have been odd little signs: a trace of unfamiliar perfume on his coat, two theatre ticket stubs tucked into his tallboy, a crumpled music hall programme in his wardrobe. She had dismissed them all. *How could I have been so naïve?* she thinks.

The next morning, she visits her friend Lydia Mayfield. Lydia always knows how to discover what's going on in Edgbaston society. A few quiet enquiries confirm Emmie's worst fears. Thomas has been seen out with several women—a widow, an actress, even a married lady or two. "What a cad," says Lydia, sympathetically. "All men are beasts."

"Oh, the shame," Emmie whispers to herself that night, lying awake and contemplating her husband's treachery. Her heart aches with anger and disappointment. But: *I will not see my daughters' lives overshadowed by disgrace,* she vows, and she begins to plan.

By morning, she has made up her mind. She will confront Thomas— but not alone. She calls on her brother Arthur.

"He's a scoundrel!" Arthur fumes when she tells him. "You can't stay with him, Emmie!"

"I always knew he was a bounder," John Peat adds, crossing his arms.

"And my heart will simply break from the scandal," Matilda declares, dabbing at her eyes with a lace handkerchief.

"No," Emmie says, straightening her back. "There will be no scandal. The marriage will continue—for the girls' sake, and for propriety. But Thomas needs to be… managed."

That evening, Thomas returns home in high spirits, breezing into the drawing room with a cheerful: "Good evening, all!" He heads for the sherry decanter but stops short when he sees their grim faces.

"Is something wrong with the girls?" he asks, his voice suddenly tight with fear, and his hand groping upwards towards his heart. Emmie feels a tiny thawing in her breast at his obvious care for their daughters, but she squares her chin and steps forward.

"No, Thomas. The girls are well. But we know what you've been up to—your affairs, your women." Her eyes are stern, her lips set in a firm line.

Thomas's face turns red, then white. He blusters, denies, then falls silent as Emmie lists names, places: the theatre, a restaurant, a certain hotel in town.

"You may take it that our marriage will continue," she advises, her voice steady. "You can carry on with these sordid dalliances if you must, but you will be discreet. If you are not, I will ruin you." Emmie pauses, takes a breath. "Your name will be mud, Thomas. I will speak to your employer, your friends, your family. And my family will stand by me."

Arthur steps forward. "We all will," he says, and puts his hand on Emmie's shoulder.

Thomas sinks into the nearest chair, his face pale. "You wouldn't," he whispers, but the tremor in his voice betrays him. Wordlessly, Arthur hands him a glass of sherry.

"Oh, we would," Arthur says, calmly.

And Thomas knows they would. He drains the glass in one swallow, his hand shaking.

From that night on, the dynamic of their marriage shifts. Emmie takes control, setting the terms of their life together.

She feels safe, but deeply disappointed. Tenderness, love, devotion—all that she had once imagined for their marriage—is gone. In its place, there is only a fragile truce. "You can't have it all," she tells herself. "I shall have my girls, my music, my art, and my garden instead."

And so, that is how it is. She has saved both herself and her girls from social scandal. But the cost is dear, because as children will, both girls absorb unconscious lessons from this debacle. Beatrice learns that marriages should be preserved at any price, and Marion learns that marriage is a risk—one that she herself may never take.

1934–1941: Thomas: Tentacles

When Thomas receives a diagnosis of heart problems, he feels something close to shame. How can his heart, of all things, falter? It seems impossible, unmanly. He's always been strong, hasn't he? He hunches over his desk at the engineering works, staring at piles of papers without reading a word. What should he do? Should he tell Emmie? No. She'd only fuss. He swallows the medication silently, folding his concerns beneath a veneer of composure.

Emmie's been loyal enough, he allows—*even after that ghastly business when my indiscretions were exposed.*

He's regretful, sometimes, about those silly affairs. The first years of his marriage to Emmie were charming, really. Then he got bored. He knows he threw away her trust. He fell out of love with her once she was his own; the thrill of the chase had been greater than the pleasure of possession. Now he stays in the marriage for comfort's sake—and for his girls.

Thomas once thought about leaving. Why not? He had prospects, friends, confidence enough to land on his feet. But what kind of future would his daughters have? How could he abandon them to an uncertain life? No, that wouldn't do. He curtailed his drinking and cut out poker completely. Too risky, too tempting. He found, somewhere, the will to master himself.

He laughs now. *I'm as straight-laced as dull Arthur always wanted me to be,* he thinks. But he feels the effort pickled him, dried him out.

Thomas is forced to retire from his job due to constant tiredness caused by the heart condition. It's depressing to be without a role. He sits in the living room with a newspaper, skulking there for hours, brooding, ruminating. He has few friends and no interests. Life isn't what he'd hoped for.

Two years later, another diagnosis hits: prostate cancer. Fear curls its tentacles around him. The treatments sound worse than the disease—each one an affront to his pride.

Briefly, he wonders if this illness is some kind of punishment for his misdemeanours. If so, then he must bear it.

1941: Emmie: A Good Marriage of Its Type

In 1941, Thomas's health declines sharply, giving Emmie pause for reflection. Looking back over the years of her divided marriage, she realises that although Thomas has been a fixture in her life, her greatest pleasures have always been her daughters and her friends.

After discovering Thomas's infidelities all that time ago, the couple settled into polite distance. The girls, Emmie feared, might be marked by this, yet they seemed to flourish. They developed interests, romances, and outlooks of their own. Beatrice fell in love and married Ernest, a nervous young man—artistic and clever. Marion surprised everyone: she struck out into a very different existence, with her modern lifestyle and steady career at Lloyds Bank. Emmie had never imagined such independence for her daughter, but she was quietly proud. Clearly, Marion had inherited Thomas's way with figures.

The arrival of Beatrice's baby was a great excitement for the whole family, who doted on this new little girl. Meanwhile, Marion's tales of life in banking provided sometimes hilarious, always intriguing diversion. The family's shared love of art and music filled their spare time with concerts and exhibitions. Emmie valued these entertainments and talked about them for days afterwards. Her book collection on oriental gardens expanded, too. That early spark endured, kindled all those years ago by a performance of *The Mikado*.

At the wedding of Beatrice and Ernest 1922. Sitting left: Emmie's mother Matilda. Right: Emmie. Standing above right: Thomas. Emmie and her mother form a strong female pairing. Meanwhile Thomas stands behind his wife, frowning anxiously.

"You're quite the Japanese scholar these days, Emmie," her friend Lydia teased.

Emmie laughed. "Japan has captured my imagination, Lydia, that's true. The gardens, the art, the Chinoiserie furniture. It's all so… mysterious and exquisite."

The 1930s rolled forward, year on year. There was tension in Beatrice's marriage to Ernest, but Emmie sat on the side-lines—present, supportive, yet unable to intervene.

Beatrice's Penny grew into a playful, intelligent child, while Thomas seemed to wane: shrinking into himself, breathless and pale. The trouble lay with his heart, he confessed, and an early retirement became necessary. After that he moped around the house, his health showing little sign of improvement despite the medicines, his mood flat and dreary.

And so the years passed. Now it is 1941—two years into Thomas's morose retirement.

This morning he has come to Emmie to admit his diagnosis with prostate cancer. "I can't face the treatment," he tells her. "It would be too much for me. The operations, you know, they're awful, dangerous even. I'd rather let things run their course."

His face is resigned, defeated, as he imparts the information. Emmie knows, then, that he will not fight it.

"Thomas, I'll support you, whatever you decide," Emmie says, and she means it. She reaches out to hold his hand. Despite everything, she feels a lingering fondness for this rather weak, vain, but ultimately good-hearted man. Thomas is unexpectedly grateful for her support. His illness brings them closer than they've been for years. Whilst their marriage is a habit, it still has some small foundations in affection. And Emmie knows that, despite everything, there will be pain when the partnership is finally over.

In the end, Thomas drifts away, his breathing failing, his heart no longer able to sustain his body. Emmie is saddened and a little adrift, but not lonely—she has grown used to being alone. Her marriage was a strange one, but not, in the end, entirely unhappy. She and Thomas rubbed along well enough once he got the other women out of his system.

A good marriage, of its type, she reflects.

1945: Emmie: Victory Sandwiches

At last definite information is circulating about victory in Europe, and it's only a matter of which day the announcement is made that holds up the celebrations. "It'll be tomorrow," asserts Mrs Sloane's son, who works in BBC radio, so he should know. "Got to be right," nods the local butcher, to his queues of customers.

On this promising morning, when peace beckons, Emmie is up early to bake and clean, and string bunting around the garden of her home in Chantry Road, Moseley. Trusting to the rumours, she's banked on today being the day and has invited her friends from the Make Do and Mend group to come over. She's made a potato and carrot cake with a few precious sultanas and some rather vintage candied orange peel. Her friends will bring baked offerings too, whatever can be scraped together from rations. Marion will visit later with her chums from the ARP Ambulance crew. *Those girls have done sterling work throughout the war*, reflects Emmie as she teeters on a kitchen chair to pin the bunting to the wall. She takes care climbing down—a fine thing, to break a leg today of all days!

The table is covered in one of Emmie's immaculately embroidered linen cloths—garlands of flowers ramble around the centre of this one and it has a deep lace edging. Emmie lays out the sandwiches, made from the tough national loaf, but enlivened with Marion's illicitly-acquired butter that comes Emmie's way once a week, plus a generous filling of marrow jam.

By 3pm she's ready—and not a moment too soon. The radio, burbling in the background, suddenly interrupts its programmes and the announcer suavely introduces the Prime Minister himself.

Winston Churchill's familiar, embattled voice rasps over the airwaves: "Yesterday morning, at 2:41 am, at General Eisenhower's headquarters, General Jodl, the representative of the German High Command, signed the act of unconditional surrender…"

One brief heartbeat of a pause and then, momentously:

"The German war is therefore at an end."

It's done! It's real! The war in Europe is over—yet the peace must still be won. Churchill is clear— forget not the sacrifices that have brought us here, forget not the work still needed to secure a safe future… but for now, make merry as well as you can.

And the whole country does so.

With a swift knock at the door, Emmie's friends pour in, clamorous with gossip, laden with buns and biscuits, and ready to wave the flags of freedom for all they are worth.

The party has been rolling along decorously for about an hour when Marion breezes in with ARP chums Betty Barker and Evette Ainsworth. The mood suddenly changes. Marion and the girls are full of bounce. They've been into Birmingham to see the crowds. "Kissing-madness," pronounces Marion, as she hangs her coat up on a hook in the hall. "I was glad to get away!"

Evette, a pretty blonde, is laughing a bit wildly—one drink too many, thinks Emmie shrewdly.

"Oh, but Marion, I never had so many chances at romance in my whole life!" Evette giggles, winking at Emmie. "Truly, I had at least three proposals of marriage in just one hour."

Emmie looks scandalised, but Betty slaps Evette on the back and cries: "Marry 'em then leave 'em, Evette my girl, that's all they're good for!"

And so the joshing goes on, until Dulcie arrives, together with her friends Irene and Vera.

Who asked them?

Emmie is mortified; her respectable friends will be appalled. Emmie doesn't at all like Vera—pushy girl—and Irene is—well, what can Emmie say in polite society? Beyond the pale, with her ribald jokes and end-of-pier dance routines.

The ladies of Make Do and Mend are transfixed by Irene. She's turned up in a man's suit, tailored to fit her slender body. Myrna Wimpole, eating a dish of rhubarb crumble, pauses her spoon on its way to her mouth and goggles. The little pile of crumble teeters and falls, but she doesn't notice. For Irene is wearing men's felt braces and a flat cap— sensational!

Dreadful girl, she just means to shock, thinks Emmie. She calmly begins to pour cups of tea for the new arrivals, mouth compressed into a firm line of endurance.

"Have you been to a fancy-dress party, dear?" asks Barbara Morton, smiling fondly at the high spirits of the ARP girls and vaguely assuming Irene and Vera are part of Marion's group.

Irene chuckles. She flips her flat cap onto the back of Emmie's fireside chair, clamps a cigarette between her lips, and lights it with theatrical flair. "Sort of," she admits. "It was a party anyhow. If you don't want to get kissed by all the boys, it's best to act like one. Confuses the buggers no end."

Vera, Marion and Dulcie hoot with laughter and the ARP girls elbow one another out of the way to get to the tea table. Emmie passes around the tea with showy politeness and a stiff smile edged with frost. When she reaches Irene, she studies the woman's braces closely. "My dear," she purrs, "it's just as well you're not better endowed; those would pinch dreadfully."

Marion snorts, and Irene throws back her head with laughter, then takes the cup of tea and thanks Emmie warmly. *After all, Mother is equal to whatever comes her way,* thinks Marion, rather admiringly.

It is a skill both Emmie's daughters will absorb into their lives in different ways—the art of dealing with uncomfortable emotions. In Beatrice's case, she learns to wear the armour of masks and deflections that her mother employs, while Marion chooses instead frankness and directness.

In the end, Emmie judges the VE Day tea party very jolly, Vera and Irene aside. After the party debris is cleared away that evening, Emmie reflects on life as she sits by the fireside. She wonders whether the world will ever return to the shape it once held—or whether, like the girls crowding her tea table, it has already passed out of her grip.

Marion comes in with a laden tray—tea, sugar, black-market milk, and some late-night biscuits. They discuss the rickety state of Beatrice's marriage—is it any better since that affair of the slap? Yes and no, replies Marion. Beatrice is always a little on edge, and though Ernest tries to behave better, it's as if his hold on his temper remains just beyond his reach.

"Never the same since Ceylon," says Emmie, thoughtfully, sipping her tea. Absently, she picks up her embroidery. It's based on a Japanese design and is very splendid indeed.

1946–1957: Emmie: The Socialite

Once the war is ended and the ordinary world starts up again, Emmie enthusiastically returns to her lively social life. Even Japan's wartime reputation can't dim her fascination with the East. She takes up Japanese flower arranging—ikebana—and pores over picture books to grasp the essentials of its style. It's an ambitious skill to acquire from a book, but with her natural flair for art, Emmie has some success, winning occasional prizes at the Women's Institute.

Only one thing troubles her: Beatrice's future. Emmie considers advising Beatrice to leave Ernest and set up home with her. But in the end, she cannot recommend what she herself never had the confidence to do.

"You can always count on me, Beatrice," she reminds, from time to time. "And on Marion."

"I know, Mother. I do," Beatrice always replies.

Unexpectedly, it is Emmie who moves in with a daughter, rather than the other way around. Noticing her mother's growing fatigue, Marion invites Emmie to share her cosy home. Emmie eagerly agrees. Their life together is comfortable, though there are compromises on both sides. Occasionally, Emmie wonders about Marion's love life. Has she got a beau? Did she ever? But Marion keeps her secrets close, and Emmie never presses her for answers.

One evening, at the age of eighty-seven, Emmie says she's feeling light-headed. "I'll go and lie down," she says. "I'll be right as rain in the morning."

But when morning comes, Marion finds her mother gone. It is unexpected, but not a tragedy. Emmie had a good life—well-lived, stoical and full of grace. Marion sits by the bed and holds her mother's hand. Emmie's face is peaceful, almost joyful. She was as ready to die as she had been to live.

Marion sighs, strokes her mother's hand one last time, and stands. From the lacquered oriental letter rack that Emmie had loved so well, Marion takes the doctor's number. As she places the call, she begins to think, calmly and clearly, about how to organise her own life now that she is free once more.

Afterlife Encounters
Emmie: visited 2025

Beauty and Talent

When I meditate on Emmie, I feel a lingering sadness from her soul—almost like a sigh—a calmness, and an unrealised spirituality buried deep inside. She radiates artistry, elegance, and grace. I sense that she has already passed through the soul-realm, though it was a slow and reflective journey. During that time, she often turned back towards the earthly realm to check on her daughters' safety and happiness. Now, she resides in the spirit-realm, distant but still watching over her family with deep affection.

Inessa studies the sepia portrait of young Emmie (depicted earlier in this chapter): the high-necked lace collar, her carefully arranged hair, the air of assurance in her steady gaze. Every detail speaks of the comfort and self-possession of her Edwardian world.

"She's spirited," Inessa remarks, "and surprisingly independent for her time. She had her own financial means, which gave her some freedom, but she couldn't realise this freedom during her life. What limited her wasn't her gender—it was the social conventions she could not transcend."

I nod. Emmie, like her daughter Beatrice, remained bound by tradition, even when her marriage proved difficult.

"She has a beautifully developed soul," Inessa continues. "Artistic, cultured, and deeply connected to beauty. She expressed herself spiritually through music, painting, embroidery, and gardening. Her devotion to family life was strong. She did not have a naturally religious orientation, but her spirituality flourished through her love of beauty."

Emmie's passage through the soul-realm was unusually slow, taking twice the average time. Partly, this was because of her devotion to her daughters, but there was another, unexpected reason—she lingered to revisit the beauty she had known in life. During her life-review, she immersed herself in the memory of every museum visit, every beloved object of art, and every illustrated book, savouring them once more. "I've rarely seen a soul take such deep pleasure in those memories," Inessa muses.

There was also something more painful holding Emmie back—her struggle to forgive Thomas. His infidelity left a deep wound, and although she tried earnestly to move past it, forgiveness took years. Finally, she found a way to transform her pain into compassion, and generously extended help to Thomas before continuing her journey.

Inessa senses that Emmie is now gathering new impulses for her next life, particularly focused on developing her intellectual capacities. "In this recent life, she didn't have the chance to study very much, or learn about spiritual matters. Her life was lived in the realm of feelings," Inessa explains.

I learn that, in Emmie's forthcoming life, she'll be attracted to cultural forms of spirituality—perhaps meditation or a deep study of Eastern traditions. Buddhism looks to be drawing her interest, and certainly she casts her eye over Eastern artistic traditions.

"Did she have an interest in the Far East?" asks Inessa. "Because there is a deep longing for this part of the world held within her spirit."

From somewhere within, the word *Japan* rings clearly in my mind. Suddenly, I remember the lacquered oriental-style letter rack I inherited from my great-aunt Marion. I bring it to the camera and show it to Inessa.

"Yes," she says, "that belonged to Emmie. She was enthralled by Chinoiserie—the exotic images of pagodas, cherry blossoms, and bridges. In her next life, she may well incarnate in Japan as a student of meditation. Let's hope she knows it's not quite the land of her fantasies anymore," Inessa adds with a smile, "otherwise she will have a disappointment."

Finally, Inessa gives one more insight: "In her next life, Emmie must learn to claim her own freedom. Despite her financial independence, she felt trapped by convention and couldn't transform her situation. That will be her challenge next time."

I cross my fingers for Emmie and wish her well in her next adventure.

Afterlife Encounters
Thomas: visited 2025

Lost Love

When Inessa views the 1916 Autochrome Lumière glass-plate photograph of Emmie and Thomas, Marion and Beatrice, she immediately senses the cracks in the marriage. Thomas's weaknesses and regrets lie thick in his soul. By then, his love for Emmie has faded, while her devotion to him endures. He has stayed with her out of affection for their daughters and a preference for the comforts of family life.

"Thomas was tempted by physical pleasures—whisky, gambling, women," Inessa explains. "He indulged because he could afford to, but in the end, his better nature helped him pull back from the worst of it. He's a good soul at heart, with stability and persistence as gifts, which mitigate against his other frailties. But a fear of being overlooked made him a social climber and gave him an air of arrogance which masked his insecurities."

He's rather a dry character, Inessa indicates, an intellectual type who believed himself amusing—yet in reality he was not. Thomas saw himself as destined for great things, but, in similar fashion to Emmie, he was unable to rise beyond the bounds of society's expectations and to embrace a different sort of life. His attempts to break free manifested as extra-marital affairs and risky pastimes, rather than as a prestigious or exemplary life.

"Thomas was meticulous about his appearance," observes Inessa. "He liked to wear finely tailored clothes and jewellery—quite the fashionable man about town."

At dancing, he excelled. He was surprisingly graceful, with a natural elegance in his movements, adding to his precision and style. Dancing drew him like a magnet—and so did dance halls. Glamour, sensuality, flirtations, and excitement were like oxygen to him. "But he had the strength to resist the charms of such places," adds Inessa, "which is one of several things to admire about him."

Professionally, Thomas was diligent but not passionate. His career as an accountant and later, as company secretary at the Graham James Engineering Works suited his methodical mind. Interestingly, Inessa notes that he found engineering fascinating—what luck, then, to gain a position in an engineering works! He retired early due to heart issues and passed away at seventy, after refusing cancer treatment. He had feared the surgery would be emasculating. In the end, both illnesses combined to claim him.

Sticky Stuff

When I look for Thomas, I see a still figure, glued in place by something sticky. It looks like caramel.

"He is certainly stuck," confirms Inessa, "but I see him more as tangled in a sort of web, with sticky stuff coating it. The web is made of ropes that tug his soul in many directions at once."

"What could the ropes represent?" I wonder.

"They're all the attachments that still bind him—alcohol, gambling, infidelity, illness, and morphine." Inessa pauses and considers. "We'll need to help him clear these attachments before he can move on."

Fire and Water

Together, we work to free Thomas. Inessa suggests that I visualize a fiery energy burning away the sticky substance surrounding him. Slowly the substance reduces, softens, and melts away. To my eye, this leaves Thomas looking less constricted, but there are still ropes of attachment clinging weakly to him. Inessa cleans and purifies these attachments, encouraging them to fade, one after another. Passions, desires, and illnesses—perceived as binding ropes—now dissolve and vanish.

Author's impression: Emmie reaches to help Thomas escape his sticky web by dissolving, with her forgiveness, his betrayal of her during their earthly life. Media: Acrylic paint, collage.

The progress is good, and Thomas begins to stir a little. After his immersion in purifying fire, I now perceive Thomas as being dry and rigid. An image of a digestive biscuit floats into my head and I smile, saying to Inessa: "He needs dunking, like a biscuit in a cup of tea." We both chuckle at the homely picture.

At Inessa's invitation, I start to wash imagined light through his soul and then a refreshing stream of water, warm with human affection. "That's helping, let's continue," affirms Inessa, and we repeat this process several times.

Thomas stands more freely now. Gone are the ropes binding his limbs, the shadows of emotion and illness, the sticky substance that held him fast. His dryness is eased, but now he looks up. *I'm thirsty*, he seems to say.

Then I see an arm shoot out and grab what looks like a whisky bottle!

"No, no," I laugh, "it will be better for you to drink some water, Thomas."

In my mind, I hand him a glass, and he drinks the refreshing draught. A smile forms in his soul—it was a joke, I sense! Now his soul takes on a cheerful aspect, as if he's delighted that his humour landed so well.

What is all this? he then seems to say to me, looking around him. Or perhaps it is: *Where am I? Who are you?* His questions and puzzlement float towards me. I try to respond but my answers are too complex for him to follow.

Thomas is scratching his head, bemused. As far as we on earth are concerned, Thomas has been snoozing since 1941, but for him, it is just a few minutes or so since he passed away. "It must be bewildering for Thomas," I say.

"Yes," confirms Inessa, "time is quite different in the soul-realm when compared to time on earth."

Thomas is now awake and aware. Inessa can tell that he's sending gratitude towards Emmie for her help when he was trapped. He stands on the brink of learning and self-development, ready to move forward.

"That's a big improvement for him," encourages Inessa. "We can hope that it's all a self-enlivening process from this point on."

Thomas will now need to absorb the experience of his soul-cleansing which has just been performed, and then start to reflect on his life. Although he has much to learn, including the ability to overcome his regrets, his positive qualities shine through and draw him onwards.

"Thinking about his next incarnation, what does his soul incline towards?" I ask.

"Well, as you may imagine," says Inessa, drily, "he might benefit from being a woman next time, so that he can understand the pitfalls of his former attitude to women. He will be able to learn about the other side of the coin…

"He has a good heart, though—I can see that," adds Inessa, "and there's much he can do next time to develop himself emotionally. But his time in the soul-realm may be longer, due to the hurt he caused, and his own passionate nature."

Emmie and Thomas during the Second World War, Birmingham, in the back garden of their home in South Birmingham. The body language is interesting—Emmie leaning forward, strong, enduring, more dynamic than her husband; and Thomas leaning back, as if the wind has left his sails.

Legacies

What does this story of love, suffering, passion, and sacrifice tell me? As I ponder the story of Emmie and Thomas, I see legacy as its deepest theme.

Emmie and Thomas leave their daughters much more than money, photographs, or lacquered letter racks. What they bequeath is more subtle, insinuating itself into the lives of their two daughters, into their grandchildren and even their great-grandchildren, too. This legacy is both comfort and burden.

To Beatrice, their oldest daughter, is passed a strong sense of duty, propriety, and the importance of appearances. Raised in the shadow of her mother's choices, Beatrice grows up graceful, loving, but fearful of scandal, and protective of her family's social standing. It is this fear—this deep reluctance to step outside the bounds of respectability—that binds her to her unhappy marriage with Ernest. Though the cracks widen over the years, she refuses to walk away, afraid of the whispering tongues that would surely follow. The cost of freedom, she believes, is too high. Like her mother and father before her, she cannot sculpt nor truly reach for her own freedom. There are consequences to Beatrice's decision. These will touch her daughter, as well as following generations, in subtle ways.

On the other hand, Beatrice also inherits gifts. She is bequeathed an ability to nurture beauty—like Emmie, she uses beauty as an inner discipline, a way of bringing light to self-restraint. Likewise, she is bequeathed the ability to hold devotion to her child; and to be creative. She inherits the skill of crafting—embroideries and flower arrangements—and perhaps at some level she absorbs her mother's passion for ikebana. Such gifts bring her pleasure and nourishment during life, even when other aspects of her existence turn sour. These things, too, Beatrice passes down in delicate ways, to her descendants.

For Marion the legacy is different, but equally complex. A bright, independent girl, she watches as her parents' marriage dissolves into distrust and bitterness. What begins as caution hardens, over time, into certainty: she will not make the same mistake. She chooses safety over risk, independence over partnership. Marion never marries, determined to remain free. Yet, in the quiet moments of her life, she occasionally wonders what might have been, if circumstances had fallen out differently.

Marion's gifts are many: a soberness and wisdom, a mathematician's brain, an independence of mind, talented green fingers, cheerful homemaking, and deep family loyalty.

Kindness, too, runs through both girls' veins. Emmie has a loving heart and an ability to draw pleasure from the smallest beauty around her. Both girls inherit these qualities, which remain with them always. Finally, they inherit Thomas's hard-won self-mastery—leading both girls to remain strong, loyal, and affectionate despite all difficulties.

These are the true legacies of Emmie and Thomas. They flow down the generations like rivulets of water, carrying challenges and blessings alike.

Turning the Page

The richly woven tale of Emmie and Thomas now draws us further back in time, to Emmie's grandfather, John Lunn. We've already glimpsed him through Matilda, who relished her father John's local fame. We have also seen him through the fond eyes of his granddaughter, Emmie.

John Lunn first appeared to me as an unidentified figure in an image of an oil painting tucked among the suitcase's photographs. In seeking to uncover his identity, I unearthed the remarkable story of his life—and, later, his afterlife.

Let us now meet this inventive and resourceful soul and see what further insights he offers to my family's unfolding story.

10:

THE ENGINEER OF FAITH

JOHN LUNN 1812–1892

My Great-Great-Great-Grandfather,

grandfather to Emmie

"Oh Lettie, I am so envious of the suit that Mr Stanwick pays you. He's such a clever young man and will surely go far," gushed Miss Fosdyke-Brown.

"Ha! Mr Stanwick," exclaimed Lettie. "It's all very well everyone talking of his cleverness with water pumps and drainage channels, but the man is an absolute silly when it comes to affairs of the heart!"

The Coffee House Indiscretion, Lorenzo Ebrio (2020)

1828: Riots

Young John stands transfixed with dread, as the crowd of angry men seethes around him and his father, Nathaniel, outside the Griffiths carpet factory in the centre of Kidderminster. The weavers have been laid off for eighteen weeks, and their fear of starvation and homelessness boils over into rage.

"They're only trying to protect their families, son," murmurs Nathaniel. The two have come out to help Jacob Griffiths protect his small 'carpet hall'. Nathaniel, a machinist, counts Jacob as friend and fellow brother within the church. A few years ago, Jacob entrusted Nathaniel with weaving a magnificent altar frontal for the new St George's Church in Kidderminster. Young John, who had watched this piece come to life, was struck by its brilliant colours and elegant design depicting Christ's descent from the cross. It felt to him like a visionary sign that he himself might one day contribute to Kidderminster's manufacturing power.

249

But tonight, the looms are silent, victims of a depression in the carpet market. The crowd presses forward, volatile and loud. Someone stumbles, cries out as he's kicked. There's a smell of sweat and fear. It hangs in the air as boots clatter on the cobbles; a brick crashes against the iron railings. Then a sudden surge—they're making for the Griffiths factory entrance.

Oil painting of John Lunn, Kidderminster, aged about fifty. A serious and steady gaze looks out at us. John is a soberly dressed man with an intense look to him, painted against a plain ground—no frills or folderols.

Nathaniel steps forward, hands hanging loosely at his sides. He stands still and silent. Inside, he's quaking, but outwardly he's calm and solid as a rock. His peaceable demeanour works. Just as John fears his father will be overwhelmed, the men seem to melt backwards a few paces.

"Now, lads, be calm, be patient," Nathaniel appeals, his voice steady. "You know the trade's bad at present. What can the factory owners do? They can't magic things better, but they understand your concerns and want to help where they can."

Nathaniel, always a man of practical kindness, has convinced Jacob Griffiths to provide food baskets for the men, and he directs the crowds to the back gate to collect bread, sausage, and cheese.

"Bless you, Mr Lunn," shouts one man, and another tugs his cap. Not all are appeased, however. There are some shouts of: "Trying to buy their way out of this, are they?" and "We don't take charity, it's work we want," but these voices are soon shouted down.

John slips through the small side gate and hurries to help distribute provisions. As he works, he thinks about how fear and hunger make people dangerous.

"Why don't we organise things better?" he asks Nathaniel later that evening, after the crowds have dispersed.

Nathaniel shakes his head. "If I knew that, John, I'd be a rich man," he says. "But there's sausage and cheese left over for us tonight!" They smile at one another, though John sees his father's brave face hides a shaken man.

That night stays with John. He admires his father's courage, yet the riot undermines his belief in the fairness of society. He starts to consider how good organization and fair-mindedness could change the world. Jacob's generosity spared the Griffiths factory; elsewhere, three thousand pounds' worth of damage tore through the town.

At sixteen, John is already a sober lad, and stalwart of the Wesleyan Sunday School. He entertains the children with Bible stories. His consuming interests come to the fore as he does so. In his stories, a hot air balloon is liable to appear above the Sermon on the Mount, or a steam-driven machine whisks away lucky families, while others are left to suffer the ten plagues in Egypt. Minister Dawson, a tolerant man, is amused by John's inventive touches. He displays the children's resultant illustrations with glee—Jesus on a traction engine is his especial favourite.

Machinery is John's passion. He tinkers with cogs and rods abandoned by the carpet factories, out of which he constructs tools and household items. Nathaniel encourages John in his talents. "He's going to be an inventor, Sarah," he tells his wife. "If we can get him an apprenticeship somewhere, he could go far."

1840: Cogs Turning Slowly

On leaving school, John had joined the local foundry. Here he began to learn more about machinery, as well as about efficiency in manufacturing processes. He absorbed knowledge with the appetite of a hungry dog at supper. In time, though, he started to hanker for a move to his father's industry, in the fascinating carpet weaving factories.

One Sunday, at the chapel, he spied a newly arrived young lady called Matilda, who, after some weeks, expressed keenness to help with the Sunday School. In truth, Matilda was keen to be near John, Sunday School be hanged, but it was the only way she could draw John's attention towards her. She and John toiled alongside one another in pursuit of raising the children's spiritual knowledge, and many were the enjoyable Sundays they spent in this fashion. John came to look forward to his Sunday School days with more than a little frisson of pleasure.

It was some time, however, before it dawned upon John that something additional—other than the Sunday School pastimes— might be required of him regarding the lovely Matilda. It was Nathaniel who finally awakened John to the real world of courtship.

This is how it happened:

"John, lad," says Nathaniel one day as he's cleaning his boots on the kitchen mat, "don't you like that pretty girl, Matilda?"

"Why, of course I do, father," responds John, in some surprise. "Why do you ask?"

"Because, son, she's been patiently waiting for you to notice her for three years now, and I can't see her waiting around for much longer!" asserts his father.

"Waiting for me, father? In what way?" asks John, absently winding the handle of a small cog-driven machine he's building. He wants it to slice string beans evenly. His mother would be so pleased if she didn't have to chop them by hand anymore.

"For goodness sakes, John, lad, marry her, or she'll marry someone else as sure as eggs is eggs," explodes Nathaniel, and John almost drops his spanner in astonishment.

Now, the cogs of his brain start to whir. Marry her? *Marry Matilda?* Why yes, yes, of course, he wants to marry her.

Suddenly John is infected with panic. Oh, why hasn't he thought of this before? Now he ceases what he's doing, and hurries to change his oily clothes. His hands tremble. What if he's too late? Ridiculous as it sounds, he suddenly pictures pretty Matilda driving away with a stranger. It could happen, he reasons, it could be happening right now! He dashes from the house, hat gripped in his hand and coat flying in the wind.

Naturally, Matilda says yes. "Oh, Tildy, I could burst with happiness!" shouts John, as he races off to tell his father the good news. The wedding follows, a small and friendly affair, and the couple settle to a contented married life. Matilda suffers John's absent mind and fascination with machinery kindly and patiently. When children bless the marriage, her world is replete with joy.

1850: Pride

Little Matilda Lunn, offspring of the famous John Lunn, is very proud of her Papa. Very proud indeed.

One afternoon, Tildy comes upon her dressed in a cardboard crown, an old satin curtain, and cotton gloves that are reserved for summer walks in the park. She is parading up and down the stairs, with the curtain trailing perilously underfoot. The small figure of her young brother Reginald shuffles along behind, carrying the end of the curtain by its corners.

"Whatever are you doing, Matilda?" asked Tildy. Matilda, an imaginative and highly-strung child, is forever dreaming up new games and inveigling her little brother into taking part by bribing him with sweeties.

"I'm the Duchess of Lunn, Mama, and I'm saying hello to all the children of my workers at my carpet mill. I'm giving them all sweets, to show them I'm kind and charitable."

Matilda, born on a Friday—*Friday's child is loving and giving*—feels the weight of philanthropic responsibility on her small, seven-year-old shoulders. She must do as her Papa does through his chapel and distribute kindness to the poor. She practices her wave, her benevolent nod, and her grand distribution of barley sugars. The hall furniture, upon which she presses her gifts, seems suitably grateful for the largesse.

"Are you playing Fine Ladies too, Reginald?" asks Tildy encouragingly.

Reginald sticks out his tongue on which rests a red aniseed ball, takes out the sucked sweet, and looks at it. At four years old he is fascinated by how everything works. How does a sweet disappear? That is his interest today.

"She's showin' off," he says, reinserting his aniseed ball, "because Papa is a famous man. Nellie says she's all 'oity-toity.'" Nellie, the maid, never minces words. The children pick up all sorts of unrefined expressions from her.

Telling John about the exploit later, Tildy paints a comedic picture. She's chuckling as she tidies tablemats and candlesticks from the dining room table. "You should have seen her, condescending as a queen in a palace!" she exclaims.

John looks concerned, even horrified. "A daughter of mine should never act as if she's better than others," he exclaims, thinking of the sad state of his daughter's character.

"Pride goeth before destruction, and an haughty spirit before a fall," he laments, quoting his Biblical Proverbs.

"Oh, let her play, John, she's so proud of you," laughs Tildy, as she deftly picks from the arm of the dining chair a sticky, half-sucked aniseed ball.

The next day, John frowningly admonishes little Matilda about her pridefulness.

"I think you must write out the Proverbs saying in your copybook five times," he decides, "and we'll have no more displays of such airs and graces."

"Yes Papa," agrees Matilda, humbly, but that very evening, when John asks to see her copybook, she has not done her task as prescribed. Instead, she has boldly interwoven the proverb into a condescending speech of thanks to the mayor of Kidderminster. In her copybook she has headed the speech: *My Speach* under which is inscribed: *To be givvin by me on the ocaysion of my receept of the key to the town of Kiddyminster on beharf of my faymous Papa, John Lunn the Invenntor.*

There is nothing to be done with Matilda. Her la-di-da ways accompany her into adulthood where she becomes a seeker of social status. But it is all done with the most proper decorum, as she herself would say. With such a father, one must keep up standards, and Matilda does so, for the rest of her life.

1852: The Lunn's Stamping Machine

In time, John moves on from the foundry and into the carpet weaving industry. In his middle years, he gains a machinist job with a factory in Kidderminster run by gruff industrialist Edward Smith.

John's inventive mind impresses Edward, whose own brain teems with thoughts of novelty textile machinery. Edward lacks the technical skill to realise his own ideas, and John becomes his salvation. Together, they innovate, but it's John's stamping machine that makes waves.

It so happens that, during part of his working week, John finds himself positioned next to the card-stampers. These men work all day on the meticulous, skilful task of stamping holes into the Jacquard loom mechanism-cards. Intensive concentration is needed for this role. A single hole mis-punched and unnoticed can mean yards of wasted material, a costly error that no factory can afford.

*A nineteenth-century power loom fitted with the Jacquard mechanism.
A continuous chain of punched cards passes over the card cylinder, each
card lifting selected warp threads through a system of needles and
hooks. In this way, the loom weaves complex patterned cloth with
remarkable precision. The accuracy of the punched cards
is vital to the whole operation.*
Internet Archive Book Images, no restrictions, via Wikimedia Commons.

John notes that many looms run the same pattern, yet every card is
still punched by hand on the piano card-cutter. One of the new lads,
Sidney Sikes, is a menace on this machine. His attention wanders to
the clacking heddles and the steady pulse of the shuttles as they fly to

and fro. The result—his cards are regularly mis-punched or tumble muddled to the floor. What problems this then causes! John can see how vulnerable the fortunes of the whole factory are to this one process, and so he begins to think.

"Edward," John exclaims one day, "this is madness. We stamp identical patterns over and over by hand, when we could batch-stamp them instead." He explains how his idea would work. A master set of pattern cards is stamped by hand, then multiple copies are accurately replicated in batches at a fraction of the cost and time. "We'll steal a march on every other factory in Kidderminster and beyond," he finishes, unrolling his sketches as he speaks.

Edward peruses the plans. It's a cunning-looking item, he has to admit. That machine could copy any Jacquard pattern onto countless cards, and it could spit those cards out as fast as can be. The looms need not stand idle any longer than necessary, and there'd be no more sloppy mistakes by copy card-cutters. Edward's eyes gleam.

"Let's build it, John," he cries, and he slaps the table with his palm. "Let's build the bugger and beat everybody to the bloody finishing post."

John cannot condone swearing, yet he has to grin at Edward's forthrightness.

They strike a bargain together. Edward will fund the machine's production, John gets the patent, and they'll split the profits. They seal the deal with a glass of port and a cup of tea. "You Wesleyans never have any fun," comments Edward, knocking back his second port in one go. John laughs. "I'll not have a headache in the morning though," he teases, sipping his tea. They go their separate ways, both well-pleased with the day's outcomes.

The Lunn's Stamping Machine is a runaway success. The factory's reputation soars, and John's invention brings prosperity. With his share, John repairs the headstock on the Wesleyan chapel bell, and then commissions a second bell with a beautiful tone, that rings out merrily over the neighbourhood.

Further inventions follow and John begins to be modestly wealthy. Mindful of the perfunctory schooling available to most working people, he decides to fund a small library for the parish. He begins with a children's library of Bible stories and follows up with a range of books for adults.

Patient Matilda eyes up his latest choices of books doubtfully. On his desk are neatly piled: *An Introductory Treatise on Locks, A Handbook of Steam Engines*, and *Bishop Abney's Encyclopaedia of the Old Testament.*

Tactfully, she tries: "John, I'm sure those could be quite interesting to some readers, but perhaps something lighter as well?"

John looks baffled. Surely his chosen books are fine indeed, and will fly off the shelves?

Matilda gazes at him for a moment. "What about the ladies, John?" she prompts. "They'd certainly be glad of a book of household hints, not to mention recipe pamphlets. And novels, John, novels are extremely popular…"

John blinks. Ladies? *Ladies*? Will they go to a library? He scratches his head. "Well, Tildy," he finally decides, "you know best. I'm a hopeless fellow to choose books for the ladies of the town." And he gives Matilda the very enjoyable task of setting up a lending library for ladies.

His biggest project, and one that lasts for the rest of his life, is his idea to train ex-prisoners in trades. He recalls those desperate men, the rioters, condemned to prison. Most never recovered their fortunes or reputations.

"These fellows come out of prison, Tildy," he explains, "and they end up on parish aid. It's not dignified. It's not practical." With Edward's help, he offers apprenticeships in a variety of trades. In good faith, he states his intention to make an accompanying study of the Bible mandatory, but is rapidly overruled by Matilda and Edward— diplomatically on the one hand, and firmly on the other.

"Not everyone loves the Good Book like you do, John," says Edward. "Let's leave that choice to the men themselves."

Some say John's daft in the head, others that he's seeking to bargain his way into heaven, but John believes that the good sense of his scheme is worth any jibe.

1888: The Portrait

John yawns and stretches his stiff limbs. It's been a lengthy meeting at the Union, and as president for the past fifty-five years, he's rather glad to be handing over the baton. Today marks his retirement, and a celebratory lunch is being held in his honour.

So much water under the bridge now. So many years since, at the tender age of twenty-one, John first accepted the unlikely role of Sunday School Union president—a surprising appointment for a young man obsessed with engines and mechanics. Yet the responsibility had been good for him. It had steadied and matured him.

Sunday School had long been his delight, though he'd never been priggish about it. When his boisterous brace of cousins, George and Jenkin, came bowling in from Wolverhampton, they'd ribbed him for his studious piety. He wasn't above giving them a punch on the jaw in return—in what he called his 'rash youth'. Once, he tied puny Jenkin to the garden tree and read aloud from the Bible—juicy Old Testament stories about fights and blood. Jenkin had to admit, there were some decent tales in that old book after all.

Then there was the time, aged six, when John overheard the minister wish aloud for illustrated hymn books. That afternoon, John crept into the chapel, took down all the hymn books, and drew pictures of Jesus on as many fly leaves as his hand could bear. Later, he told the minister the chapel could buy them off him for a halfpenny each. The adults had roared with laughter and called him a 'chip off the old block'. He'd had no idea what they'd meant.

Back in the present, John notes that the buzz of conversation in the room is growing. Suddenly there's a kerfuffle at the doorway and several men appear, carrying a large object draped in a curtain. John is intrigued. All eyes swivel to Oswald Hurlston, who's clambered up on a chair. He raises his hand.

"Dear friends!" he cries, in his special-occasion voice. "We are gathered to celebrate fifty-five years of service by Mr John Lunn to our Sunday School. He has lived a life of active love of God through service to our Union. On this historic day of his retirement, we present our compliments with this specially commissioned portrait."

The curtain falls. To John's astonishment, he finds that he's gazing at a large version of himself, but painted in oils. Depicted in his younger days, he looks keen-eyed, upright, slightly stern, with a wry lift at the mouth, and a quiet kindness in the eyes. John is, for once, almost speechless. Matilda, seated next to him, gasps with excitement, and seventeen-year-old Emmie claps her hands with delight.

"Go on, Papa, say something," hisses Matilda urgently, prodding John in the ribs.

"Friends… dear friends," John begins, then falters. Matilda frowns.

A pause, then John blows out his breath and grins.

"Well, you might have painted me atop a steam engine, fellas!"

The room erupts with laughter.

"Seriously—thank you, from the bottom of my heart," says John, and the applause that follows is warm and prolonged.

He smiles around the room, pondering the turns his life has taken. Kidderminster has grown grander in his time. The railways have arrived. The early 'carpet halls' have become humming factories, now powered by steam. Stylish new Axminster designs pour from the looms, alongside the Brussels, Wilton, and Kidderminster patterns he knows so well. Once he marvelled at the Brussels loom—now it is just a workhorse. He shakes his head in wonder.

After lunch, John walks home on the arm of his son-in-law, John Peat—'young John', as they all call him. He's a kind man, doing well with his decorating business. He seems to rather enjoy his wife's dramatic ways—Matilda is nothing if not colourful and larger than life. Young John, raised in the countryside, is still round-eyed at town life, and happy to let his wife lead in all social affairs.

Living in their house, John has been comfortable. The rooms are spacious, the hospitality gracious, the décor carefully tasteful. Still, he must mind his Ps and Qs—no tobacco crumbs on the rug, no books left open on the floor. But his beautiful granddaughter Emmie is a treasure. She reads the Bible to him when his eyes grow tired. It does an old man good. She reminds him of Tildy—his late wife—in the turn of her head, her milky skin, her wide blue eyes.

As they near home, John glances up and sees a shaft of light piercing the heavy skies. *A finger of God,* he thinks, nodding to himself. The moment stirs a memory. Some years ago, he had taken Emmie to the recently opened Art Gallery in Birmingham. They had stood, hand in hand, marvelling at the colourful paintings—especially one depicting a divine ray of light pouring from a figure in the clouds.

"Is that God, do you think, Grandpapa?" Emmie had asked, eyes wide.

"Yes, sweetheart. God's light shines upon us, each and every one," John had replied, smiling. "We call those shafts of light that break through the clouds the Fingers of God, you know."

Emmie had looked thoughtful. Then: "If God has so many fingers, Grandpapa, I shouldn't like to have to knit him a pair of gloves."

John had pealed with laughter and regaled the family with the story on their return.

That evening, after all the excitement of the celebratory lunch, John is a little weary. He blows gently on his cocoa and stirs it to stop the skin from forming. Tomorrow is Sunday, and he looks forward to the Mill Street Methodist Church service, where he'll see his friend Ambrose Slade, a great scholar of religious texts. Together they'll dissect, with many a scholarly groan, the muddled messages of Reverend Cartwright's sermon.

Perhaps the congregation will sing his favourite hymn—*Rock of Ages*.

That's a grand tune, he thinks drowsily. It reminds him of Nathaniel, all those years ago, standing like a rock while the rioters surged.

For now, today has been pleasure enough. He'll sleep well tonight, thinking of dear Tildy, whom he misses every day. She waits for him in Heaven, he believes. He's not far from crossing over himself. What a happy homecoming it will be when he spies his dearest girl again.

He climbs gratefully into bed, closes his eyes, and rests in the dim hush of his bedroom. Somewhere downstairs, behind oak-panelled walls and velvet curtains, music begins to drift upward. Emmie is practising Schumann's *Träumerei*. The rivulets of notes pour delicately from her hands, travelling the length of the hall, climbing lightly up the staircase, floating along the landing, and stealing into his chamber.

The cadences entwine him in soothing tendrils of peace. His breathing deepens and softens.

Going home, he thinks, as his soul drifts away to be with the angels, until the morning's light awakens him to another fine day.

He sleeps. And in this sleeping, he feels blessed. In the background, the music plays on—serene and pure, like the voice of another world.

Afterlife Encounters
John: visited 2024

Seek and Ye Shall Find

Where shall we look for John Lunn? His obituary makes him sound like a latter-day saint, but then, obituaries of this era were often flowery and effusive. Souls can be found in surprising places, regardless of their earthly reputation. "I suspect he's in the spirit-realm," I suggest, because I can detect no feeling-based presence, no trace of a feeling-and-emotion body. I believe this might indicate that his soul is no longer lingering in closer realms.

"It seems likely he's in the spirit-realm," Inessa agrees.

Searching in the spirit-realm is different from searching in the soul-realm. In this higher world, a being has shed the physical body, then the life-force body, and later the feeling-and-emotion body (soul). What remains is the enduring self: the essence that has absorbed the soul's personality—together with many others shaped across previous lives. Such a being is less emotional—more a luminous presence.

Inessa concentrates deeply, focusing on John's oil painting and then on an engraving of his face as an old man. "Where is he?" she murmurs.

A shimmery presence seems to gather in my meditation: a figure standing quietly, looking about with gentle curiosity. Joy seems to radiate from him in soft, light-filled waves. "I see him," states Inessa.

"As with your great-grandfather Arthur, he's in a kind of spiritual school."

Another scholar, I think. As in life, so beyond: John continues his studies.

"I feel he's amazed and humbled by what he has met since death," Inessa adds. "He longed to return quickly to a life of religious devotion, but he was not yet suited to such a path. Why?"

She listens inwardly again. "His angel indicates that he must deepen the heart forces. In life, John's thinking had the clarity of something almost spiritual, but it lacked warmth. That is his next lesson."

Travelling Well

John's spirit is now working towards cultivating more feminine qualities of heart-love and warmth of thought. These are the forces he'll need to deepen his spiritual growth.

"What a nice soul he is," declares Inessa. "I like him very much. There's a high element in his make-up. I see that he already carries a part of his emerging spirit-self, one of the three aspects of our future higher selves. This is remarkable!"

Asking for more information, I learn that humans are on a long path towards their spiritual potential. En route, we will all develop further spiritual parts of ourselves, higher elements that will nourish and mature our eternal inner being.

Inessa considers: "Yes, he is highly spiritual already, and yet, I think he's also a little dry, strait-laced, and intellectual. He needs some warming up—humour, expressive artistry—qualities he lacked during his life as John. So now, this is his mission."

John's obituary speaks of cancer, yet Inessa observes that no illness weighed on his journey after death. "He's travelled well," she comments. "His strength and integrity carried him through the soul-realm and on into the spirit-realm. He needs no help from us."

"I imagine he'll return as a woman," I venture, picturing how a more feminine life might aid John's growth.

But Inessa surprises me. "No," she says, "I believe he'll come back as a man again, but with the challenge of developing warmth and artistry. In a way, it would be too easy for him to cultivate these qualities as a woman. This path will strengthen him more."

She adds, with a smile, "I see poetry or story-writing in his future. Even, perhaps, romantic poetry!"

I imagine the machine-obsessed inventor transforming into a sensitive bard. "He'll need all his powers of invention to earn his keep as a poet!" I laugh.

How has John done so well for himself, despite his flaws? Inessa reflects that his devotion to an ordinary life has been key. "We don't need to be saints to progress spiritually," she explains. "A life devoted to work, friends, community, and family—with integrity and willingness—is as valuable as any religious vocation. We can gain profound spiritual initiation simply by dedicating ourselves to our work, without greed or aggression. That's what John has done."

So John Lunn has found his way, in clear consciousness, to the blissful heights of the spirit-realm. Ahead lies the schooling of warmth. He will surely learn to weave that quality into his spirit.

Author's Note: The Mystery Man: Finding John Lunn

I discover John by chance. In a stack of Jimmy's pictures, a black-and-white print of an oil painting stares back at me—an upright man, stern yet kind, mid-nineteenth-century clothing—but unlabelled. I study his features for family echoes. Who does he resemble? Emmie? Perhaps.

In the spirit of conversation, I say to his portrait: "Please tell me who you are, if you'd like to be re-united with your family." Silence... but who knows? Perhaps something may come of my request.

Some weeks later, I unearth from Jimmy's suitcase a small mother-of-pearl scrapbook inscribed: "To my daughter Emmie from JP" (John Peat—Emmie's father). Inside lie clippings and oddments. I flip through, and there—yes!—near the back I find an engraved portrait of an elderly man. I laugh—it is the same face as the oil painting. And there's a name; even an obituary. *John Lunn is found!*

*John Lunn in old age—a kindly and wise face,
earnest and serious.
Engraving published with his obituary.*

Within the obituary, I find mention of the Lunn Stamping Machine, said to have transformed production potential within the Kidderminster carpet world. Nowadays there is no remaining record of this invention, and I have had to reconstruct its likely function from research. Its existence—though proven—now joins the many threads of knowledge sustained only through the chance recovery of a family memory. That printed obituary, perhaps snipped from a newspaper by Matilda and passed to Emmie to paste into her scrapbook, travelled across time to finally reach and speak to me. And so John's achievements are rediscovered.

Emmie was twenty-one at John's death so it is likely that she both knew and loved him. This realisation brings John closer, connects him to me, brings him into the heart of my family to take his place once more.

John had been lost only briefly. Now he sits among my invisible friends, another presence in the growing circle that has made this book possible.

Turning the Page

John's story takes us as far back as the family photographs allow—tracing a lineage of invention, faith, purpose, and acts of charity that anchor us in the divine moral stream. In his tale we glimpse the origins of the family's devotion to duty, its orthodoxy within society, its aspiration (Matilda), its intellect, and, in Emmie, its artistry.

Many years later, this legacy will enthral another—a young engineer who marries one of John's descendants. Ernest Mallory, in marrying Beatrice Gwyndaf, cleaves to the same lineage of invention and duty, absorbing its sober industriousness along with its moral seriousness. Through Ernest's careful collection of family memorabilia, he becomes the first custodian of a tradition that will, in time, pass to me, the author of this book.

John Lunn, Arthur and Ernest Mallory—each inventive and clever—continued their striving beyond the threshold of death, seeking to temper intellect with heart. To them, the family owes both forbearance and gratitude.

In completing this arc of the Mallory/Gwyndaf line with John's tale, the wheel of my forebears turns now to a road less travelled—a road that leads not backward in time, but sideways, into the lives of the Ruggles family.

The Ruggles are relatives by marriage. Jimmy Ruggles, warm-hearted and resourceful, married Dulcie Mallory, daughter of Lily and Arthur. We have seen how the Mallory line runs parallel to the Lunn-Gwyndaf thread, and how the two lineages culminated in the union of Ernest and Beatrice. These families, while distinct, are woven together through love, karma, and shared destinies.

Shortly, we shall meet Jimmy and Dulcie and follow their tale of love, destiny, and growth. But before we do, we must turn towards Jimmy's mother, Polly Ruggles.

On the surface, Polly's life appears quiet and uneventful—yet it opens into one of the most profound spiritual dramas in the book. Through her story, we encounter a hidden world of entrapment and release, confusion and grace—a drama shaped not by heroic deeds, but by the gentle power of a loving heart. Even here, an inner strength is tested: compassion and nobility of soul rise to meet their challenges and, in doing so, touch the Light.

Let us now turn the page and be introduced to Polly.

II:

A SOUL CAUGHT IN THE BLAST

POLLY RUGGLES 1887–1940

My Great-Great Aunt by marriage, mother to Jimmy

"I am here in the library at last," thought Fanny.
Her hand reached out to touch the books' spines.
Softly she stroked the embossed gilt lettering on the old leather.
She had yearned all her life for this moment.

"Take a look," called her uncle Albert. "Pull out any of 'em you like."

But Fanny could not bring herself to borrow one single book,
for she lacked the boldness to see her world changed
by the knowledge within their pages.

The Barnacle Rope, Lorenzo Ebrio (2022)

25th October 1940: Carlton Cinema: Sparkhill

The screen flickers, the pictures fragmented, incomprehensible. Colours, rich and bright, flash and change before Polly's wide-open eyes. There's a jarring noise—voices, crashing, tearing. She sits frozen in her seat, hands locked to the armrests, feet jerking as her toes scrabble for ground that seems no longer to exist.

Her breath comes in sharp little pants. She cranes her neck. The cinema is packed, the seats filled with men and women staring vacantly at the screen, their faces blank with shock or rigid with fear. Smoke curls fuggily around their heads. There's a smell of—what? A sharp, bitter stench, acrid and metallic, fills her nostrils. She wants to cough but there is no air in her lungs. She wants to vomit, but her body won't obey. The tripe and onions sit like lead inside her.

*The wedding of Fred and Polly Ruggles in Birmingham, 1912.
Polly is surrounded by Fred's family, and strikes a cheerful,
almost noble pose in the photo. Given her skill at dressmaking,
she probably made her own costume.*

The film reel seems to be stuck. It flicks repeatedly—wind, rain, people, water, Dorothy Lamour shouting one word over and again, her pretty face bulging out towards Polly. The screen seems to be ripping, and its edges billow as in a high wind.

Polly is bewildered and terrified. She cannot understand what is happening. Where is her body? She looks at her limbs. One of her legs is missing, or is it one of her arms? Her eyes dart wildly, hunting for meaning, hoping for escape. She can't remember anything. Wasn't she going to the movies? Some film about a girl and a chimpanzee on a desert island? No, that must be wrong. It sounds ridiculous.

Suddenly the lights fail. The screen tears apart and falls. There's a groan, a smash—as the ceiling joists give way—and Polly is wrenched into a vortex of blackness.

1916: Socks and Smalls

Polly stirs onions in a heavy iron skillet on the black-leaded range. Little Jim, just one year old, is slumbering quietly in his cot in the corner of the kitchen. Young Freddie, two years old, sits cross-legged on the rag rug, building towers with his wooden bricks.

Polly wipes her forehead in the steamy room. She's busy from dawn 'til dusk, being a lone parent. Her husband, Fred, in the 21st Empress of India Lancers, is holed up in India.

What use are cavalry in the trenches of Flanders?

he'd written to her, just the other day.

We'll be here for some time to come, Pol, so don't worry about me. Civil unrest is always around the corner in India. They need us lads here on the ground, to keep the Empire safe!

The onions caramelise slowly on the range, as Polly stirs and stirs, her eyes unfocused. She's coping all right on Fred's pay, with her own money coming in alongside it. Tuesdays to Fridays she runs a small shop in Sparkhill—Polly's Tripe and Meats—selling cows' heels, tripe, offal, and hot meaty snacks spooned into bowls or paper cones for the lunchtime crowd. Her cuts of meat are cheap and cheerful, but the quality is decent and local folk queue to pick up their shopping at a good price.

Life is hard, but she has Fred's family supporting her—Maud, Emma, Alice, Jesse, Kitty. What a clutch of sisters Fred has. She gets along well enough, though it can feel like one against five.

Just the other day, Kitty had breezed into Polly's kitchen with three rashers of bacon wrapped in greaseproof paper.

Polly (on the right) posing with a girlfriend in a photographer's studio, leaning on an improbably rustic stile. Their wide picture hats, fashionable walking coats, and high-collared blouses are typical of the Edwardian era just before the First World War, giving the image both a holiday air and a sense of jaunty self-presentation. Birmingham c. 1910—1913.

"Thought you and the boys might like these for your tea," she'd said kindly, then reached into the basket of freshly washed and mangled laundry and started to hang out the items on Polly's pulley airer. Socks, smalls, nappies, blouses. She'd hung them in ways Polly disapproved of—bunched too close, overlapped, and layered to cram more on the slats.

"How's your shop doing, Pol?" Kitty had asked, as she stooped and straightened, bent and stretched. "You know, you ought to call it something posher—like, use your proper name—Maria. It sounds grander and you could charge more. *Maria's Meats and Treats*. What about that?"

A vest dangled any old how, and Polly blinked hard to stop her eyes rolling in irritation. "I like the shop's name, Kitty, and my customers like the value I give them. Posh isn't what I need—it's queues of customers!"

Kitty had wiped her hands on her apron and looked around for more tasks, but Polly had hastened her out of the door with hearty thanks. Once the door had closed behind Kitty, Polly had set to, quietly re-hanging the washing the way she liked it.

1917: Cows' Heels

The big boiler pot in the back room of Polly's shop burps and spits. The cow heels roll in their bath of hot water, emitting meaty smells. They're a treat for her customers—warm, gelatinous, and nourishing, to be consumed with bowl, spoon, and a smack of the lips.

Polly's teenage assistant Ada, limp and pale as a piece of overcooked tripe, flops out the sheep's heads onto white cloths. The tripe and sheep's hearts go slithering into a big enamel bowl, the lungs—sheep's lights—into another. There's dripping and bread in the back ready to be made into sandwiches, a few slices of cold tongue for the discerning customers, and a big kettle steaming on the stove for cups of tea. Polly spent an hour this morning ensuring Ada scrubbed the floors and counters, so they're gleaming like cut glass.

Jim gurgles and babbles in his playpen in the back room, well away from the seething broiler pot. He clatters wooden cubes together and shouts gleefully when they bounce and bang on the floor. Freddie gravely rolls his toy car backwards and forwards, in and out of the table legs.

The bell jangles, and Mrs Baverstock heads for the counter, her shopping bag ready to receive the weekly pound of tripe and lamb's liver that Polly has already parcelled up. Behind her, the lunchtime queue is forming. A line of men in blue overalls gather from Green and Drake's Precision Fittings, mingling with a gaggle of women from

Ashford and Monto trinket finishers. They all hold enamel mugs, plates, and bowls, and in one case even a teapot.

"Has yer wife let yer out then, Malcolm?" shouts Elsie Evershed, gripping her spoon and bowl like spoils from a battle. "Must've polished yer boots *and* yer manners over the weekend."

Malcolm sticks his hands in his braces and smiles jauntily. "Eat some bread an' drippin', Elsie girl," he hollers. "Yer scrawny enough to go in a broilin' pot."

Two dandies: Fred's brothers, ready for a day out on the town. With glossy top hats, a walking stick and umbrella, they strike nonchalant poses for the studio camera, presenting themselves as men of the world. Birmingham c. 1908—1910.

Laughter ripples up and down the queue as they wait, shuffling their feet.

Polly's mind wanders to the letter Fred posted from India, now tucked into her apron pocket. France, he'd said. A winter with the horses on those blasted slaughterfields. Her hand trembles slightly as she chops liver and slides it into greaseproof paper. She tries to keep her mind on the job.

"Bit 'o heel in the bowl, Missus," croaks old Mr Perkins, wrinkled as a raisin, stooped as an ancient yew. She ladles glutinous cow heel, the jelly sticking to the spoon. Cups of tea, bowls of broth, pork dripping sandwiches, pigs' trotters, pease pudding with ham scraps. Polly cuts, scoops, wraps, chats, while Ada scuttles around behind her.

Fred, she thinks, *Fred in France. What if... No, don't go there.*

Farthings, halfpennies and pennies pass to and fro.

Clang-clang goes the shop bell. Through the door bustle two smart men. Polly sighs. It's Fred's brothers, Louis and Bernard—'a pair of sillies' is what she calls them, although her little boys enjoy their antics. They both failed recruitment checks for the army—Bernard has flat feet—"the flattest the recruitment officer ever saw," he assures people—and Louis is so short-sighted he struggles to find his way home. They work as bus conductors on the Birmingham buses, and maintain the public parks in their spare hours.

"Hellooo, Polly Dolly," they chorus as they push to the front of the queue, to the annoyance of the waiting purchasers. "We've popped in for some of your delectable faggots and gravy. Wrap 'em in paper for us, Pols, and we'll lick 'em up while we wait for the homnibus into Brum." They turn and pirouette for the queue, showing off their smart coats and hats. They're off to gallivant around town on their day off, ready for mischief and a drink or two.

"Ta-ra, gorgeous Pols—keep your brisket warm until our Fred comes home," they chortle, already slurping up their faggots and gravy take-aways. Chuckles and catcalls follow them, and a few winks flow in the direction of Polly.

"No chance of playing away with those two 'olding yer leash," sighs Elsie, giving Polly a sympathetic moue, and casting her eyes longingly over a handsome soldier as he strolls by in uniform.

Really! thinks Polly, with annoyance. *Those two brothers of Fred's make me a laughing-stock.*

Sometimes, just sometimes, Polly wishes Fred were an only child.

Fred poses for a portrait in his dashing uniform for the 21st Empress of India Lancers. He is aged twenty-one. The original is in colour. An investment in a colourised photograph shows how proud Fred and his family were of his posting and army career.

1922: Sparky

Fred, now an electrical switchgear assistant for the City of Birmingham Electrical Department, is known as Sparky by the neighbours. His new-fangled job seems glamorous to them. Most work in older trades—lacquerer, leather worker, chain maker—and Sparky is a novelty. He works all day with the nebulous, invisible forces of electricity and comes home alive every night.

Old Bert on the corner, a cobbler for all his life, scratches his head and says it's a miracle. "Do you store it in jars, Sparky?" he asks. And: "How's it made, that electricity?" And: "Can you touch it?"

Polly watches good-naturedly as Sparky laughs, struts, and basks in the awe of his friends. She's proud of him and admires his social ambition. But sometimes, watching him preen for the lads, Polly wonders where it's going—this drive to improve, to impress. What part of it is for the family, and what part just for Fred?

After his return from war, Fred was galvanized to make something of his life. "All that horror, boredom and discomfort's got to have been character-forming, Pol. I'll be able to get my foot in the door of a good career, as a war veteran," he says.

Out in France, Fred had kept his ear to the ground. New jobs were emerging. The lads were on about all sorts of possibilities—railway signalmen, telegraph installers, engine fitters, chauffeurs, plumbers, electrical workers. He'd written in excitement to Polly about his thoughts:

They're saying in the canteen they've got lads wiring up whole streets back home, Pol. Streetlamps, factories, houses—electric everything. No more soot, no more gaslight. I might give it a go. Learn something that won't kill my lungs or crick my back.

Through his former Squadron Sergeant Major, Wilf Andrews, he'd secured a place on a Veterans Training Scheme. Electrical switchgear worker had been SSM Andrews' idea—"Right interesting, Ruggles, you'll be a natural. You're handy and quick, and the pay's good. Get in there and build yourself a better future!"

But Fred's real desire, as he explains to Polly, is to drive cars. Not the rough old army cars he's used to, but those purring, monstrous beauties that rich people have. He describes them to his wife—shining Daimlers, gleaming Rolls Royces. He persuades Polly of his vision of himself—in a uniform of a different kind to that of the army, with a leather steering wheel in his grip, a polished dashboard before his eyes, and sunlight glinting off the car chrome. "You wait, Pol, I'll do it yet," he assures her.

Meanwhile, the post of electrical switchgear assistant for the City of Birmingham Electrical Department will do for now.

City of Birmingham Electrical Department panto—Aladdin—performed by the staff and their children. Back row second from right: Freddie as a magician. Second row, first on right: Jimmy as magician's apprentice—1922.

The job comes with perks—one week's paid holiday, a 'Christmas box' of a ham and a voucher for poultry, a works sickness fund, and a works panto for the employees' families organised by the social committee. The boys adore it. Freddie played a devil last year, and Jim played Robin Hood. This year, in *Aladdin*, they're going to be, respectively, a magician and a magician's apprentice.

Polly teases Fred about the capers last year. "You and your big feet!" she admonishes delightedly. "What chaos you and the boys created."

Fred remembers with a chuckle the whole hilarious shebang. As Polly tells it, Fred had got into difficulties with a cardboard chimney when playing Father Christmas in the panto.

"That big old work boot of Fred's was stuck in that chimney like a pig in mud, and he was about to topple head over heels when our Jim—Robin Hood—scorched on from the wings yelling fit to bust: "It's Father Christmas, and he's got presents for us! Come on my merry men!"

"Then the boys went wild, dancing round Fred, who just had time to rip the boot off. He scattered the lads, swinging his big sack—whackety-whack—left and right, and then launched into a song-and-dance routine that brought the house down," laughs Polly.

Fred's immortal song lines, entirely improvised, were:

> *I'm Father Christmas—and I haven't got a clue.*
> *I've lost me address book, so what's a chap to do?*
> *One boot's stuck in Edgbaston the other's stuck in Lye,*
> *So I think I best go home now,*
> *Toodle-oo! Goodbye!*

"Then he waddled off the stage," finishes Polly, slapping her thigh as she sits telling the tale, "with one boot on and one boot off. The audience fell about laughing at the whole crowd of dafties! They thought it was all part of the act."

Polly loves making the costumes for the pantos. She's deft with a needle. Her mother taught her pattern cutting and dressmaking. Polly never thinks of it as a talent, just something you do if you have hands and patience. But the neighbours know better. Her needlework is careful and clever, her alterations always spot on. She never charges, not really—but they bring her biscuits or buttons or a bit of cloth in thanks. Polly is a popular woman, all right, but she doesn't notice, in amongst the hurly-burly of her life.

1924: Education

Oh, I do like to be beside the seaside, sings Polly, as she scrubs the washing. She and Jim mangle the sheets first, then the pillow slips, and finally the shirts. They're all hung out to dry on lines that run across the street. They billow in the breeze, reminding her of ships' sails.

Washing is a good, steady earner for her on days when she doesn't open the tripe shop. It suits her to be at home for part of the week, caring for the house and the children. She's a house-proud wife and mothering her two boys brings her real joy.

She devotes hours to their education—homework is important, she tells them, as they try to rush out to play after school. She makes them do their sums, write their essays, learn their times tables. "You'll be grateful one day for that knowledge," she promises.

Polly is a great respecter of education. She didn't have much schooling herself, and she feels the lack, somewhere inside her, like a hollow stomach that longs for food. Her hope is that one day she can get some time to study… something… anything. She's not sure what, but she yearns for a bigger life, a wider horizon.

Occasionally, on breezy, sunny Sundays she packs a lunch basket and takes the boys to the Lickey Hills where she points out the names of trees and flowers, the points of the compass, and the direction of different cities—London, Manchester, Norwich. The boys rush to get to the top of Beacon Hill where the view is huge, green, and full of the tang of freedom. They all three run and shout in the wind, chasing the shadows of the big puffy clouds floating above them—clouds that drift far beyond where Polly ever dares to follow.

One evening after closing up the tripe shop, Polly hurries home in the scudding showers of rain, her heels clicking on the wet street. As she passes by St. Mark's School gates, she halts. There's a poster pinned to the noticeboard. The words are just about legible in the muted yellow of the hissing gas lamp on the corner.

Workers' Educational Association, Sparkhill—Autumn Term Lectures:

> *Understanding the Plays of Shakespeare:*
>> *An introduction to major scenes and characters, with special focus on everyday meaning and speech. Texts provided.*

> *The Great Thinkers and What They Believed:*
>> *A friendly survey of big ideas from Plato to Karl Marx, with time for discussion and questions.*

Looking at Art—A Simple Guide:

> *How to see meaning in painting and sculpture, using examples from galleries and local exhibitions. No drawing required.*

Our Own Village: History from the Hearth:

> *A practical course exploring Sparkhill and the local area through oral history, old maps, and parish records.*

Open to All. Small Subscription. (1s 6d per term)

"Only one and six for the whole term," Polly murmurs, eyes tracing the last line of the notice as the gaslight flickers. She can afford it—she knows how to make money stretch.

Something in her awakens, yawns, and opens its eyes. Yes, she could go, couldn't she? If Fred were back from work in time to care for the boys?

But Fred is never back from work in time. And what would he say about it anyway?

She samples a conversation in her head. "There's these lectures, Fred, about Shakespeare and philosophy and art. I'd like to go to them, and we can afford it…"

Fred wouldn't say no, exactly. He'd just blink at her. Then say something like: "Shakespeare plays? What do you want with all that, Pol?" As if interest needs permission. As if beauty must be justified.

The something in her that had stirred—that had turned its face briefly towards the light—sighs, and sleeps again.

1930: A Daimler Light Twenty

"Oh Fred, you do look glamorous—like a movie star!" Polly exclaims, casting her eyes over the light blue uniform that fits Fred so well. "Tell me again, where will you be working?"

Fred is busy polishing the badge on his new cap. He's grinning broadly, the boys hanging on to his words as Polly waits for his response.

He can hardly believe it, Fred says. He's finally landed the dream job. A chauffeur for a rich elderly gentleman. A Daimler to drive, even if it's only a Daimler Light Twenty.

"It's not top of the class, Pol," Fred explains as he dusts his uniform cap with its gold braid trim. "But it's a damn good car all the same. Walnut dash, polished grey bodywork, drives smooth as cream. Sir Lionel, see," expands Fred, squinting proudly at his brass-buttoned jacket, "he's a retired industrialist—light engineering or some such— and now he's a bit of an antiquarian. Collects old things like books, paintings, sculptures, and furniture. He's a nice old fella—lives over in Edgbaston."

Fred shows Polly a picture of the Daimler in his latest Autocar magazine—a sleek-looking vehicle, all bonnet and chrome. Polly can't get excited about it, but she nods kindly. Fred's dreams are wrapped up in those magazines, she knows. Some model called a Daimler Double Six—that's his ultimate idea of desirable. He calls it the favoured car of royalty. But for now, explains Fred, he's landed the 'big job' in getting this chauffeuring post with Sir Lionel. He'll be driving a car, yes, but he'll also be driving *status*.

The salary is good, and holidays are paid. Fred will be on call six days a week, with one day's paid holiday. It's amazing! Polly and Fred buy the family a fish supper to celebrate, and the next day Fred starts his new post.

The hours prove to be lengthy, and Polly's long-held ambition to attend WEA classes is put aside once more while Fred builds his career. Soon he's indispensable to Sir Lionel. So much so that, when Polly has to work at the tripe shop and can't get anyone to mind the boys, Sir Lionel says: "Come along, one and all! Bring the boys!"

The house in Edgbaston has a huge garden. It rambles across an acre of ground and offers copses, steps, a summerhouse, and a pond. What fun the boys have on Saturdays while Polly weighs out sheep's lights and chops liver. When the shop closes, Polly goes over to join the family at Bainbridge House—Sir Lionel's home—and they all have tea and cake in the kitchen with Mrs Crimp, the cook.

One summer afternoon, when the sun slants in through the windows of the kitchen, Polly is gathering her bags together in preparation for going home with the boys and Fred. "Would you like to look around the library, Pol?" asks Fred suddenly. "I know you like learning and books, and Sir Lionel's out until this evening. I've been set on polishing the Daimler today, no driving needed."

Polly hesitates, then, leaving the boys to continue their outdoor play, she follows Fred through the baize door into the house. Curiosity has overcome caution. Thick rugs deaden her footsteps as she treads softly through a corridor into the hall. The walls are lined with paintings—such colours, such movement! Battle scenes are on one wall, shipwrecks on another, and landscapes crowd up the stairs. "Goodness, Fred, so many paintings!" she exclaims.

"Wait 'til you see the ones in the breakfast room, Pol," tempts Fred. He pushes open a heavy oak door, and they step into a small room with windows on one side and bright flower paintings on the other. They are breath-taking—delicate, transparent, and colourful. The flowers float on the paper, filled with life. Polly thinks she could just touch their petals to feel the cool satin of their forms. "What are they, Fred?" asks Polly.

"Watercolours, Pol. Do you like them? They're painted by Sir Lionel's late wife, Maria."

Maria! Polly's own name, although everyone calls her Polly. In that moment, Polly feels a strange stirring of memory, as if she once sat and painted elegant scenes on snowy white paper, just like these. Suddenly there awakens in Polly a desire to paint, to create magical watercolours and capture the world around her.

Before she can reflect on this sudden aspiration, Fred pulls her into another room.

The library is large, square, and lined with books. The fireplace is flanked by shapely wooden figures—curvaceous, naked women and muscular men in loin cloths—apparently straining to hold up the mantelpiece. Polly wonders what the housemaids think about when they're polishing those voluptuous forms.

Above the shelves, in the carved frieze of each bookcase, words gleam in old gold leaf—*Philosophy, Natural History, Oriental Texts, Astronomy, Colonial Affairs*. Polly runs her eyes along the line, as if reading the names of chapters of the Bible, so mysterious and sacred do they appear to her.

"There's 5000 books in here, Pol," asserts Fred, striding around the room and pointing to the leather-bound volumes, slim, fat, tall and short. "And Sir Lionel's read them all!"

Polly ponders what it would be like to have so much knowledge in your head. *Wouldn't it feel like an over-stuffed chicken?* she thinks, imagining Sir Lionel's head bursting at the seams and needing a firm line of stitching to hold it together.

She pulls out a volume. *Down the Mississippi: a Journey by Canoe into the Heart of America*, announces the binding. She flips it open, and sees page after page of dense text, a map or two, some engravings of wild-looking men and women. Naked bodies again. She shuts the book quickly and replaces it.

Wandering over to the desk, placed squarely in the window, her eye falls on an unemptied waste bin in which sits a thick, stitched-spine catalogue. *Sale of Antiquarian Books from the 'Estate of Sir Godfrey Carruthers of Godolphin Manor, Shropshire, March 3rd 1922*, she reads. She picks it out and under Fred's curious gaze, she peruses it.

"No one wants it, Fred, do they, and it looks interesting. D'you think it's all right to take it?"

Fred laughs and nods. "You funny girl, Pol, what do you want that for?" Polly just smiles and tucks it into her bag, closing the clasp with gentle fingers. *Something to read. A window into the world of education*, she thinks.

The catalogue rides home with Polly, along with the thoughts of watercolour painting. The one, she puts on the kitchen shelf next to her savings tin. The other, she keeps in her heart, and when the tin is full enough she buys herself a little set of watercolour paints, a brush, and some paper.

Her efforts are clumsy and halting, but she persists. Her landscapes and flowers seem wonky, or muddy, or wrong, but some day, she believes, she will learn. In the meantime, Jim and Freddie look at her paintings, their heads on one side, and say "Very nice, Mum, what is it?" or "The colours are nice, Mum." Fred gazes on fondly. His Polly's a cut above, after all. A bit artistic, eccentric. It's one of the things he loves about her.

At night, when Polly has finished clearing up in the kitchen, she takes down the catalogue, and leafs through it. Titles on subjects general and obscure float before her.

> *The Afterbearing of Empire in Hindustan:*
> *by Colonel Geoffrey Forsythe, 1923,*

Polly reads.

> *Antient Forms and Foundations:*
> *An Illustrated Treatise on Ecclesiastical and Vernacular*
> *Architecture in the Middle Ages: by Revd. J. Pettigrew, 1862.*

> *The Vapours and Their Humoral Management:*
> *A Gentlewoman's Companion in Cases of Nervous Weakness,*
> *Hysteria, and Spleen: by Dr Silas Armitage, 1794.*

> *Jewels of the Firmament: The Moon, the Planets, and the Stars:*
> *from the journals of H.R. Biddlecombe, Esq., 1825.*

The titles draw her in. The subjects are strange, beautiful, tempting. They feel like something just out of reach, a door she cannot quite walk through. The catalogue represents for her the missing opportunities within her own education. It is never too late, though; the WEA still beckons. She'll make it there one day. One day, when Fred's hours are shorter, or the boys are older, or when she's not as busy.

Polly marks in pencil the books that catch her eye. It might be the name: *Botanical Gems of the High Tundra*; or it might be the author: *Mrs Hugo de Clavelley van Hoet presents her Treatise on...* The woman's name seems both exotic and outlandish.

There is one lengthy entry that Polly returns to again and again, pressing her finger to the text to trace its words.

> *The Substance of Soul and Star: An Inquiry into the Origins of*
> *Matter and the Divine Nature of Being: by Cuthbert N. Withers,*
> *Natural Philosopher.*
> > *Being a thoughtful explication of the principle that all*
> > *Corporeal Substance is but Condensed Light, and that the*
> > *Human Soul—immortal and radiant—is formed of Celestial*
> > *Love. With references to Newton, Swedenborg, and the*
> > *Doctrine of Correspondences. Published London, 1832.*

How can a thing be made of light? ponders Polly. Except for the movies, she can't think how anything could be made of light, and even the movies involve cellulose film strips. As for the soul, what is it, in fact? Does she have one? How can it be made of love?

Yet inside her, there is a glow of happiness at the thought that the love she herself readily feels for others is something special.

The catalogue gets more and more lines, notes, and ticks on it as her imagination flourishes. Zoology, botany, geology. The words are like spells. They conjure a half-seen vision in her mind, like a place she's always wanted to visit, without even knowing its name.

Always, at the end of Polly's quiet cup of tea with her catalogue, she folds it up and places it carefully back on the shelf, where it sits, a fat promise of learning, month after month and year after year. It becomes a catalogue of a life that never quite begins.

March 1939: Maid Marian's Kiss

The situation in Europe is a terrible worry. Polly thinks about her boys and what they might experience should there be a war.

Jim is now a fully-fledged plumber. From school he'd gone straight into an apprenticeship at the local foundry where he'd done well. But the work was heavy and grimy, generally unhealthy. He'd got out as fast as he could to train as a plumber with Evans Brothers in Sparkhill.

Freddie had followed his father into the electrical industry, training to be a meter reader and engineer.

"Trust you to get a clean job!" Jim had complained, as he scrubbed off the oily filth of the foundry in the kitchen sink.

"Get yourself over to the City of Birmingham Electrical Department and ask for a job," recommended Freddie, combing his hair in the kitchen mirror before going out to meet his girl. But Jim liked using his hands to make and mend, so Polly had known he would stick with the foundry work until something better came along, that something being plumbing.

Polly has spent the last nine years in a suspended state of unfulfilled ambition. She still hankers after evening classes, but she never seems to have the confidence to act on her hopes. *What use is philosophy to a seller of tripe and liver,* she thinks? Her spirits have progressively sunk as she's found her narrow life less and less satisfying. Her watercolours sit neglected on the dresser. Her catalogue, now dog-eared and tea-stained, is crumpled up on the top shelf of the larder.

"Shall we go to the Birmingham Art Gallery, Fred? There's more than paintings—historical and scientific displays too," Polly asks one wet Saturday, as she paces the living room. Fred scratches his head.

"I suppose so, Pol, but it'll be full of things we won't understand. And our feet will get wet!"

"How do you know you won't understand the exhibits, Fred, if you've never been?" asks Polly. ""I read in the paper they've got some watercolours on—country landscapes and floral studies. Really delicate and pretty—I'd love to see those."

They set out for the Gallery, but a mile from Chamberlain Square the bus gives a heave and a sigh, smoke belches from the engine, and the vehicle grinds to a halt. Fred, car-expert to his bootstraps, leaps out and engages the driver and conductor in a long conversation about the possible causes of the problem. Polly sits disconsolately in the bus with the other passengers as the afternoon ticks by and her chance at cultural nourishment dwindles.

Fred eventually comes around to the back of the bus to pick Polly up and they step over to the nearby Lyons Tea House where they order tea and crumpets with butter and jam.

"Never mind, Pol," consoles Fred, spreading the jam on his crumpet and licking butter from his thumb. "That Gallery would probably have been beyond us anyhow."

Polly nods wanly and stirs sugar into her tea. She notices that her saucer is chipped—a sharp little dint that irritates her eye as she looks at it. Around her, crockery and cutlery clacks and clatters. Customers huddle over their meals, their faces—animated, tranquil, disappointed—mingling into one blur of humanity.

Why is she so depressed, wonders Fred? "What is it, Pol, love? You're like a wet weekend in Weston these days. Aren't you happy? We've got a lovely little house, and the boys are doing well. And we're fond of one another... aren't we?" he ends, with an encouraging smile.

Polly can't quite name the longings. They hover inside her—not feelings exactly, more like absences—an ache for something richer, wider, deeper. How can Fred, who is so happy with his lot, understand that she feels this lack, this emptiness? He loves her so, but he doesn't understand her.

"Tell you what, Pol, if we can't have the Gallery and all its pictures, let's have our own pictures—*Robin Hood*'s on at the Empire just around the corner. Fancy it? Swashbuckling, music, romance?" Fred's eyes look warm and almost pleading.

He wants me to be cheerful, Polly thinks. *He needs me to say yes*. "Yes, all right," she agrees, "that'll be lovely, Fred." In that moment, something in Polly turns away from the world, and chooses to follow the shimmer of the imaginary instead.

The ticket girl barely looks up as Fred drops coins into her palm. "Two for *Robin Hood*."

Inside, the air is thick with perfume and cigarette smoke. Polly squeezes past legs, handbags, and shopping to sit in vacant seats in the centre of the row. Fred settles in beside her, and they unwrap barley sugars from a paper bag of mixed sweets. Polly's mind is still on the failed gallery visit.

"We can see paintings another day," Fred says, as if reading her thoughts. "Next weekend if you like."

The film starts with a blare of trumpets. Cymbals crash, drums roll. Polly shrinks a little. It's too loud when her thoughts have become so quiet these days. Errol Flynn swings into view, sword aloft, eyes blazing. The crowd cheer, someone claps, and she feels Fred relax, reach for her hand, and squeeze it. "All right, Pol, love?" he whispers. She nods and smiles.

Polly tries to follow the plot, but her thoughts keep drifting off to that old library at Sir Lionel's house, the books all in rows, the mysterious words *Cartography... Rhetoric... Theology* picked out in gold against the old oak shelving.

Fred has long ago moved on to work for a wealthy widow in Balsall Heath—a Mrs Shepherd, widow of a doctor of medicine. She's a pleasant, kind employer, although she's apt to call for Fred's driving services any time day or night. Once, a telegram arrived at midnight summoning Fred to her door. "She wants to see the sunrise over the sea in Brighton," explained Fred as he shoved arms and legs into clothes, feet into boots, and clattered out. He gets well paid for his trouble though, so he puts up with it.

Polly thinks of the day last April when Fred arrived home looking like a mother bird whose chickens have just hatched. "Come with me, Pol," he'd called from the front door. He'd taken her out on the street, and there she saw a handsome little maroon car, twinkling with polish and love. "Austin Seven 'Chummy'," Fred had informed her, stroking the bonnet. "Rexine seats, too," he added, as if announcing padded leather covers.

Polly had clambered in at Fred's insistence. "I'll take you for a spin," he'd offered, and jumped in the driver's side. The Rexine seats felt cold and hard. Bits of the covers had cracked and peeled away, snagging on the cloth of her fine wool skirt. There was a musty, chemical smell mixed with petrol.

"You've got to give the door a bit of a slam, Pol, but not too hard, she's delicate!" Fred had warned, caressing the steering wheel. "Now you'll see what's she's made of!"

Fred started the engine whirring, and off they set. Bowling along the streets of Sparkhill, they headed out to the Lickey Hills. As they glided past terraces, then suburban properties, and finally hedgerows and fields, Polly thought of *Botanical Gems of the High Tundra*.

What is a tundra? she had pondered. *Would Mrs Hugo de Clavelley van Hoet enjoy seeing one?* And: *Is a tundra made of light?*

Polly in middle years, in one of her own handmade dresses. She emanates a weariness and a gentle sadness—a hint that her life is beginning its downward arc.

The car had made a splash at Freddie's wedding that same month. Fred had driven the bride to the church in style, her two bridesmaids crammed in with her, filling the car to overflowing. Polly had judiciously warned Cynthia, Freddie's bride, to mind her dress on the old seats. "You don't want to arrive with a rip in your skirt!" she'd smiled. Despite the pouring rain, it had been a grand day. Everyone so merry! Even bossy Kitty had been as happy as a cow in clover, and those two sillies, Louis and Bernard, had been three sheets to the wind and tacking around the headland, as Fred had laughingly told

Polly. Now Jim's met a nice girl called Dulcie. Older than him, sensible and well-off. A good match. They seem happy enough. She hopes they'll marry. *Will I be there to see it, though?* thinks Polly. Then, surprised at herself: *Don't be daft, Pol—course you will!*

Fred hands Polly a toffee. On the screen, Errol smacks a kiss on Maid Marian's waiting lips as they teeter on top of some castle battlements. Polly blinks and comes back to the present. The flicker of the projector catches dust motes in the air. They look like falling stars. *Jewels of the Firmament: The Moon, the Planets, and the Stars.*

The film is fun, after all, and she's feeling better with all the laughter and company pressed in around her.

"Happy, Pol?" enquires Fred, leaning closer.

"Yes," she whispers. "It's a good film."

She accepts another toffee and quietly unwraps it. In the dark, she does indeed feel happy for the first time in several months. The movies enchant her from that day onwards, beckoning her into their stream of colour and light. She becomes a regular attendee at the Carlton Cinema, just near their home in Sparkhill. Three times a week, sometimes more, she walks to the palace of dreams and sits, enraptured by the faces, the colours, the music, the romance. She doesn't think of it as giving up. Just drifting a little. Letting the pictures carry her where the world never will.

1st October 1940: Malta

Polly sits, staring at the sheet of notepaper before her. She's written nothing in ten minutes. What do you write to a son who's trapped in a siege? Malta is blockaded by sea and bombed from the air. Rumours circulate that the islanders and the British forces will starve to death together, if the Italian and German bombers don't get them first.

Dearest Freddie,

writes Polly, at last. She nibbles the end of her fountain pen. She thinks of him, brown, sun-scorched, smiling. She imagines his days spent in nameless barracks. She hears the air raid sirens in her mind, sees the island folk and the soldiers dashing for cover, the bombs raining down on them.

Polly presses on.

We've had the sirens three times this week. I go down the Anderson Shelter with Jim and your dad, or we go under the stairs if it's wet. We keep the radio on but we can hear and feel the bombs falling. Don't worry though, we are all surviving just fine.

What else to say?

I think of you night and day and pray to whoever can hear me to keep you safe. I hope you have enough food and water. I hope you are warm and well. When you look up at the stars, think of us at home, and we will think of you.

Your very loving Mother.

Polly feels the letter is insufficient, but she doesn't have the words to speak her deep love for her son, her dread and pain at his suffering, or her sadness at the waste of his youth. She seals it, addresses it as she's been directed, and places it on the mantelpiece ready to stamp and post.

Her mind wanders to the paper today.

Island Fortress Holds Firm Under Fire: Malta Bombed but Unbowed!

shouts the headline in the Birmingham Post.

Then the story:

The island of Malta, vital to Britain's operations in the Mediterranean, withstood its most intense aerial bombardment yet, this week, as Italian forces stepped up attacks. Despite limited supplies and constant threat from sea and sky, the garrison and local population maintain high spirits.

"We are not giving an inch," one officer reported. "Malta stands."

All Polly's customers know of Freddie's situation. When Elsie Evershed comes in for tripe and lights, she shakes her head sympathetically, seeing Polly reading the newspaper.

"Awful, in't it, about Malta? Heard from yer lad, 'ave you?" she enquires, grasping her waxed paper parcel of meat.

Polly nods, wiping her hands clean on her apron. "Yes, Freddie says he's all right—but it's dreadful now. Bombs every day."

"God 'elp 'em," exclaims Elsie with feeling. "Poor things. No food, no rest. Can't even bury their dead, someone said."

Polly blinks and breathes in and out slowly.

"I worry about him, Elsie, all the time, and Jim too. But what can we do? And the poor islanders. Their homes are being blasted away from under them. The children, Elsie, can you imagine? It must be terrible."

"You've always 'ad a soft 'eart, Polly," says Elsie, "In't it enough to worry about yer boys?"

Polly gives a wan smile. "I don't know, Elsie. I just feel we must remember one another's suffering somehow. It keeps us human, don't you think—remembering we're all in it together?"

Jim has joined the Royal Army Ordnance Corps. He's already been sent off to somewhere or other in foreign parts—but of course his whereabouts are a secret. At the end of last year he proposed to Dulcie. What a pleasure, what a joy! Polly hugs the thought of another wedding to her heart. They'll have to wait until the time is right, what with army service and so on. But still—what a happy prospect. War or no war, the family will try to make it a day to remember.

Dulcie's family are a bit stand-offish but Jim's won them over with his plumbing prowess. It seems he bailed them out of a crisis with their hot-water cylinder and now everything's violets and roses. Polly doesn't expect that Dulcie's family will ever want to socialise with the Ruggles. They're educated, wealthy, like gentry. But Dulcie comes to visit Polly now and then, with a homemade jam tart or a loaf of bread. She's learning to cook, and her efforts are worthy if not inspiring, but Polly makes much of every gesture Dulcie offers. It's second nature to Polly, with her loving heart beating within her. She wants to make Dulcie feel as welcome as spring sunshine.

The soul is made of love… Perhaps I have a soul after all, thinks Polly.

25th October 1940: Carlton Cinema: Sparkhill

"It's that Dorothy Lamour film, *Typhoon*, at the Carlton tonight, Pol," says Maggie, Polly's neighbour. "We could go and see it together. What do you say?"

Polly's always up for a trip to the movies. Anything will do, but the more colourful and romantic, the better. Maggie finishes work at the munitions factory at four o'clock, Polly's back from the shop at five, and there's a screening at six. Just time to swallow down a bit of tripe, onions, and bread, and get to the cinema door in plenty of time.

The two women meet at the fancy half-domed entrance and pay for tickets in the stalls. There's a long queue for the lift to the balcony—quite a crowd in tonight. Groups of youngsters pack the lobby, some of whom are known to the women—Joyce Murcott and her young man, Douglas Parfitt, together with his mates Hal and Bertie. Then there's fifteen-year-old Ted Byrne, a gangly Irish youth who grins at Maggie and waves his ticket in the air like a flag. "It's me sister's bottle-return money!" he shouts. They wave back, smiling their understanding that Susan Byrne had returned a pile of bottles to the Antelope Pub in exchange for cash, which had then passed into Ted's keen hands.

Polly and Maggie take their seats. Polly removes her coat and eases her feet out of her thick boots. The chill of the clear-skied autumn evening doesn't penetrate the thick fug of the heated cinema. Outside, the moon rides high in the sky. Polly had overheard someone, as they walked into the cinema, say: "Look at that, it's a bomber's moon," and she had shivered.

Settling down, Polly and Maggie take out their paper cones of sweets—sherbet lemons and pear drops. Not the best, but sweets are becoming an endangered species. All around them there's rustling, giggles, whispering, and a sharp slap from the back row. Maggie winks at Polly—"A little of what you fancy going on over there!" she murmurs.

Now the velvet curtains sweep back majestically to reveal the big screen. The lights dim, a hush falls, the Technicolor world springs to life and Polly allows herself to relax into escapism. Part of her awareness seems to leave her body and hang, mesmerised, before the bright moving pictures. She seems taken away from herself, and it feels like a relief.

Rain squalls across the screen as Dorothy Lamour clings wetly to brawny Robert Preston. Her skimpy, flowery sarong hugs her figure flatteringly. *Where would a wild-girl brought up by chimpanzees get the fabric for that?* wonders the dressmaking part of Polly. Never mind, it doesn't matter. Polly is lulled by the film. She takes another pear drop and sucks it contentedly.

Suddenly a thin wail becomes audible through the sounds of the artificial typhoon. "Oh no," cries Maggie, "it's the sirens!"

The audience members start to boil out of their seats, grabbing bags, coats, dropping cones of sweets. Birmingham hasn't experienced many raids as yet and no one's very practised at what to do. The manager comes running down the aisle waving his arms. "Ladies, gents, kiddies, get up quietly and file to the back of the cinema under the balcony," he shouts. And up at the balcony: "Down the stairs quickly and quietly. Don't use the lift. We'll get you under the balcony. We'll all stand under cover."

Some people make a dash for the exit. The nearest air raid shelter is a good step away, though. Polly hesitates. What should she do? She and Fred have the Anderson shelter in the garden. Could she get there if she ran? But she's towards the front of the cinema. Forward and backward she looks, but she's blocked from a fast escape route. She'd never get out in time. She and Maggie scramble back with all the other audience members, cramming themselves into the space below the balcony. More people file into the stalls from the upstairs seating area. The space is fetid now with fear. Polly feels claustrophobic, hemmed in on all sides.

This is where it ends, she thinks, from out of the blue. No! She gulps down her anxiety, and fumbles for Maggie's hand. Maggie's eyes are hollow with terror. "All right, love, it'll be all right," Polly shouts, as the thud of falling bombs begins. The cinema shakes, the roof timbers seem to shift. Someone screams but it's cut off short.

Whoosh. Wham. It's so sudden. The cinema roof tears apart with an ear-splitting wrench. Through the ceiling a dark shape comes rushing and roaring. It's an incendiary bomb. It hurtles downwards, making for the orchestra pit. There's a flash and roar as it lands and bursts into flames. The carpet catches, the seats bloom with licking tongues of fire. Screams erupt all around. There are explosions now somewhere outside. Inside, roof beams tilt and topple, slowly, as if in a dream. The balcony above the pressed-in bodies begins to disintegrate. Polly's body seems lifted—clean off the ground, up and up, as if the typhoon on screen has claimed her. *I'm flying*, she thinks. Then a massive stake of wood pitches towards her, intent, murderous. She sees it, curls up instinctively—but it's useless. *Jim and Freddie will never know how much I love them*, she screams, inside herself.

The falling beam, heavy and sharp, pierces her small, fragile body through and through. With its own force, it drives Polly downwards, pinning her to the ground. Masonry falls on top of her. Bodies, flung upwards, drop back in ragged pieces, like monstrous snowflakes.

Polly is trapped. Oddly, she can feel nothing in her body, only a gaping hole where her body's life used to be. She turns her head. What has happened? Is she alive or dead? She watches in horrified fascination as another incendiary smashes through the roof, taking the big screen with it. Clinging desperately to one another as the typhoon roars around them, Dorothy Lamour and Robert Preston are ripped apart, their cellulose bodies splintering sideways, their big faces ballooning into the shattered auditorium. Are they made of light? Or are they made of love? Polly cannot remember. An explosion rips the air apart. Its reverberations settle, and outside, there is more pounding, shaking, roaring.

Finally, there is an eerie quiet. Polly lies in the demolition around her. The quiet is punctuated by debris cascading through the air, the rattling of loose bricks tumbling. In the distance there is sobbing, calling, and scrabbling. Polly lies, unmoving. She stares upwards. She stares outwards. She feels herself once more sitting in the cinema seat. Around her, a vortex of terrifying shapes swirls and weaves, grabbing at her, biting at her. But she cannot move to escape them. She is pinned by the beam that has become one with her. She must carry this beam everywhere with her now.

On all sides sit the other audience members. They gape slackly at the ripped screen.

Their eyes are glazed. Their mouths are still. They are frozen.

And there they sit, on and on, for hours, for days, for years, for decades.

No one sees them.

No one rescues them.

Because no one knows they are there.

A visual reconstruction of the Carlton Cinema interior after the bombing raid, generated using AI (ChatGPT/OpenAI, 2025) based on surviving historical photographs.

Afterlife Encounters
Polly: visited 2025

Vortex

"What an unusual death, to die in a cinema!" exclaims Inessa, as she ponders Polly. "Can you get a sense of her?"

I pause and concentrate. To me, Polly Ruggles seems to be absolutely still—like a kind of rag doll, limp and inert.

"Yes, you're right, that's how I perceive her too," says Inessa. "And the reason is most fascinating."

As always, I'm intrigued. Polly's manner of death—a violent one associated with war—has troubled me ever since I first learned of it while researching my great-uncle Jimmy's family. Sudden deaths can shock the soul so deeply that transition across the threshold becomes compromised. Polly is no exception.

To aid our research, Inessa has discovered startling images on a local history forum: photographs of the ruined Carlton Cinema after the incendiary bomb attack. In these photos, sunlight bleeds through the shattered roof, lighting up the devastation below with appropriately cinematic drama.

Rows of plush seats are covered in debris, much of it deadly-looking in appearance. Part of the balcony—under which many audience members had been sheltering—appears to have collapsed. The walls are torn and scored. The screen lies in a crumpled heap on the floor of the stalls. Yet the velvet curtains hang oddly untouched.

The Carlton was a splendid cinema with an impressive entrance, a lift to the balcony, a cinema organ, and a large seating capacity. That night, it was full. Local people had flocked to see *Typhoon*, starring Dorothy Lamour and Robert Preston. A silly plot about a girl raised by chimpanzees on a desert island was likely offset by lush romantic scenes, dramatic licence, and visual spectacle. Popular in its day, escapist, ridiculous, and exotic—it was exactly the kind of film Polly would have loved.

The Carlton was rebuilt after the bombing raid and remained in service until its final closure in 1980. It was eventually demolished and replaced by a memorial garden. The nineteen people killed that night, along with others who were injured, are commemorated there, in that small patch of green.

When I view it on Google Maps, it's a rather tired-looking grassy space, with a little memorial stone at its centre. Local newspaper reports speak indignantly of litter and dog mess, and of efforts by local volunteers to restore some dignity to the place. I wonder whether Polly—and perhaps some of the other casualties—might still be tied to the spot, supersensibly, waiting for a kind of spiritual ambulance crew to come and give first aid.

Inessa, smiling at the phrase, studies the little memorial garden carefully.

"Yes—totally fascinating," she murmurs. "Because I can see that your hunch is correct. Polly is still here, along with all the others who died. What's even more extraordinary is that some of the injured are partially here too—supersensibly speaking—even though most of them didn't die."

How can that be?

I learn that trauma on this scale—absolute terror from out of the blue—can sometimes cause even survivors to leave a part of their life-energy behind. These energy imprints remain tethered to places of suffering.

"The troubled atmospheres we sometimes sense in battlefields or hospitals, or ruined places," explains Inessa, "are often filled not only with those who died, but also with those who survived—though the survivors' life-energies are not intact, not whole. Just a part of a survivor's life-energy might remain, tied to the trauma."

Inessa is familiar with this, having worked supersensibly at several former Second World War concentration camp sites over the years.

"Let's take a look at the state of the cinema audience right now," she suggests, turning her attention to the images of the bombed cinema.

Even to me, these images seem full of anguish. But Inessa sees more.

"There's a vortex," she says, "a dark, twisting structure—right over the seating area in the stalls, around rows five or six. It's filled with a tangle of disordered spiritual forces—beings that are very dark and undeveloped who seek only to harm."

This may sound strange, explains Inessa, but such impressions are consistent across many sites of sudden mass death, from many commentators. Beings like these—voracious, anarchic—are drawn towards violence. They cross into our realm when hatred and fear explode. In locations like the Carlton, where trauma and terror converged, supersensible doorways open, and such beings seize their chance. They are not evil in a fully moral sense, but undeveloped. One day, with help from the divine realm, humanity will work to redeem them.

Meanwhile, Polly, along with many others, is still sitting in a cinema seat. These souls are not fully conscious, nor are they fully dead. As with young Eric, the First World War soldier in chapter 4, their life-force bodies and their feeling-and-emotion bodies remain tethered to their physical forms, long after death. The shock of sudden, violent transition has left them trapped in a strange half-life.

While researching the Carlton, I came across an astonishing testimony by the son of an ARP ambulance driver. It describes how, on the night of the bombing, his mother drove her ambulance to see what help was needed at the bomb-struck cinema. What she saw was chilling. Rows of people sat, as if enchanted, slumped in their cinema seats, gazing at the empty screen, silent and frozen.

I retold this moment within Marion's story (chapter 6), imagining it as a quiet exchange between a group of female wardens, as they awaited the sirens that betokened another air raid.

Now I ask Inessa—was this vision real?

"Yes," she replies after a pause. "It sounds like a supersensible impression, a real supersensible perception. The sirens would have sent people scrambling—not calmly sitting in their seats, waiting for death. So what your ambulance driver was seeing wasn't physical. It was spiritual."

Even now, Inessa can see the same sight. There they are—rows of people, eyes blank, faces slack, limbs unmoving. They are present, but unseen. For decades, they have sat in silence, their souls dislocated by trauma, repeating the last moments of that night like a broken reel of film.

"I can see that some people perceived these poor souls, sitting in the cinema or in the memorial gardens," Inessa adds. "They would have appeared as ghosts. Some were bloodied, or badly damaged. They must have terrified those who glimpsed them."

Poor Polly is one of those ghosts. Her injuries were massive. A ceiling beam drove clean through her body. Part of her physical form was lost—perhaps an arm, or a leg—and was never recovered. In such deaths, remains are often mingled and incomplete. The authorities did what they could. Bodies were buried with dignity, but not always with certainty about whose parts were whose.

Inessa can see that although Polly's body was buried, it was not wholly hers. Some remains were interchanged. The blast had made everything indistinguishable. These souls were, in a terrible sense, united by destruction.

And so Polly remained at the Carlton. For perhaps forty years she wandered supersensibly through the ruins. Step by step, she dragged her invisible form, still pierced by the beam, looking for the limb she had lost.

Something then happened to transform Polly from being bound to the physical realm. Perhaps an event occurred within the family—the deaths of her two sons would have taken place around this time, for instance. Polly might have been inspired to move on, seeking to be with them. Somehow, she moved forward, but once more became stuck before she could reach the soul-realm.

Strange to say, even now Polly doesn't understand that she has died. Her consciousness is dim, confused, and vulnerable to the swirling negative forces that hover over the site.

Around her, the other post-mortem souls are in a similar state. They cannot move on. They seek completion, understanding, and release.

Inessa now turns her gaze to Polly's inner life. She sees much to admire.

"Polly was a warm-hearted woman. She adored her boys," Inessa explains. "She was loved by her husband Fred—but he didn't understand her. That made her lonely. She longed for something richer, though she couldn't name it."

Inessa tells me that Polly once lived as a member of the nobility in a distant past life. Her soul carried memories of refinement and aspiration that this life as Polly couldn't satisfy. She began with joy, but by mid-life something was missing. A low depression set in.

"She longed to study," says Inessa. "She painted, she sewed. But none of it quite fulfilled her. Fred—poor man—was baffled. He kept asking—What's wrong? You have a home. A husband. Sons. What more do you need?"

But none of it touched Polly. She declined slowly. And in time, her soul saw that the arc of this life could not be completed. So it took a different route.

"If Polly hadn't died in the Carlton," says Inessa, "she would have died another way. It was her time."

The Spiritual Ambulance Crew: Polly's Rescue and the Redemption of the Carlton Souls

"Let's see what we can do to help these souls," announces Inessa, as if rolling up her sleeves.

There are layers of difficulty we must now address. The vortex of negative beings—like a dark swarm of wasps—must be cleared from the space. The gateway to their realm needs to be sealed, and the souls trapped in the cinema require forces from the divine world to support their release.

"I suggest we invite the fiery energies of Archangel Michael and his angelic legions to step forward. They are ideal for cleansing and purifying a space such as this," says Inessa.

Into my mind comes the image of Michael's radiant angels, their swords raised. Divine fire rushes through the Carlton Cinema like a cleansing wind, followed by waves of pure, crystalline water. In the stream, I see the residue of long years—the fear, confusion, and pain—being washed away.

The space grows bright and clear.

"This first cleansing has separated the souls from the negative beings," Inessa explains. "What remains now is an abyss—an empty, exhausted space. Let's now imagine a majestic waterfall, filled with the Light and Love of Christ. His spiritual presence can fill and restore anything. This space is His to heal."

A column of brilliant light begins to pour down. It flows like a waterfall, soaking the parched souls below with warmth and life. I pause to think how Polly will respond, once she is fully conscious—her rescue is being wrought through Light and Love. It is, quite literally, the pot of gold at the end of her rainbow.

"The situation is much improved," says Inessa, "but I can now perceive another layer. An interesting challenge."

She falls quiet, sensing.

"The guiding angel of each person who was crushed, injured, or pinned by fallen beams is likewise caught," she says at last. "I can see each soul still accompanied by their angel. All are motionless—all are stuck within the cinema."

I wait as Inessa considers further.

"I believe we need a different kind of help," Inessa says. "There is a particularly compassionate gesture that we can invite, one that can reach both the souls and their angels. It is embodied in the being of the Blessed Maria—the mother of Christ Jesus. This gesture can complete what we've begun."

Together, we concentrate and extend a silent request—one formed not in words but in intention. We invite graciousness and Love to flow towards all those who suffered at the Carlton: those who died, those still partially bound, and the angels who faithfully remain beside them.

A beatific presence arises. The air within my imagination becomes infused with blue, gold, and violet. It is—to me—something like standing inside a loving embrace. Slowly, the souls begin to shift. I see them now as ovals of soft, intense colour, and behind each one, its angel—bright and glowing.

The ovals begin to move. They circle one another gently. Then they begin to rise—first one, then two, then five, then ten. They move more swiftly now, like a great release of birds, streaming upwards, as if drawn by a powerful force. It is a coordinated dance of Light. The cinema begins to empty.

And at the end, just one soul remains.

"Oh dear," I say, "I can see that Polly hasn't moved."

"Yes, don't worry," replies Inessa. "I asked her permission to be the gateway through which the others could pass. She is the one we can work with—we know her story, we have her picture. The others are unknown to us. But through Polly, we were able to help them."

I marvel at this. That Polly—modest, cheerful, emotionally neglected in life—should become the conduit for release is entirely fitting. Her warm-heartedness made her a spiritual touchpoint—a catalyst for collective healing.

"She is not fully conscious," Inessa adds, "but her good heart made this possible."

At that moment, I see Polly rise. Her soul lifts like a shooting star, soaring up and up towards the sky, with her angel beside her. She travels swiftly and surely into the soul-realm—finally released, finally free.

As I lose sight of her, I think of Polly, realising her dreams at long last. I imagine her stepping through the library door into the learning she so longed for, to join the *Jewels of the Firmament: The Moon, the Planets, and the Stars.*

Author's Note: The Bombing of the Carlton Cinema

In this story, we encounter real individuals who perished in the bombing of the Carlton Cinema—names drawn from historical newspaper reports. The tale of the fifteen-year-old boy—the youngest casualty—who bought his cinema ticket with bottle-return money is also true, recorded in local oral testimony.

I first discovered the tragic manner of Polly's death while researching the Ruggles line of the family. Until then, I hadn't realised that Polly was, in fact, a civilian casualty of war. In seeking more detail, I explored maps of wartime Sparkhill and Sparkbrook, official reports, local histories of the Carlton Cinema, and present-day views of the site—now the modest memorial garden.

These sources allowed Inessa to perceive Polly's supersensible location with clarity, enabling a rescue that not only freed Polly's soul but also permitted the release of many others caught in the spiritual wake of that catastrophic night.

This is a moving story. But it is more than that. It is also a story of Light and Love—of how even a quiet life can become a vessel for the healing of others.

The tale carries several motifs, introduced through the book catalogue that Polly finds in the library. The most important of these motifs is drawn from Rudolf Steiner's spiritual research: that matter is condensed Light, and that the soul is formed of Love. These two truths weave gently throughout Polly's story, shaping its symbolism. They reflect her yearning, her unfulfilled inner life, and the quiet reality of her goodness—qualities that, after death, allowed her to become the point of passage for so many others.

This tale has a hopeful ending—but many such tales of trauma do not. If you ever find yourself at the site of a past disaster, even decades later, a quiet prayer or gesture of blessing may offer unexpected help. Some souls may still be waiting, just as Polly and her fellow cinema-goers once were.

Turning the Page

Polly's story reveals how a seemingly ordinary life can become a vessel for extraordinary spiritual service. Her loving heart enabled a profound act of rescue after death—showing that even the overlooked can hold sacred roles.

As a wife, mother, neighbour, and worker, Polly lived with quiet dedication. She inspired her sons to become happy, capable men, and gave freely of herself to those around her. Yet behind this practical goodness was a soul that longed for more: for learning, beauty, and meaning.

Over time, her inner life fell silent as her resources to sustain hope failed. Surrounded by the bustle of family, Polly's unfulfilled aspirations faded into a kind of soul-hibernation. It is one of the poignancies of her story that she lost her inner vitality before her physical life was taken. But the love she had sown, quietly and without expectation, became a spiritual lifeline for others. Like Lily, maternal warmth was her gift, and purity of heart her inheritance. These two qualities became opportunities in Polly for spiritual service.

In the realm beyond death, Polly's soul became the point through which others could pass to freedom. That is her greatest offering. It gives me confidence that Polly has indeed fulfilled something essential in her incarnation, and will find deeper growth in lives to come.

Although not directly connected to Ernest by blood, Polly's soul belongs to the wider constellation of love and striving, frailty and strength that shapes this family's destiny. From a spiritual perspective, family may extend far beyond earthly lineage, forming a great community of souls, all working together toward healing and revitalisation.

Through her son Jimmy—whose loyalty and warmth echo his mother's nature—Polly's influence enters the main current of this story and, from the margins, begins to lift it upwards. Jimmy's marriage to Dulcie, Ernest's sister, creates a bridge between the Ruggles and Mallory lines; and over this bridge step a lightness of love and a fidelity of partnership that begin an ascendent arc of restoration. It begins to balance the wounds carried by others.

Polly's life stands as a metaphor for love's power to heal unseen damage, a quiet force moving beneath the grander dramas. Alongside all the other players in our story, Polly contributes to the greater work of redemption that has unfolded through this karmic detective story.

Now we turn the page, to see that love, having passed through darkness, prepares to walk once more in human form. For we come to Polly's son, Jimmy, and his wife, Dulcie—the pair whose tale will complete the arc of the characters in this book.

Jimmy is the man who left me the suitcase—the very object that began this journey into the examination of my family—their lives, their deaths, and what lies beyond. It feels fitting that his and Dulcie's story closes the circle.

We return now to the beginning: to the one who unknowingly handed me the key.

12:

A QUIET TRIUMPH OF LOVE

JIMMY RUGGLES 1915–1993 & DULCIE MALLORY 1905–1987
My Great-Aunt and Great-Uncle
Dulcie: Sister to Eric and Ernest

"I am not romantic, you know. I never was. I ask only a
comfortable home; and considering Mr Collins's character,
connection, and situation in life, I am convinced that my
chance of happiness with him is as fair as most people can
boast on entering the marriage state."

Charlotte Lucas in *Pride and Prejudice*, Jane Austen (1813)

And fare thee weel, my only luve!
And fare thee weel awhile!
And I will come again, my luve,
Though it were ten thousand mile.

A Red, Red Rose, Robert Burns (1794)

1912: Dulcie: King William's Oranges

Dulcie's small fingers struggle to span the chords, as Lily teaches her
the new piano piece. The jaunty rhythm of *Beethoven's Ecossaise in G
Major* makes Dulcie smile. It brings thoughts to mind of kings and
queens trotting along on fine horses. Dulcie is keen on royalty, due to
her favourite book: *Our Island Story: A History of England for Boys and
Girls*. How exciting the stories are! Eric, too, loves English history and
often tells Dulcie historical tales—a fat king called Harry with a trail of
wives following after him; someone called Bloody Mary chopping
people's heads off with a big axe—"Euch!" says Dulcie and wrinkles
her nose. "That Mary must have been strong!" Dulcie's seen the
gardener chopping wood. She knows what she's talking about.

Eric laughs and ruffles her hair. "She was a titch, dear Dulcie, but she had a big executioner!" and he pretends to wield an imaginary axe while she squeals with excitement.

Jimmy 1939, Birmingham
—this photo cost him fifteen shillings, which
was a considerable sum at the time.

Dulcie enjoys studying with Miss Ludlow, her governess. When Glenda Ludlow first arrives in Dulcie's life, Dulcie recognises *History* in her tutor's name. "I know all about Ludlow, Miss," she pipes, on the first morning. "It was where poor Prince Arthur Tudor went to die of the cold. He was planning to be King Henry the Eighth, but in the end, his little brother had to be King Henry the Eighth instead. And they both married Catherine of Harborne, who lived just up the road from here. In Harborne," she finishes, with conviction.

Miss Ludlow gives a tinkling laugh and corrects: "Catherine of Aragon, Dulcie, not Catherine of Harborne." Dulcie is a bit disappointed. Not a queen from Birmingham after all.

This morning, as Dulcie strives for musical accuracy in the *Ecossaise*, the warm breeze puffs the scent of lilacs into the front room. When Miss Ludlow arrives at 10am, it will be time for reading and writing.

Dulcie as a young girl c. 1922
Erdington, Birmingham.

Dulcie is not a slow child. On the contrary, she is quick-witted with a sharp memory and a vivid imagination. How else could Catherine of Harborne have come into existence? Her work is deemed good in all subjects. She works hard, feeling that she must measure up to some invisible quality standard that hovers in the air around her father, Arthur.

Now Dulcie takes out her copybook, ready for copperplate handwriting practice. Handwriting is her bête noire. Miss Ludlow always pronounces her writing messy, no matter how hard she tries. The copybook is a lovely blue leather-bound volume of sweet-smelling paper with rough-cut edges. It was a present from Father. On its cover it says: *Blessings Often Come In Humble Disguise*. She likes this phrase. It makes her feel that blessings are all around her, just out of sight, if she could only see past their camouflage.

Between the frontispiece and first page lies a dried daisy chain. She keeps it there because it makes her feel warm inside. Eric always makes her a daisy chain for her birthday, and places it around her neck with a kiss. It is a little ceremony that they both enjoy.

The book looks promising, as though it invites secrets and imaginative stories—perhaps something about a puppy who saves his mistress from drowning, or a plain girl who grows up to be a beautiful duchess. But really, it is full of mottos that Dulcie has to copy out five times.

She looks at today's motto. It is one she has seen several times before. *Perseverance conquers all things*. She runs her finger over the cursive script, and then falls to her task of copperplate writing. Her tongue sticks out with concentration. Tomorrow's motto is: *There is nought as pleasing as God's work*, to which she would like to add *except for a kitten*.

After lunch is history, and that's the best. There is half an hour of stories, and then half an hour of drawing pictures. In this way, Dulcie has created a beautiful book of illustrated tales full of knights, monarchs and horses. Eric always leafs through her drawings, turning straight to the one about King William's Oranges and whooping with laughter. She has sketched the fruits stacked in piles around the small King with his wonky crown. He has a greengrocer's sign pinned to his palace door, that says: *Oranges for sale*. It is not Dulcie's best, she thinks, so why does Eric always turn to it with such relish?

"My sweet, wondrous girl," he says, using his pet name for her, "you're a caution!"

1915: April: Jimmy: Tiny Toes

Baby Jimmy squeals with delight as his mother, Polly, bounces him up and down on the sprung rocker outside the front door. His tiny toes wiggle gleefully. *He's an adventurous one*, thinks Polly, as she breathes the sharp autumnal air. Her husband, Fred, is with the 21st Lancers. He's posted to India. *So very far away*, thinks Polly, dreamily. *It must be hot there*. She goes indoors to write him a postcard about their lively young son, thanking God that Fred's unit remains in India, far from the terrible war in France.

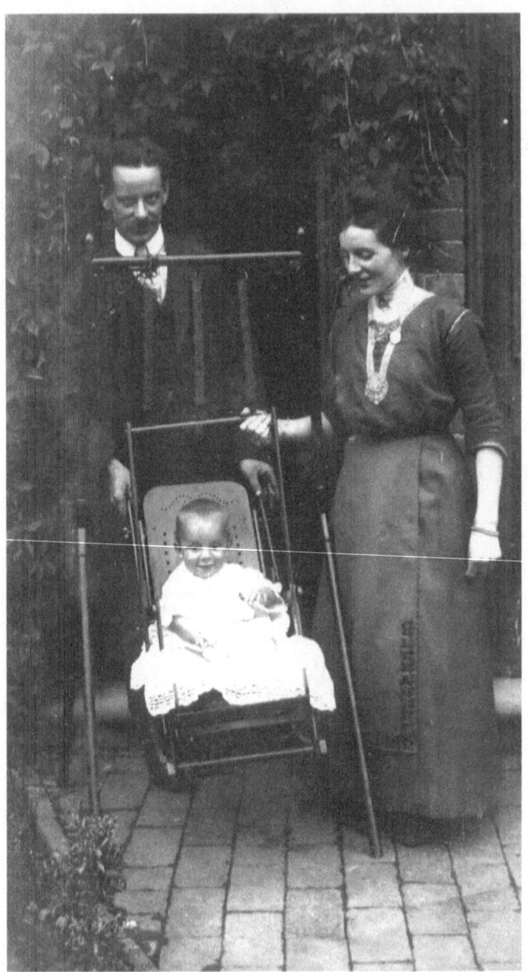

Polly and Fred, Jimmy's parents, Birmingham, 1914, pictured with Freddie, Jimmy's brother.

1915: August: Dulcie: The Daisy Chain

Wonderful Eric is dead. Beautiful, kind, funny Eric is dead. Dulcie stands forlornly in the schoolroom, crying quietly. She strokes her book of historical illustrations and stories that Eric so liked to look at. Eric had always paid her attention. As other family members had become both more busy and more distracted, Dulcie had felt herself shrinking in importance even as she grew in physical stature. But Eric had always had time for her. Now she fears she will be overlooked completely.

The house is in a state of emotional collapse. Poor Mother is almost hysterical. Father has locked himself in his study. Ernest has gone for a walk, grief in every line of his face. In the peculiar silence of disaster, Dulcie treads warily over the landing to Eric's room and pushes open the door. She tiptoes to the tallboy and slides open the top drawer. There are Eric's cotton handkerchiefs, snowy white and crisply ordered, nestled upright in a leather box. She reaches in her fingers and takes out just one. Just one handkerchief. She folds it into her pocket, slides the drawer shut and creeps back out of the room.

In the schoolroom once more she opens her book, takes up a pair of scissors and snips out the picture that had made Eric laugh so much, the one of William's Oranges. She knows now why he chuckled. What a goose she had been, to think Prince William had sold oranges from his palace front door.

She shakes out the handkerchief, smooths it, and places the snipped-out picture in its centre. She adds the pressed daisy chain, gingerly removed from the front of her copybook. She folds the handkerchief carefully, following its pressed lines, and places it inside her small wooden chest of treasures: the mother-of-pearl hair clip from Ernest, the gold chain from Mother, and now this—a memory of Eric to keep forever.

1921: Jimmy: The Wonder of the Universe

Jimmy stands solemnly in his Robin Hood costume, bow and arrow poised, feathered hat at just the right angle. His collar itches a bit, but he has the discipline to stand still and pose until the photo is taken. His Mum and Dad smile pridefully. They always encourage him and his brother Freddie to take part in their father's Works panto. Jimmy has played a couple of small roles already, even though he's only a nipper. This year, at six years old, he's going to be Robin Hood, and that bow and arrow are perfect for capering around the neighbourhood and teasing the girls. The other day he shot an arrow clean into Mrs Watson's shopping bag, and a trail of flour from the pierced sack followed her down the street as she ran after him, clutching her shopping and trying to box his ears. He's a scream—everyone says so. "You've got more sauce than my gravy boat," says his Aunt Katie.

Jimmy in his panto outfit c.1921 Birmingham.

His life is stuffed full of cousins and aunts. Dad's one of ten, and apart from Uncle Harry, who died in the War, they're all alive and kicking. Jimmy likes the rough and tumble of playing with his cousins, and he's always mending their broken toys for them. As only a six-year-old's mending can be, his is resourceful—full of string, corks, and wire. Jimmy can see money's a bit short, both at home and in the wider family.

"How does he do it?" wonders Aunt Maud to Aunt Emmie. "He's only a little scrap of a boy, but he's as inventive as that Thomas Edison!"

When he's not doing that, Jimmy's helping Dad fix things in the house or turning the mangle while Mum squeezes out the washing she takes in to make ends meet. Jimmy delivers it to people in an old pram.

Everyone knows him. "It's that cheeky Jim," someone's bound to shout after him as he careers along with his load.

He's always on the lookout for 'treasure', as he calls it. Once he found a broken bracelet in the gutter. He cleaned it, tied the broken parts together with embroidery silks from his mother's workbasket, and gave it to Polly for Christmas.

"You're the wonder of the universe!" says Aunt Maud.

Life's busy and a bit hand-to-mouth, but he couldn't be happier. He's a tornado of energy, and life's for the living.

The months and years rattle along in this way. But what Jimmy cannot foresee is that his mending skills will be needed in a quite a new way, one day. Mending broken hearts is not yet in his toolkit, but give him time, say the Fates, and the opportunity to learn.

Spring 1922: Dulcie: A Sugared Almond

Oh, the fuss. Dulcie is fed up with it. It's only a wedding, but you'd think it was a Coronation, the way Mother and Father go on. Ernest's marriage to the beautiful Beatrice is going to be a society event, it seems, and Dulcie must play her part by acting as bridesmaid.

Dulcie looks in the mirror. It is seven years now since Eric's death, and few people have given her compliments in the interim. Dulcie has come to think of herself as a plain girl. Her eyesight, like Ernest's, is weak, and she must wear glasses. *Girls who wear spectacles are never the popular ones,* she thinks, wryly.

The cream silk satin bridesmaid's dress is fashionable, with its rosettes of silk flowers at sleeve and hip, carnival style. But Dulcie thinks it makes her look wide in the girth. The hat is rather nice, though, with its flowers, and her neat T-bar shoes shine with newness. As they wait for the bridal car, Dulcie glances across at Marion, Beatrice's sister. They match one another: same dresses and hats. But Marion has added to her outfit a stylish silver arm cuff and a pair of bohemian criss-cross ballet shoes with heels. Why had Dulcie not thought of such a personal, unusual touch?

*Dulcie as bridesmaid at the wedding of
Ernest and Beatrice 1922, Birmingham.*

Too late now, it's time to go. The gleaming Daimler, with its white satin ribbons and white posies of flowers, purrs into the drive, its soft hood open to the delicate April sunshine. Dulcie and Marion clamber into the back and perch carefully so as not to crease their frocks. Beatrice sits regally between them.

The Daimler slides away up the road. Soon they are at the church, where the ushers hover anxiously at the door. Beatrice is fashionably late, by ten minutes. It is not too much and not too little. Dulcie watches as Marion smooths the lovely ankle-length silk of the bridal gown and pats at the cloche-style veil with its flowery hair pins and perfectly-formed folds of gauzy lace. Oh, how she would like to look like Beatrice, thinks Dulcie. Just once, she would like to look that elegant, that poised.

The music strikes up, and the doors swing open. Thomas Gwyndaf takes his daughter's arm, and they step forward into the unknown future. Dulcie hears, with a shiver of excitement, the daringly modern choice that escorts the bridal group down the aisle: Vaughan Williams' *Come Down, O Love Divine*. For an instant she senses its rich, rolling cadences unfolding like patterns beyond human sight—a tidal pull of immensity against the smallness of one's interior world. Then she shakes herself from the reverie and concentrates on walking in step with the bride.

That piece of music had caused some arguments, she recalls.

"It is perfect for an elegant, modern, stylish spring wedding, Mr Mallory," Emmie, mother of the bride, had declared, firmly.

"My dear Mrs Gwyndaf," exclaimed Arthur, attempting a charming yet commanding smile, "far better to have something traditional in my view! I recommend *O Perfect Love*—that's what Lily and I had, and it's done us well enough."

"That is a dreadfully old-fashioned, dreary piece, Mr Mallory," Emmie had sniffed aristocratically, effortlessly batting aside Arthur's imperiousness. "But I suppose it is entirely suitable for those who like that sort of thing."

Arthur had turned a light puce and was about to reply when Beatrice leaned forward and said: "We shall have both pieces, of course. They are both lovely," and she had, for once, quelled her mother with a single look.

Dulcie keeps firm hold of her bouquet, in case she drops it. She longs to take off her new shoes. They pinch horribly. She stands awkwardly, feeling gauche and rather miserable. *Who would ever look at me*, she wonders. *This bridal business will never be for me.*

Later, at the wedding breakfast, Dulcie sips champagne and toys with her pâté and melba toast starter. The dainty printed menu card at her table place promises poached salmon with cucumber, roast beef, sliced ham, and minted peas. Normally she would think this a delectable spread, but melancholy sits upon her, even though she pins a smile to her face and forces merriness into her chatter.

As the trifle with cream arrives, decorated with sugar roses, she glances up and sees a young man watching her. He's handsome, smartly dressed, with a pleasant and open face. His eyes meet hers, widen amusingly, then blink. He smiles. Dulcie, on the point of plunging her spoon into her dessert, pauses uncertainly. Is he flirting with her? She can't quite believe it. *Sweet, wondrous girl*, breathes Eric's memory in her ear, *smile back, before he looks away*. So she does.

After the cake, and the toasts to the King and the happy couple, the best man—Perry Tremaine—rises to his feet to make the customary short speech in praise of the bridesmaids. "Two such girls as we have here today… bridesmaids who look as beautiful as iced wedding cakes in their rose-bedewed gowns… smiles like sunshine, lighting up the day…" waffles Perry, who has had too many glasses of wine. He wipes his brow, and looks set to carry on for some time, until Ernest nudges him and frowns with annoyance. "Hurry up," Dulcie hears her brother hiss, and Perry hastily proposes the toast and falls back down into his seat. The guests start to stretch, move, mill around.

Now, to Dulcie's amazement, the handsome young man strolls over and introduces himself as Charles Westwood, a friend of one of her cousins.

"My word, Miss Mallory—who made you wear that dress? It might be the latest thing, but I'd have put you in soft powder-blue, with a drop waist and a clean boat neckline."

Dulcie's mouth drops open. *What?*

"Erm—yes," she manages, wriggling her feet around to find her discarded shoes. "I don't think the dress suits me as well as it suits Marion…"

"It doesn't suit her either," says Charles, eyes glittering with mischief. "I hope you don't mind my saying so, but I work in a draper's shop, and I'm forever advising young ladies on their dress choices." He winks. "I'll wager you've some much nicer gowns at home."

Dulcie blushes, then laughs out loud, and admits she has very few gowns. Most of her clothes are serviceable, although nicely cut and of good quality. "Mother is always telling me to buy more feminine outfits," she confides. "But really, my tennis outfits are my favourites. They're so easy to wear, so modern, so… liberating!" Dulcie realises that she is burbling but she is unable to stop herself and feels horrified at her own temerity. What is she thinking of? *Liberating?* Her face reddens.

But to her gratification, he exclaims with pleasure: "Tennis, Miss Mallory, how splendid! That's my own game too. What club do you belong to? Perhaps we could team up with another lady and gentleman for some mixed doubles? If you wouldn't think that too presumptuous?" His brown eyes twinkle at her, and she cannot help but laugh.

"I do play mixed doubles Mr Westwood, but…" she demurs, "I am really rather good so you will have to run to keep up." *What has got into me?* thinks Dulcie. Charles's eyebrows raise and then he chuckles, and Dulcie's own face relaxes into laughter.

"Why Miss Mallory, your smile lights up the day like sunshine," says Charles, his face twitching with suppressed amusement. Dulcie stares, then a gurgle of merriment escapes her as she recognises the gentle aping of the best-man's gushing speech.

"But my forehand is jolly fine, Miss Mallory," says Charles. He snatches up a sugared almond, laid aside from the table settings, and tosses it high into the air. He brings his other hand behind his head and… swipe! He strikes the nut enthusiastically and it sails across the room in a steady arc, landing with unnerving accuracy, and a loud *plop,* in Arthur's glass of port. The drink slops up and spurts onto Arthur's white cuff. He curses and looks around angrily for the perpetrator. Convulsed with laughter and horror, Dulcie ducks behind Charles, who is gazing innocently around the room without a care in the world.

"Must be that idiot best man throwing food at the guests," Dulcie hears Arthur mutter, and she chokes back her mirth.

By the end of the evening, she is no longer Miss Mallory but 'Dulcie' and he is 'Charles'. *Well, it's 1922 after all*, thinks Dulcie. She knows what her father would say of such impropriety. But, daringly, she doesn't care.

Autumn 1922: Dulcie: Frostbite

The fresh spring weather gives way to a golden summer. To Dulcie, launched on her new voyage of love, the birds sing all day long, the sun shines, and the skies are cloudless.

Charles writes to Dulcie several times a week at first. His letters are witty, scattergun affairs, full of barely connected thoughts and ideas. He doodles drawings in the margins, and adds newspaper cuttings, magazine clippings, and snippets of cloth. *To tempt you,* he notes. *This one will bring out the blue of your eyes. This one will enhance the glorious red of your lips.*

Dulcie hoards the letters like jewels, and pores over them at night, wondering what to write back. Her own letters are shorter and less polished, but heartfelt and charming all the same. And they are full of tennis.

Tennis is Dulcie's great pastime these days. Both her parents play—slightly sedately, it must be said—but Ernest is a dab hand at the game. It was inevitable, once she grew up, that Dulcie would catch the tennis virus too. Her backhand is sharp and strong, her forehand fluid, her serves varied and cleverly placed. She's hard to beat, and always in demand for mixed doubles tennis matches.

At her club, Dulcie blooms in the knowledge that Charles admires her. She plays all the better, dresses all the smarter, pinches colour into her cheeks, and has a shine in her eyes. Her friends, Portia and Dorcas, can't help but notice. "Who is he, Dulcie?" asks Dorcas, as she clips her racket into its press and changes her tennis shoes. "He must be something special, for you to look so peachy!"

Dulcie blushes. "I don't know what you mean," she tries, but Dorcas and Portia brush aside her doubts and winkle out all the juicy details.

"Invite him to the club match on Saturday, you silly sausage!" chides Portia. "It's the perfect chance to shine. You're bound to win the ladies' singles."

Dulcie goes home and pens the invitation. Nervously, she posts the bold request and awaits a response. *I thought you'd never ask*, comes back by return, and it's all arranged.

On Saturday, Charles bursts upon the Court Road Club, racket in hand, in dazzling whites and a striped blazer. With charm and ease, he befriends everyone he meets, letting himself be ribbed by the chaps because of his too-short trousers—"Oh but I grew overnight!" he says, rolling his eyes. "Doesn't it happen to you?"—and complimenting the girls on their strokes. "First-rate Miss Fisher... crackerjack shot Miss Sykes... tip-top Miss Mayberry!" he smiles, fitting the modernity of his language seamlessly to each girl's preferences. Oh yes, Charles is a great success, and Dulcie glows with pride.

Dulcie (second from left, second row) in the late 1920s, pictured with fellow players on an outdoor deck (exact setting unknown). The photograph highlights her sporting confidence and cheerful composure.

It's the first of many happy Saturday afternoons. Once the draper's is closed, Charles is his own man, he declares. "Or rather, I'm *your* man, Dulcie," he corrects with a wink.

What fun are those tennis days! When Dulcie looks back later, they are as if powdered with gold dust and kissed by the sun.

When she plays mixed doubles against Charles, he showers her with his guileless, generous compliments: "By Jove, you've got a backhand like a cannon!" he shouts, or "Suppose you give me a couple of games' lead, to save my dignity?" And once, he throws down his racket, puts his hands on his hips as he tries to catch his breath and gasps: "You're a corker on court, Dulcie—if I can't beat you, then perhaps I'll just have to marry you instead!"

He laughs uproariously, as does Dulcie, but his words make her fingers and toes tingle, her heart beat faster, and her legs go weak.

That was then of course.

As the summer lengthens, events shift. Tennis matches broaden out to other activities: walks, bus rides, theatre trips, a dance or two, morning coffee and afternoon tea taken in pretty park cafes. But after a few months, Charles begins to be unreliable. He cancels dates at the last minute, changes times and locations, and, unnervingly, sometimes fails to turn up at all. The first time this happens, Dulcie stands forlornly at the Six Ways tram stop in Erdington for an hour, before she finally gives up. "Back so soon, darling?" asks Lily, absently, as she mends one of Arthur's socks, but Dulcie slinks up to her room where she cries into her pillow, and then goes out to see Portia for some moral support.

"Oh, too bad, Dulcie," sympathises Portia, and "He's a rotter to do that, Dulcie," asserts Dorcas. Dulcie is determined to give Charles a second chance, then a third, and a fourth, but even she has to admit, eventually, that he's running out of chances. The letters stop coming, the invitations stop arriving, and the tennis matches revert to singles.

All too soon, summer fades into a flat, dull autumn. Cold winds suck the moisture from the leaves, then toss them down to the ground, desiccated and shrivelled like spoiled wedding confetti.

Dulcie's shimmering summer of Being-Important is over. Her hopes wither into the lengthening nights. Like a gardener who closes his greenhouse for the winter, she shuts her emotions down, protecting what is left of her fresh green youth from further frostbite. It will be years before any tender shoots re-emerge.

1934: Dulcie: Baba

Dulcie browses the bright shelves of toys, feeling a little wistful. She's using her lunch break to buy a Christmas gift for her little niece, Penny:

> *A little girl, as sweet as pie,*
> *So fresh in the world, her paint's not dry.*

Dulcie smiles. Those lines are so touching—one of Ernest's poems. He's very apt with his word-pictures.

What would I buy for a daughter of my own? she wonders, stroking a finger over the silky curls of a doll with wide blue eyes and a pink-and-white broderie anglaise dress. This one? Or this one—long dark hair, red hat and coat? She sighs.

She picks up a pull-along wooden dog, painted in warm browns and creams. It wobbles so comically that she bursts out laughing. Her own little fox terrier, Pip, walked a bit like that as a puppy.

Buying herself a dog had been an act of rebellion. Living at home with her parents, Dulcie feels hemmed in by their opinions and weighed down by their lop-sided relationship—Arthur sitting so heavily on one side of the marriage scales, Lily so lightly on the other. Dulcie needs to flex her wings—*if I have them,* she thinks.

Sweet, wondrous girl, you can have wings if you want to, whispers the memory of Eric. Dulcie feels fleetingly bereft. But Eric is gone, and life plods on.

Arthur was set against the idea of another dog—"That terrier of Lily's provides quite enough mud and hair," he had pronounced. Dulcie was determined, though. One day, having seen an advertisement in the newspaper shop, she went out and came home with a puppy in her handbag. Part of her was delighted by the horror on her father's face. She cannot say what makes her do these things.

Pip goes everywhere possible with Dulcie. He's her excuse to get out, be alone, live a life for herself. If Lily says, "I need some help compiling the AGM papers for the Ladies' County Club, darling," Dulcie can say, "But I have to walk Pip, Mother." It's marvellous what freedom little Pip has earned her.

Even having her own job doesn't save Dulcie from the rigours of living under someone else's roof, but she accepts that it is so and gets on with her life with good humour.

Dulcie's great comfort is meeting Beatrice's sister, Marion. They work quite close by one another, so it's a once-a-week treat: a long lunch at the Kardomah Cafe—egg-and-cress sandwiches and coffee. Family gossip, office gripes, and amusing tales make the hour swing by. Neither woman says it, but together they form a sort of unmarried, childless luncheon club for two. It helps to have a compatriot in the family.

Penny with a toy, aged about two and a half,
in the back garden of her parents' home, Celandine.

Marion is glamorous and pretty. Dulcie, cup of coffee resting in her hand, watches Marion's eyes sparkle as she talks. Today it's a funny office story—about her boss and his appalling memory for his wife's birthdays. Marion is sent out every year, regular as clockwork, to buy a present, order flowers, and pick up a card. "It's a wonder he doesn't get me to write it as well!" she laughs. Dulcie hears Marion's elegant bangles chink as the coffee is sipped and the cake eaten to the last crumbs. There's time for Dulcie to admire the restrained but expert make-up Marion wears, and the fashionable high-heeled shoes she always complains about. "They give me bunions, Dulcie, but what am I to do? I am so small that I must have extra height," Marion says, widening her eyes, "or none of those pompous Big Bankers would see me when I enter the boardroom to take shorthand." Dulcie splutters coffee down her front as she starts to laugh. Marion is of average height but cannot resist painting herself as the butt of her own jokes. It's something Dulcie deeply likes about her.

In Lewis's Department Store, Dulcie decides on the little wooden dog, but thinks: *Something more?* Her eyes come to rest on a fabulous mohair teddy bear. What a beauty, and soft as a cloud. Should she? It's very dear but... why not?

Impulsively, she goes to the counter with both toys and pays before she can change her mind. She cannot wait to see Penny's reaction.

At Christmas, Penny unwraps her gifts, ripping away the paper, which she puts in her mouth. Her eyes are round when she sees the toys. She squeals and grabs the teddy. "Shall we call him Rupert?" asks Dulcie, laughing at Penny's delight.

"Baba," Penny announces firmly, patting the teddy's head with her small hand. "Baba mine." It begins a lifelong love of teddy bears for the little girl, although at the time, Dulcie has no idea of the impact of her gift.

1936: Dulcie: Affordable Adventures for All

1936 rolls around, and Dulcie feels the fresh energy of the coming year. An almost optimistic air gathers about her as she contemplates possibilities.

It's in the Graham James Engineering Works canteen that Dulcie meets Vera. They're waiting in line for hotpot when Vera strikes up a conversation. "Good day, Miss Mallory. Isn't it warm today in the offices?" Dulcie turns. She's seen this girl in the typing pool—slightly younger, strikingly elegant, popular with the other typists.

"I'm so hot my feet have swollen up and I can't get my office shoes back on," confides Dulcie, smiling as they shuffle along. She is, indeed, walking about in stockinged feet. *How daring is that?* Dulcie thinks, almost hoping her father, prowling the Works floors, will come upon her in such déshabillé.

They chat about where they live—Dulcie in Erdington, Vera in Gravelly Hill. "Oh, we're just up the road from one another!" exclaims Vera, and somehow, they end up eating lunch together. Dulcie learns that Vera is unmarried and aims to be a career girl. She'd hoped to be a photographic model, but dreams fell away after she left home and needed to earn her keep. The typing-pool job came up; she applied at once. She likes it, she explains, because it's a chance to meet people and improve herself.

Dulcie's ears prick up. So Vera has left home and is living alone... *Interesting,* thinks Dulcie. Soon they're fast friends, going to the pictures at weekends and indulging in light shopping trips to Beatties Department Store, where the crowds are sparser and the prices a bit lower.

It's clear there's another girl to add to the lonely-hearts club to which she and Marion belong.

Vera is up for fun, and the three begin to live it up a little. She tempts them to try one of the Great Western Railway's 'Sunday Mystery Excursions.'

"Oh, go on, girls—it's only a few shillings and they go to some lovely places," she pleads. "I've heard it'll be the Cotswolds this Sunday and the forecast is sunshine all day! Think of it—us three sauntering down quaint little streets, popping into the Cottage Garden Tea Rooms, browsing that nice row of antique shops. It's ever so genteel, you know. I've been before—I think you'll love it."

Dulcie and Marion capitulate and book their tickets. *Mystery Destination,* the tickets tease. *Affordable Adventures for All!*

When they meet at Moor Street station on Sunday morning, Marion and Vera look like fashion plates: elegant town coats, sweet little hats, high heels—Marion's are suede, Dulcie notes, dubiously—snap-smart patent handbags, and *no* packed lunches. Men's heads turn in their direction, and they're not admiring Dulcie's utilitarian outfit.

*Dulcie with Pip—Dulcie's mechanism to gain freedom,
as her mother once used a car to gain
independence from Arthur.*

Dulcie, of course, is a Mallory. Not for nothing has she endured wet vacations in the Lake District and long hikes across the Cumbrian hills. She has Come Prepared.

When she mentioned the trip, Arthur looked at her approvingly. "Well done, Dulcie! That sounds just the job for blowing away the cobwebs—and you deserve a bit of fun." He is in benevolent mood, given that Dulcie stayed late the previous evening to type, in record time, the notes from a lengthy Board meeting. He smiles and slips her a ten-bob note. "For spends," he says, to her astonishment. "Enjoy yourself—and make sure you take your walking boots and some sandwiches."

After bending to pat little Pip, whose entire body is one big wag, Marion now looks askance at Dulcie's grim-looking cleated leather shoes. Then she eyes the flask of tea stuck into a serviceable haversack, which bulges with sensible provisions, including a rain cape.

"Darling, what are you thinking of?" says Marion, puffing daintily on her cigarette. Her lips leave little lipstick kisses on the filter, Dulcie notes idly. Puff, kiss, puff, kiss... No wonder men think she's special. "You look like a refugee!"

Dulcie laughs. She has taken the trouble to research likely destinations and is betting on the Malvern Hills or the Hope Valley, as it's an all-day tour.

Vera giggles. "Oh, Dulcie dear, how will you manage in the Cottage Garden Tea Rooms—your boots will never fit through its weeny door!"

"We'll see who's right," says Dulcie, merrily, and they climb aboard. The guard steps into the carriage. "Three All-Day Adventure Excursions—and sixpence for the little doggie, Miss," he intones, clipping their tickets and issuing one for Pip.

And they're off.

It's a longish journey with two changes—Leamington Spa and then onwards towards Derby and the Hope Valley Line, where a connecting train whisks them north. Dulcie smiles serenely as her companions' faces fall further with every passing mile.

"Oh, my word," moans Marion, "where are the tea rooms?"

Dulcie shares her flask of tea and sandwiches, carefully wrapped in waxed paper. Meat paste and cucumber—rather tasty, though she says it herself. Vera wolfs hers down, but when Marion takes a bite her nose twitches comically. "Meat paste, Dulcie, darling? Dear God— the heathens are upon us!" she pronounces, theatrically replacing her sandwich in its nest of paper.

Dulcie, chuckling, gives her a playful kick. "Oh heavens, Dulcie!" Marion cries, "those boots of yours have broken my leg!" And the journey continues in like fashion, to everyone's satisfaction.

On arrival, a damp, squally wind has sprung up. The gusts whip the jaunty feathers in Marion's little felt hat, sending them crosswise.

Dulcie cannot help but think of a small sailing yacht tacking in the breeze.

She strides along the platform confidently, Pip tugging on his leash, ready for the off. Dulcie has a map and a book of walks. "Shall we try a one-, two-, or three-hour walk, girls?" she asks—though she knows the answer. Vera and Marion wobble delicately to the station cafe and disappear into its steamy warmth. "Railway cake and an iced bun," wails Marion, "that's my Sunday lunch?"

As they laugh and talk, the weather clears, and they decide to risk a small stroll.

Mud soon clumps onto the spiky heels of Vera's court shoes, which she wipes with a handkerchief from time to time. Marion's Lotus shoes—"softest navy suede, darling, and as comfortable as a bed of nails!"—sink into one puddle after another, but the two women soldier on, Dulcie pulling them out when their feet get stuck.

After a while, Vera and Marion cease caring about appearance and breathe in the fresh, energising air.

"My, it's really rather fun," admits Vera, delving in her handbag for another handkerchief. "But I shall listen to you next time, Dulcie, and dress more wisely."

"Nonsense, Vera," declares Marion, loftily. "It behoves a lady always to dress for lunch! I shall not be vanquished by the needs of the English climate!"

As she turns back towards the footpath, her heel slips in the mud. She skids sideways, arms flailing, and teeters for a moment on the grassy bank of a mud-filled trench. She gasps. Dulcie grabs, Vera reaches… but too late. Marion slides neatly from their grip and lands, quite ingloriously, on her bottom in the ditch.

Pip, transported with excitement, leaps in after her.

"Great heavens!" shrieks Marion, batting at the dog with her hand. "He's after my Asprey handbag, Dulcie! Help, help—it's an ambush!"

But Dulcie and Vera are helpless with laughter and cannot move a muscle.

On the train home, Marion holds up her shoes mournfully. "Well, darling, they're going to a better place when I get home," she sighs, peering suspiciously at a brown stain on the toe of the left shoe.

Dulcie settles back in her sensible shoes and warm wool skirt and jacket. It's good to be in company, she reflects. What a wonderful day it's been. In her heart, a door that had long been closed cracks open—and through it tiptoes Freedom.

1937–1938: Dulcie: The Outsiders' Club

The 'Three Musketesses'—Marion's invention—are now on a roll. They attend art-gallery openings together, admiring the beautiful and giggling at the pretentious. They cram into packed cinemas to see the latest Fred Astaire and Ginger Rogers, taking the opportunity to dress up and dine out afterwards. And they dance.

There are plenty of fashionable, respectable dance halls to try. Tea dances, evening dances, dinner dances—everything is in their sights. The trio sweep in together, drawing admiring glances and ample invitations to foxtrot, quickstep, and even the Charleston—although Vera says it isn't very chic anymore.

Dulcie is an elegant dancer and a popular partner, but she knows—without resentment—that Marion and Vera are the stars. They twinkle around the floor with small galaxies of gallants trailing behind. Neither girl takes the flirtations further. Dulcie watches, and wonders.

"I'm fit to drop," sighs Marion, flopping into her seat and fanning herself with a drinks menu. "Let's have a Dubonnet cocktail!"

Dulcie glances across the room at Vera, who is talking to a young man she's never seen. As they turn towards the table, Dulcie stares: the 'young man' is a woman—in a man's suit, with a man's haircut. She presses her foot on Marion's toes and swivels her eyes towards the approaching pair. Marion is alert at once. She almost sniffs the air. Her posture says: *What have we here?*

"I want to introduce my dear friend Irene," breathes Vera, anxiety edging her voice, her eyes not quite meeting theirs. *Will it be all right?* The three girls have been friends for months, and the name Irene has begun to drop from Vera's lips: a friend, a companion, a lodger.

"You must bring her along to one of our dance evenings some time," Marion had suggested—without much interest. But now here Irene is, in the (surprising) flesh.

Vera has been a great success for Dulcie. The friendship carries parental approval, even though Vera is a working-class girl. "You're a typist at our works, I believe," says Arthur, greeting Vera at the Mallorys' one sunny Saturday. Dulcie nods and smiles, mentioning Vera's words-per-minute—nearly as good as Marion's—and Arthur murmurs approval. Vera bats her eyelashes, smooths her skirt, and stretches her ruby-red lips into a smile of such innocence coupled with allure that further words vanish from Arthur's lips. He is putty in her hands; it is almost comical—and most satisfying for Dulcie to see.

From that day, Dulcie is encouraged to bring Vera home. Vera is a diplomat, not above social climbing, and keen to be included in the Mallory orbit, as she has no family of her own.

It's as if a spell is cast over the family with Vera's arrival. Like a fairy godmother, she brings gifts: the easing of tensions, the softening of Arthur's set ways, the soothing of Ernest's tetchiness, the fluffing up of Lily's feathers as she receives compliment upon compliment about her beautiful home, garden, food—even her table linen. "Family heirlooms, dear," says Lily, stroking the crisp linen embroidered by dexterous Plum women now long departed. Yes, Vera knows the benefits of empathic communication. She could run courses on it.

Vera sets the right tone with whomever she meets and wins the hearts of the entire family—barring Emmie, who terms her "a jumped-up girl from nowhere." *But Emmie is old-fashioned and obsessed with social status*, thinks Dulcie. *One cannot expect anything else—she has had to guard her own status so carefully.* Everyone knows about Thomas, her philandering husband. Emmie has had a lot to put up with.

And now, here is Irene to add complexity—or relish. Dulcie greets her cordially and shakes her hand. She asks Irene to sit; Irene needs no second invitation. She slides into her chair, takes out her cigarettes, lights up, crosses her legs, and starts talking.

Marion, a woman of the world, knows instantly that her suspicions about Vera are confirmed. Vera and Irene—yes, they're a couple. She watches and listens as Irene rattles out racy stories from the world of variety theatre, where she once earned her living. She is hilarious.

"Oh, Miss Gwyndaf, I must tell you this one. I once borrowed a fellow comic's top hat for a dance routine. We'd quarrelled over who'd drunk a bottle of port. I got on stage and discovered—too late—the rotter had stuffed an old smoked kipper inside the hatband as revenge. The stink hit the front row like mustard gas. Curtain down. Exit Irene!"

"Not really?" laughs Marion, tipping down her second port-and-lemon and calling the waiter. "And please call me Marion."

"Oh, yes, really, Marion. They're a rum lot in theatre. And you've got to think on your feet—fast," says Irene, eyes gleaming. "I was at the Empire once, done up as a toff in tails—big solo, spotlight, high kicks, the works. Just as I hit the highest kick—*ping!*—my braces gave up the ghost and the trousers hit the floor. Clean drop. Instant death, unless you turn it to gold. So I threw my arms wide, gave the audience a wink, and yelled, 'Well, ladies and gentlemen—this really *is* the full revue!' Brought the house down. I got flowers. And a written warning."

Still puzzled by Irene's outfit, Dulcie seizes the trousers story to ask the question burning in her head. "Irene, I see you're wearing an unusual outfit. Is it... more comfortable to dance in trousers?"

Irene smiles. "Dulcie, after years as a male impersonator, I can honestly say yes—trousers are king in my wardrobe, on stage and off. Now, have you seen the latest hiking trousers for women? My dear, they're delightful. Just the thing. Vera tells me you're a walker. We'll take you shopping and get you to try some on."

Dulcie is scandalised by the idea of strolling the hills dressed as a man—even while seeing the practicality. She demurs politely, and the conversation flows on.

After that first meeting, Marion has a quiet word. Dulcie's ears stand out on stalks and her face flushes red as a beetroot. *Fancy that,* she thinks. After a pause, all she says is, "Well, it takes all sorts," and that's the end of the matter.

At Mallory family gatherings, Irene is absorbed into the melée. Vera is so beloved that any friend of hers is welcome—especially one so entertaining. "Go on," they say, "tell the story of the flaming wings, the boiled knickers, the duchess who proposed to you." Or, "Irene, sing us a song—something we can join in with," and Irene obliges.

"Evening, gents—keep your hands on your ha'pennies! And keep your eyes off your wives!" she cries, sipping a drop of brandy from her hip flask and striking up a tune, Vera at the piano and Pip barking under the stool. It livens up afternoon tea no end. If the wider family understand the situation, nobody says so—and there are no objections. It astonishes Dulcie. To think, her father who is so stuffy, and her mother who worries about others' opinions—entertaining two confirmed bachelor girls! It's enough to make Dulcie and Marion chuckle for months.

Dulcie with her friends, standing in the gardens
of her parents' home in Erdington.

They watch, mesmerised, as the Mallorys slide gently into the twentieth century, the older generation taking the path less travelled by their contemporaries—tolerance of the unconventional.

Dulcie's status changes, too. Now she is Dulcie-who-introduced-Vera-and-Irene. It's like a gold star in her copybook.

And suddenly there are four women in the lonely-hearts club—though Dulcie must rename it, as neither Irene nor Vera is lonely. *The Outsiders' Club,* she terms it privately. Childless and unmarried they might be, flying in the face of convention, but the four women contrive to enjoy themselves just the same.

And there's another thing. Dulcie hugs this secret like a mouse with a cobnut. She's met someone. A man. He's called Jimmy Ruggles, and he says Dulcie is the best thing since the invention of the flush lavatory. Is that romantic? Well, it is to a plumber—which is exactly what Jimmy Ruggles is.

1938: Jimmy and Dulcie: Why Not Fall In Love with Me?

Jimmy, Archie Fields, and Walter Cox are out on the town. Tonight it's the King's Ballroom, and they're dressed up swanky, with cash in their pockets.

The dance band is in full swing. *Puttin' on the Ritz* floats across the hall. Jimmy's foot taps as he waits for his beer at the bar.

He and the fellows are often out on Saturday nights after the plumbing firm lets them go and they've spruced up. It's what life's about, isn't it? Meeting girls, tripping a light fandango round the dance floor, putting a few beers down the hatch.

Jimmy's doing well. After leaving school at fourteen, he was taken on in a foundry—casting and fettling. Heavy, hot work—grubby and sweaty—but it taught him how industrial processes function. With a practical turn of mind, it suited him for a while.

At nineteen, through his Aunt Maud, he met a journeyman plumber seeking an apprentice, and grabbed the chance. Timothy Evans is strict but fair, meticulous in every detail. This suits Jimmy. He's keen, quick, skilful with his hands. Soldering pipe joints is his speciality. "Never had one leak on me yet," he'll say. "I seal 'em sweet as a nut." He relishes the tougher jobs too—installing or replacing a hot-water tank, for instance. "It's the problem-solving, d'you see?" he explains to his mum, Polly.

*Jimmy in 1939, dressed to the nines for a dinner dance.
Taken in Birmingham.*

Polly Ruggles is that proud of her boys, Jim and Freddie (a meter reader), she could burst.

With a good wage, suave looks, charm, and a light-footed grace, Jimmy pulls the girls without a hitch. There's been Ava, Lena, Freda… best not to go on. They've come and gone. He regrets some, not others. He's untethered, as he puts it, and his eyes comb the room for a likely partner.

His attention is caught by four girls coming in. Two are strikingly good-looking, one is plainer but with a lovely smile, and the fourth—well— Jimmy reckons she's not the marrying type. He sidles over, beer in hand. "Jim, Jim Ruggles. I'm a plumber—always ready to tend to your pipes," he jokes. The one called Vera chokes over her drink; her masculine-looking friend slaps her heartily on the back and winks at

Jimmy. Marion—posh, that one—looks a bit arch, and the one with the smile—Dulcie—blushes furiously. Something warms in Jimmy towards Dulcie: steady, pretty eyes behind the glasses, open face, the modest way she stands, letting the others take the glory. Yes, she's rather nice.

Jimmy holds out his hand. "Dulcie, would you like to dance?" *Isn't It Romantic?* has just struck up. He's confident he'll impress—until she glides onto the floor and leaves him trailing. She steps with rises and falls, turns gracefully, follows his lead flawlessly.

"Dulcie, you're a regular Ginger Rogers!" Jimmy exclaims. "Wherever did you learn to dance so well?"

"Oh, you know," says Dulcie, straight-faced, "my private dance tutor used to teach Ruby Keeler. He's awfully good." Jimmy gapes; Dulcie giggles. "Got you!" she says, and he laughs out loud while the singer purrs into the microphone.

As the night wears on, they swap tales. She tells him about tennis, Pip, walks in the country, her job at her father's engineering works, and lunches with Marion. He tells her about his mother's shop, his father the chauffeur, and his own work with Timothy Evans. His stories make plumbing sound interesting—even socially important. Dulcie, raised with engineering in the background, can grasp the usefulness of stop-valves, pipes, and siphons; but Jimmy's emotional way of telling draws her in.

"Fitted a new bathroom for a widow down Balsall Heath," he says. "She hadn't had a hot tap since her husband died. Five years. Carried kettles to the bath every week." He pauses. "When the water came through, she just stood with her hand under it. Said it was the first time she'd been warm to the bone in years. That... that was a good job."

Or: "I put an inside lavvy in for a lady in Sparkbrook this Monday. Do you know, Dulcie, it almost made me cry. She wept actual tears of joy over that lavatory. Told me she'd fallen on ice going out to her privy last winter and lay there eight hours in the dark until someone found her."

Dulcie feels safe with Jimmy. He's attentive, kind, enamoured, very polite. He never oversteps the mark. She worries that Arthur will veto the friendship—on account of Jimmy's background, and of his being younger than she is—but Marion says, "Let Arthur say what he wants. I see you and Jimmy having a glorious future—if that's what you want." She leans forward. "Dulcie, it's up to you."

Is it what I want? Dulcie wonders. She's fond rather than deeply in love; Jimmy's fond of her too—perhaps a little enchanted by her social status. Would it be so bad?

"It's not a wild romance, you know," Dulcie confides to Marion, as they sit one lunchtime in the Kardomah Cafe with coffee and cake. Chocolate cake is a must, Dulcie finds, when one has a problem to solve.

"Wild romance isn't all it's cracked up to be, darling," advises Marion, placing her cup in its saucer and wiping chocolate from her finger. "So uncomfortable—all that passion and pain. No—a good partnership, Dulcie. It could be enough. Think about it. He's a nice man. Genuine. Steady."

Dulcie does think. It's tempting to fasten her hopes upon this young man as a means of escaping the humdrum, repressive life she leads. But is that reason enough? On the other hand, she's aware that for Jimmy a relationship with a middle-class girl is a step up; she's pragmatic enough to realise—part of his attraction towards her is social aspiration.

Vera sympathises. "Oh, the twists and turns of the heart, Dulcie. It's hard for us girls!" It turns out that she gave up an affair with a young man, even though they were set to get married. "But he was only a coal man, Dulcie, he would never have amounted to enough for me," adds Vera, wistfully. "I wanted more from life." When she met and fell for Irene, she knew she was giving up everything—marriage, convention, children—all the 'more' that she had desired. She could not help herself, though—it was love.

"If you like him, Dulcie, and you want children, well, why not?" concludes Vera, painting her nails one evening as they sit in Vera's little flat in Gravelly Hill. Dulcie reflects, considers, weighs up the alternatives. And really, she can only agree with Vera. There is no argument against Jimmy.

The following Saturday, the Outsiders' Club meets Jimmy at the King's Ballroom. They sit awhile, enjoying the music. This band are big on tangos, which Dulcie doesn't much like, so she and Jimmy fall to chatting about the new dance styles they've heard about—latin— something called a rumba, very modern, says Irene. "You've got to have hips that wiggle like jelly on a washboard," she adds, blowing a smoke ring. "Birmingham's not ready for that sort of thing." Jimmy snorts with laughter.

Marion taps out a cigarette from her silver case and snaps the lid shut. "I once tried the rumba, you know," she says, "with Jeremy Newberry—but I fell into a plant pot in his mother's conservatory. A good thing, really—he was all hands."

The band launches into a foxtrot: *Why Not Fall In Love with Me?*

"Now, that's more like it," cries Jimmy, taking Dulcie's hand and leading her onto the floor. As they sweep around the ballroom, the singer croons:

> *Why not fall in love with me?*
> *Let your heart sing—set it free.*
> *The night is short—let's take the chance;*
> *Before the dawn, our hearts could dance.*

Jimmy's arm tightens around Dulcie. His eyes become serious. He smiles at her and breathes, "Dulcie, girl, I've something to ask you."

Dulcie almost holds her breath.

He pauses, swallows, then—courageously: "Will you marry me?"

This is it, Dulcie, don't fluff it, she tells herself.

The singer carols:

> *Oh darling, take my hand—we'll try,*
> *To waltz up to the moon, to fly...*
> *Let's take a chance while stars are high,*
> *For love waits not—it passes by...*

Dulcie takes a deep breath. "Yes, dear Jimmy," she whispers. "I will. I will happily marry you," and she gives him a little kiss.

Hearts may be shy, but they long to be true—
Say yes to the moment—
I'll dance it with yoooou...

trills the singer artistically, and the audience claps with enthusiasm.

Dulcie feels almost like the applause is meant for her.

1941: Jimmy: Rosewater and Peaches

Dulcie and Jimmy on their wedding day 1941.

Jimmy stands at the altar table on a pleasantly warm July day. He's on leave from war service and glad of the break from army routines. He and Dulcie have managed to squeeze the wedding in—long overdue, as his mother would have said, had she been here.

His parents, Polly and Fred, were ecstatic about the engagement. What a chance for their boy! What a lovely girl Dulcie is! That was before Mum died in the air raid. Terrible. Such a shock. The Carlton Cinema—two bombs, nineteen dead, many more injured. He misses Polly's warm-hearted presence. He wishes she were here, hair piled up, an elegant handmade dress gracing her petite frame.

Jimmy clasps and unclasps his hands. He's wearing the morning suit he bought before the war for his brother's wedding—a posh do. Freddie married Cynthia Grey, daughter of a bank manager, no less. The Ruggles boys are doing well. But now poor Freddie is trapped in the dreadful siege of Malta. Who knows if he'll come back? They say everyone is starving. Cynthia is beside herself with worry.

Walter, the best man, inspects Jimmy, straightens the tie, secures the carnation, brushes the lapels. "Dashing," is his verdict. Walter used to work with Jimmy at Timothy Evans; now he's in the Navy. They keep in touch as best they can. Jimmy stretches his toes in stiff, shiny shoes as he awaits Dulcie's arrival. *Nice not to be wearing army boots*, he thinks, after months of tiring parades, exercises, and manoeuvres.

The registry office smells of lilies, polish, and floral perfume. Guests greet one another and murmur quietly.

While Jimmy waits, his mind wanders.

It took a long time to wear down Arthur's resistance. A plumber was not good enough for Dulcie, in Arthur's eyes. They could have married anyway, but Dulcie wanted to keep good relations with her parents. "We're not in a hurry, Jimmy. Let's wait a while, take it slow. Mother and Father are stuffy, but they'll get used to it. Short-term pain for long-term gain."

Fortuitously, a plumbing emergency arose at the Mallorys' house on Apple Tree Road. Jimmy to the rescue.

What happened was this.

Padding over the upstairs landing one day, Lily lets out a cry. "Oh no, Arthur! Water! The rug is wet through. What on earth is happening? Tilly, Tilly—bring towels!" At the same time there's a growl on the stairs as Arthur appears, complaining of drips through his study ceiling and onto his important documents. "How is a man to work under such conditions?" he demands, as if Lily has orchestrated the problem herself. Tilly, the daily help, heaves into view with bucket and towels, and she and Lily begin mopping the rug.

At Dulcie's suggestion, Jimmy is called in. She senses it's his moment to shine.

He comes on his bicycle, toolkit aboard, whistling. Arthur, red in the face, tells him to hurry up, while Lily flaps her hands and laments her poor Axminster. Dulcie smiles and goes to the kitchen to make a brew. Tea and biscuits—always the thing.

Arthur grumbles about the cost of redecorating and rug-cleaning. "Now then, I'll bet we can fix it all just fine, Mr Mallory," soothes Jimmy, "but I'll have to make an assessment first."

He mounts the stairs in his unruffled way, surveys the old hot-water tank, and realises it's worse than he'd hoped. Arthur, hovering at his elbow, is shown the corrosion at the joints, indicative of blocked pipes elsewhere. "I'm afraid it's a new copper tank, a complete drain-down, some new piping, and a bit of rerouting to improve flow," explains Jimmy in his most reassuring plumber's voice. "Not too bad—just the bother of getting the tank out and in."

Arthur's face draws into a frown. He's on the brink of argument, but Lily hushes him, and he huffs off to his study.

Jimmy swings into action. He pulls some strings, explaining to his boss the gravity of the situation. "It's an emergency, Timothy, of a very sensitive nature—if I were to say it's my future in-laws' water tank, you'll get the picture," he says, winking.

A new copper tank arrives next day. Meanwhile the system is drained, floorboards neatly lifted, new piping installed, soldered, and ready, and the boards replaced. In less than thirty-six hours, the hot water is up and running. Jimmy beams as he checks it over.

"That's a nice job, if I do say so myself," he grins, glancing up at Arthur, who stalks over to inspect.

"Well, let's see... hmm." A poke at the pipework. "Erm, yes... You seem to have done an efficient job... Yes, I'd say that's a very fair job... in fact, excellent." Arthur smiles, relaxes, and holds out his hand. They shake. Arthur is all contradictions, reflects Jimmy later—one minute furious as a gnat, the next mellow as honey. The truth is, Arthur respects good workmanship, and he recognises it when he sees it. Jimmy's star is rising.

The wedding is small: close family and a few friends. On one side sit the Mallorys; on the other, the Ruggles, including the aunts and uncles that pepper Jimmy's life. Looking around, Jimmy has the feeling that after the roast mutton the two sides of the aisle will never speak again.

The piano strikes up *Sheep May Safely Graze*. Tender, lilting notes cascade through the room. A ripple as the guests crane their necks; everyone stands as the doors open and Dulcie sweeps in, radiant, on Arthur's arm. She wears a flowing velvet gown in forest green and a pert little turban hat perched at the back of her head. Her hair is nicely pinned in soft waves. Very pretty, appreciates Jimmy. The whole effect is unusual—chic, modern, with a traditional twist. Vera and Marion must have had a hand in it.

Dulcie carries an artistically tumbling bouquet arranged by her sister-in-law, Beatrice, whose flair with flowers is remarkable. Young Penny sits quietly beside her mother, good as gold, eyes like saucers. Marion is maid of honour in a graceful leaf-green dress, and Vera and Irene are the witnesses. Perfect. *The Outsiders' Club* is all there. Jimmy grins quietly; he knows Dulcie's name for her closest friends.

When Dulcie and Arthur reach him, Jimmy takes Dulcie's hand and they stand side by side. She smells of rosewater and peaches—a wonderful summer scent he breathes in deeply. Her dress rustles softly as she breathes; petticoats stir beneath velvet's heavy folds. It reminds him of Polly, always smart in her carefully crafted frocks. Poor Mum. *Where is she now?* Looking down on him, he hopes, although he isn't really a believer. An odd dark shadow seems to flit at the edge of vision as he contemplates his mother and a soft sadness touches him.

The registrar's nasal voice delivers the formal words at speed, as if he's got a train to catch. In no time, he's on to the vows.

Jimmy goes first. "I call upon these persons here present to witness that I, Peregrine James Ruggles, do take thee, Mireille Dulcie Mallory, to be my lawful wedded wife," he states, feeling anew the sublime awfulness of his first name, chosen by his ambitious father to sound grand. Thank God for Mum's common sense in adding 'James'.

"And you, Miss Mallory?" the registrar mumbles, absently scratching his ear.

Dulcie has already begun repeating her vow while Jimmy is wool-gathering. He jerks his attention back to the over-warm room, sweating slightly in his morning coat.

"I now pronounce you man and wife," mutters the registrar, glancing at his watch and snapping his book shut.

It's done.

Jimmy looks into Dulcie's eyes and drinks in the wide-open, honest candour of his new wife's gaze. *A sensible match,* he thinks. *A good match. We'll get along fine. No pretensions, no castles in the air—just a pleasant life together.*

Dulcie, contemplating her new husband, thinks fleetingly of Charlotte Lucas in her beloved *Pride and Prejudice*. The young woman's clear-eyed appraisal of a pragmatic marriage has always struck Dulcie as commendable good sense. Now she wonders—would she characterise herself, or Jimmy, as 'Charlotte Lucas' in their own alliance? Who is marrying whom, for what benefit? After all, each will help the other, it seems to Dulcie.

She tells herself: *It's not a grand romance, but I believe Jimmy and I will make a good life—not fanciful, perhaps, but kind and true. And that may be the better part of happiness.*

The wedding breakfast is at the Royal Hotel in Sutton Coldfield. The polite formality Lily has designed descends into cheerful anarchy with the arrival of Jimmy's tribe of relatives. They feast on tomato soup, cold roast mutton and tongue, steamed pudding with custard, and a Victoria sponge got up as a wedding cake. It has that horrible icing they make nowadays of margarine and powdered milk.

"Not sophisticated—but it *is* wartime," declares Lily to anyone who will listen. Anyway, the guests are well pleased.

"I haven't had such a delicious feed in years!" cries Aunt Maud, rubbing her tummy and downing her third sherry.

Then she's up and off round the room, bestowing wisdom on all and sundry. Her hat is a little skewed, her face flushed; she's having a high old time—chatting up Arthur, encouraging Irene to tell rakish stories. Jimmy can hear her "Well, I never—"s and "Go on with you—"s from here. Dear Auntie Maud. Always a kind word.

When she reaches Jimmy, she clasps his arm. "Well done, Jim—your Ma would be proud. Now, don't forget us once you're off on your new life!" A little hiccup. Then, leaning close: "I'll tell you something, Jim. We all hold the keys to our family memories, don't we? But for some of us, Jim, that's our special job." She looks at him keenly; a shiver runs down his spine. She pats his hand.

Then she's off to discuss the merits of patent-leather handbags with Vera, and that's the end of it.

Her odd words stay with Jimmy. He ponders them for years. One day, he'll act on them—though he doesn't know it yet.

1943: Jimmy: Gaskets and Gravestones

Jimmy in uniform. His cap is worn at a cheeky angle,
giving him a slightly rakish appearance.

Jimmy straightens up and wipes sweat from his brow. He's a soldier in the Royal Electrical and Mechanical Engineers, posted to the 7th Armoured Division—the famed Desert Rats—through a Light Aid Detachment: the REME's on-the-spot repair crews.

The hot Egyptian sun bakes down. "That'll do for the cylinder gasket," he grins to his pal Billy, wiping oil from his hands. Billy has sauntered over to rope him into another play to 'raise morale.' This time it's the role of a sheikh. "Go on then, if I must," says Jimmy, mock-reluctant but secretly pleased to entertain the lads.

Jimmy in theatrical costume.

The show brings the house down. Jimmy, ad-libbing madly, is chased by Billy in full harem get-up—headscarf, cotton-bag bosoms, and all. Mid-chase, the stuffed bosoms burst, showering the front row in sand. The lads are spitting it out all evening. In the finale, Jimmy's sheikh is lashed to a camel (two blokes under a blanket) and sent packing. "Farewell, you naughty wives. Smethwick, here I come!" he calls, swaying into a crudely painted sunset.

The camel gag comes from an incident now famed across the unit. One afternoon, flat on his back under a field generator and swearing at a seized bolt, Jimmy feels a shadow fall. He looks up—and there's a camel, calmly chewing through the generator cable. "Oi! You thieving sod!" Jimmy shouts, leaping up as it trots off, the cable dangling from its mouth like a liquorice bootlace. "You're not on the payroll!" he yells after its retreating rear, while his mates look on, laughing uncontrollably. From then on, the camel is known across the unit as 'Ruggles' Apprentice'.

The camaraderie suits Jimmy perfectly, and his flair for cobbling together props and costumes earns him a reputation as the man who can make anything happen. Sometimes he sweet-talks the local ENSA lot—'the Luvvie Squad', as the lads call them—into handing over a few film reels. He rigs a makeshift cinema with scavenged projector parts and blackout curtains slung across the motor pool. Beer mats become numbered tickets, each scrawled with *J. Ruggles, Impresario*. He stands on a crate and booms, "Gentlemen, tonight's double bill—*The Lady Vanishes*, followed by *My Tank's on Fire!*"

"How much, Ruggles?" someone calls.

"Two cheese crackers and a bit of fuse wire—or the shirt off your back if you're skint," replies Jimmy.

The REME engineers are expected to fix anything, anywhere, anytime—and fast. It's the perfect fit for a resourceful man who loves tinkering and problem-solving. Jimmy's skills are used hourly; he's always head in an engine or under a Valentine tank. The pace is relentless.

When he writes to Dulcie, he includes the funnier side of stories but hides the raw, dangerous nature of his life.

The other day, the lads were called to fix a Sherman damaged by a mine. They raced out in their Scammell Pioneer, knowing abandoned tanks can be booby-trapped if left. The location was close to the front, the crew had scarpered, and though they judged themselves out of artillery range for now, the roads were studded with German reconnaissance patrols itching to pick off a recovery crew.

Jimmy's REME crew on a Caterpillar crawler tractor in Europe during the Second World War. These heavy tracked machines were the workhorses of wartime engineering: clearing wreckage, hauling equipment, and keeping the Allied advance moving. Jimmy's service took him from Egypt to Europe, where his duties were as varied as the machines he worked with.

"Let's get to it, lads!" said Jimmy, and they hitched the winch. The Sherman was heaving out of the sand when the crack-crack of rifle fire snapped across the air. A sniper, maybe two. They dived under the Scammell, swearing and panting, firing off shots to deter more.

Jimmy crawled flat on his stomach to peer at the underbelly. "Damn— the drive sprocket's shattered!" Working fast, he improvised a patch with the gear ring from an old Italian truck, cutting, filing, drilling, and fashioning a sleeve to braze in place. It was hot as hell under the tank; sweat ran into his eyes. Thankfully the snipers seemed to have found other interests.

Billy, keeping low, handed tools, nuts, bolts, and bits of advice. "Take yer time, Jim; we've got 'til next week," or "Give it a polish, Jim—got to look good on parade!" Gordon lay on his stomach, rifle cocked, alert for any threat.

Thirty minutes later, the Heath Robinson device was fitted. "It's not pretty," said Jimmy, crawling out, "but it'll get us back."

Gordon scooped the tools and jumped in the Scammell. Billy and Jimmy scrambled into the Sherman, slammed the hatch, fired up the engine, and limped to base with the racket pounding their ears and smoke trailing from the rear.

A job like this Jimmy describes to Dulcie thus:

The lads and I went to pick up a tank sunk in sand. We patched a repair with old tin cans and a soup spoon, but we got it started. You should have seen me and Billy riding back with the hatch up, waving like generals in a victory parade.

He doesn't want Dulcie to worry.

Dulcie's letters are a real pleasure: family news and all the latest about life on the home front. The pair keep up running jokes and a store of funny stories for one another.

In this letter he reads that Arthur is busy annoying Ernest at Graham James by forcing a new filing system on the office. Beatrice has knitted a dozen hats for orphaned children, but the daily help accidentally put them through the wash and shrank them small as mouse bonnets. Aunt Maud has sprained her ankle demonstrating the hokey-cokey to a bemused vicar and is directing her husband hither and thither from the sofa.

Dulcie is being worked like a navvy by Arthur, doing the tasks of five secretaries because the others have gone to work in munitions— better pay and more radio music, apparently. In her sparse spare time, she meets Vera at St Martin's Church Hall to sort and parcel donated clothing and provisions for bombed-out families. Here she comprehends the devastation of one's home being obliterated. "Nothing," she hears one lady say to another. "Grace and Cyril— nothing at all left. Literally. They've got to start again. Just the clothes they stand up in."

Dulcie writes:

It's the children's toys that tug at my heart—little dollies, teddies, bunny rabbits. Some new, some scruffy and well-loved. I imagine a child, inspired by generosity, letting go of a prized teddy for another— unknown—child. A tender gift of selfless kindness.

Ernest's Air Raid Warden work has been a revelation. He seems calmer, happier, more at peace. Polly Ruggles' death in that dreadful attack brought them all up short; Ernest signed up for the ARP shortly after.

It's brave,

writes Dulcie,

to enter bomb sites and rescue the injured. He pulled a little girl from rubble the other day—she was just Penny's age. It gives you pause.

News of Marion, the ambulance driver, follows. Everyone was surprised when she volunteered. She began with soup kitchens and temporary canteens—"A chance to meet the masses," she joked—but there was genuine commitment there. As the raids intensified, a stronger calling grew. Now she rattles around at the wheel of an ambulance, picking her way through flattened streets to ferry the Luftwaffe's victims to emergency first aid stations.

Marion might appear frivolous and flirtatious, but she's really a down-to-earth girl, Dulcie knows. It's all an act. Flapper she may have been, in her early youth, but Marion has her head screwed on all right. She works hard, abandoning her handbags for shopping bags, and her high heels for sensible lace ups.

Jimmy drinks in the news like a pint of stout. What a correspondent his Dulcie has turned out to be!

But wait. There's a postscript, more serious. Knowing Jimmy's near Alexandria, Dulcie asks him to visit Eric's grave. She still mourns her brother, who died so far from home in the last war. Would he—could he—take a flower? *A daisy,* she writes, though she doesn't know if they grow in Egypt. *A daisy for all the daisy chains Eric made me.*

Jimmy knows about the daisy chain and King William's Oranges. Dulcie showed him once. He was touched to the core. He dislikes cemeteries, but he will go, of course.

What can I do for the boy? he wonders. After some thought, he crafts a daisy from tinplate and fuse wire. He pierces the centre with a pattern of holes describing a heart. There. That'll be for old times' sake.

At the gates of Chatby Cemetery, Jimmy pauses, sniffing the dry, dusty air. He walks in. Poorly tended during the war, the grounds look shabby, though laid out with care. He finds Eric's grave and stands, staring at the inscription. A slight breeze wafts the smell of hot stone and earth. An ant crawls over his boot as he contemplates the youthfulness of this lad and the waste of life the grave represents.

After a minute, he bends and tenderly wipes away sand gathered in the engraved date of Eric's death: 14th August 1915. A shiver runs down his spine. There's something chill about this place, hot though it is. He turns quickly—it's as if someone's watching. Is there someone in the corner by that tree? No. He's not given to flights of fancy. Probably a stray dog or cat shrinking into the shadows.

He shakes off the impression and places the little metal daisy upon the sparse tufts of grass. What now? Say something, perhaps? He clears his throat. A fly drones past his ear; somewhere a metal gate squeaks.

He speaks softly into the empty air: "Your family still remembers you, Eric—Dulcie remembers you. She sends her love. They all send their love."

Then, awkwardly, he pats the stone once, twice—as if to comfort it— and leaves.

1953: Dulcie: These Are a Few of My Favourite Things

When Jimmy had returned from the war he'd been a more sinewy, tougher version of himself: still bright and merry, but now extra-confident and resourceful. The war had done him good.

Arthur saw it too and spoke to Ernest.

"You know there's a vacancy for a workshop foreman?" says Arthur. "You could do a lot worse than appoint Jimmy."

Ernest rubs his chin. "The men might feel it's nepotism."

"We're not talking about a favoured son-in-law," replies Arthur. "We're talking about a man who repaired tanks under fire. If Jimmy can keep a Desert Rat rolling in battle, he can manage a few valve castings in peacetime. He knows metal, he knows pressure systems—and he knows people. Let's see what he can do."

And so it is. On his first day Jimmy turns up, toolbox in hand—though he suspects he won't be using it much. The smell of oil and hot steel greets him like an old friend. A dozen men glance up as he's introduced—some nod, some narrow their eyes.

"Morning, gents," Jimmy says cheerfully. "Let's see what you've got for me."

He walks the line with quiet attention, asking about output targets, snag rates, lead times. He notices a sticking point on the overhead conveyor and asks to see the breakdown log. By tea break he's helped unjam a casting jig and advises one lad to reposition a lathe guard— "unless you fancy playing the piano one-handed for the rest of your life." Laughter breaks the ice.

By clocking-off time, Jimmy knows every man's name, every machine's temper, and that the tea made by Ron in Bay Four should be avoided—reused teabags tinged with the flavour of grease are never the best.

The years tick peacefully by. Now it's the couple's twelfth wedding anniversary. Dulcie smiles as Jimmy offers a little gift-wrapped parcel on the breakfast tray he's carried up—complete with a red rose in a tiny silver vase.

"Oh, Jimmy," says Dulcie, yawning and stretching. "What a delightful husband you are!" It's their ritual on birthdays and anniversaries: breakfast in bed with a rose and a gift—not just any gift though. Dulcie anticipates this anniversary gift each year, yet it is also a yearly surprise.

Ever since Jimmy made that wire-and-tin daisy for Eric's grave, he has created a new daisy for each wedding anniversary, using the traditional material of the year: paper, cotton, leather, and so on. First a delicate paper sculpture, then a daisy painted onto cotton, followed by one embossed into leather. For the fruit-and-flowers year, he mounted Dulcie's original dried daisy chain between two sheets of glass in a silver frame. It hangs in the dressing room; each morning Dulcie touches the glass and murmurs a greeting to Eric.

This year it is silk. She opens the gift: a daisy embroidered in stranded silks onto pink taffeta, made into a lavender bag. "How do you think of these ideas, Jim?" says Dulcie, stroking its contours with a fingertip. "So lovely. Thank you."

This practical, capable, amenable man is the steady heart of her life. Not in a rose-covered-cottage sort of way, but more in a comfortable-semi-detached-in-the-suburbs sort of way. She and Jimmy have a great deal in common. They play bridge and golf with friends, take walks around Sutton Park and Cannock Chase with their Border Terrier, Bonnie, and are both learning holiday Italian in preparation for a second walking tour in the Tuscan Hills, planned for next year.

Their first trip abroad together, to Tuscany, had been marvellous. With a little income to spare—and no children to consider—Jimmy and Dulcie decided to splash out on a holiday in the land of romance.

"Something like the Lake District—only warmer," Jimmy had said, when he proposed the idea.

They took the boat train to a modest pensione above Greve, arriving on a sweet spring morning. Swallows swooped, cherry blossoms clustered around the old stone walls, and bright yellow arnica lined the path to the door.

"Oh Jimmy, they're just like daisies!" Dulcie had exclaimed, bending to stroke one.

Days were spent walking, with sandwiches and a flask of tea on board. Evenings brought simple meals: toasted bread with cured ham, rabbit casserole, almond biscotti, coffee. The beaming landlady spoke not a word of English, but her gratitude for Jimmy's repair of a dripping kitchen tap was clear in the portion sizes alone.

Now Dulcie looks out from their Sutton Coldfield house onto the sparkling July day. The golf course behind their house is already dotted with keen figures working on their swing. She and Jimmy are booked for a game later with Janet and Harold Norris, followed by lunch at the clubhouse to celebrate their anniversary. After that, the cinema for the Queen's Coronation showreel—so sumptuous she wants to watch it again—and the new British comedy *Genevieve*. A treat of a day.

She counts the kindnesses in her life with a grateful heart: their pleasant house and garden, the dog, holidays, friends, family—with all its ups and downs—and of course, dear Jimmy. She is lucky. And these are just a few of her favourite things. She hasn't even started on the intimate chats over coffee with Marion or Vera, the uproarious evenings with Irene in full entertainment mode, or the pleasure of seeing Penny's life develop. Many more benedictions will surely come, she hopes—even if children will now never arrive.

1965: Dulcie: Blessings Often Come in Humble Disguise

As Dulcie examines the conveyor belt carrying valve fittings from one construction process to another, she thinks about life. This jostling line of valve parts seems like a metaphor for her own life—functional, no-nonsense items being built up out of constituent parts, and becoming something quietly useful. What was that motto on the front cover of her old copybook? Ah yes: *Blessings Often Come In Humble Disguise*. She'd always liked that phrase, and now she understands it too.

Life with Jimmy has been full of blessings. Somehow, without her noticing, a seepage of romance began to flow into her comfortable Charlotte-Lucas marriage. It began many years ago. Gradually, her marriage turned into one of deep love. How did that happen?

The valve parts float past her eye hypnotically—black, silver, shiny, sleek. She blinks and moves on.

She's here for a special Open Day at Graham James Engineering Works. The company has just been granted a Royal Warrant for supplying specialist plumbing valves to Buckingham Palace. What an honour! All the directors' wives are invited to a celebration: tour of the factory, display of the latest valves, cold buffet lunch.

"It sounds like one of the lesser circles of hell," Marion comments when Dulcie rings to say there are two spare places. "Take Vera and Irene instead, dear. Or Janet and Harold. Or anyone, really."

Now Dulcie stands before some gigantic valves. They hang from an overhead monorail conveyor, swinging slightly. *They look a bit like models of the female reproductive system,* thinks Dulcie, absently.

Dulcie mesmerised by the large industrial valves travelling along the overhead monorail at Graham James Works. Surrounded by the precision and weight of the machinery, she slips into private thoughts about her marriage.

Jimmy strolls up to her, in a very natty suit that has a subtle tartan weave. He steers her towards the buffet table. "Vol-au-vents, Dulce, they're bound to go first, let's grab some," he murmurs.

Snatches of conversation drift towards Dulcie as she balances her plate of finger food and sips from her sherry glass.

"We so love *Dr Finlay's Casebook* that we're off to Scotland this year for a camping holiday!"

"*My Fair Lady*—you must go and see it. Divine, just divine and the costumes are absolutely heavenly."

"My eldest just passed the eleven plus. We're so proud. Now he can go to King Edwards."

And so on. Dulcie herself is engaged by a tall lady in a spotted dress and bowler hat, to discuss recipes. "Have you tried adding tinned mandarins to prawn cocktail?" asks the lady, poking at the devilled egg on her plate. "It's surprisingly nice." A detailed recipe follows, with several variants on the theme of tinned mandarins.

Dulcie is mildly bored but polite. Then she overhears someone say: "That's our Production Director, Jimmy, over there. Always calm in a crisis, he is, and a fantastic chap to have as your boss."

She glows with pride. Jimmy now catches her eye across the crowded floor. He winks, smiles, then very slowly he touches his hand to his heart. Just for a moment.

His attention is sought by another, and he turns away.

There was a time when Dulcie might have missed that small gesture, dismissed it as a habit. But not now. Now she sees it for what it is.

In that moment, Dulcie knows that Jimmy is the best thing that ever happened to her—and that she is the love of his life. Such a grand romantic insight to have while eating a slice of Battenberg is unexpected. She coughs delicately, dabs her mouth, excuses herself to get a glass of water, and goes in pursuit of her delightful Jim, to tell him a thing or two about mandarin oranges.

1978–1989: Jimmy and Dulcie: All Good Things

Jimmy and Dulcie's move to a pretty dormer bungalow in the Cotswolds coincides with acquiring another dog, this time a Norfolk Terrier named Sukey. "Great walks, Dulcie—you'll be in your element," says Jimmy, as they house-hunt in the rolling countryside of Gloucestershire. Now that Jimmy has retired and Arthur has passed away, they are free as birds.

Dulcie regards Arthur's twilight-years-incursion into hers and Jimmy's household as deeply ironic. "I spent years escaping the parental home," she remarked to Marion, "only to have it follow me here in the end!"

"I know your pain, Dulcie," winked Marion. "Living with my own mother wasn't always a walk in the park!"

*Arthur enjoying his breakfast at the home of
Dulcie and Jimmy.*

Arthur had mellowed, mind you. His irascibility and sniping criticisms faded as insight into his own life grew. "Reflection, Dulcie dear girl— it's all there is left to do now I'm a fat old man," he'd sigh, good-naturedly.

That is, apart from growing vegetables in her flower beds, scattering newspapers over the living room, turning the morning room into his smoking parlour, and blasting the radio news morning and evening. *What happened to his military tidiness?* wondered Dulcie, as she scurried around picking up after him.

All that's behind them now. They gave Arthur a good send-off—better than Lily's, whose wartime wake was scanty—and settled down to their new life as retirees.

Cruises now feature large—a far cry from those wet Lake District weekends of Dulcie's youth. Lisbon, the Canaries, Cadiz—and once, the Madeira wicker toboggans, the couple's laughter tumbling down the hillside in the wake of their breathtaking descent. Always, there is dancing. Jimmy and Dulcie are statelier now, but still lithe enough to turn heads on the dancefloor. As they glide, dip, and turn on board the cruise ships, the oceans of the world slip past the ship's windows in long velvet streaks, and they are young again, dancing in the King's Ballroom with all their lives ahead of them.

But as all good things do, these times dwindle as health deteriorates. Jimmy suffers from emphysema and now finds travel too much as his breath diminishes.

The years slip onwards, bringing quiet contentment but also loss. First Beatrice, then Irene—both to cancer. Ernest passes away, worn out by disappointment, mental ill-health, and loneliness. The great shock for Dulcie is losing Marion; without her, the world sheds some of its lustre and flamboyance. Vera tips over the edge next, dying of pneumonia brought on by the damp and cold of her large flat in Handsworth Wood. Rented for its splendour, it was housed in the wing of a Victorian mansion, the ballroom being the bedroom. Very hard to heat in winter.

Dulcie takes on the household and garden chores. Her old cookery lessons come into their own, and she cares devotedly for Jimmy, encouraging him to sit in the sunshine or tinker in the back bedroom with his jewellery-making. Last month he made a stylish ring for his great-niece—a hammered design topped with decorative beads of silver. Next he plans coloured-resin pendants. His ingenuity never fails to move Dulcie's heart. Jimmy still makes her a daisy every anniversary. She has a treasure trove of them by now.

Evenings are restful: chatting, reading, sifting through old photographs stored in the dormer bedroom. "Look at Father in this one, Jim," Dulcie might say, holding a print from a walking holiday in the Lakes. "He's squeezing Mother and me out of the frame entirely with his swaggering pose!"

Or: "Look at me as a kiddie in this family photo, Dulcie," Jimmy might say, chuckling. "I look like I'm about to smack someone in the face!"

They love their home in Chipping Campden. Dulcie believes she would be quite happy to die here when the time arrives—and in 1987, that is what comes to pass.

Jimmy's heart breaks at the loss of her. Once, he thought it was just a phrase; now he knows it's true. A broken heart feels like carrying a splintered bowl in one's chest, the shards sharp, piercing the soul with agony and suffering. He and Dulcie were quietly devoted; life is utterly meaningless without her. He has no spiritual beliefs, no feeling that Dulcie watches over him. For all his practical skills, this is one problem he can't solve.

He sits in the little back bedroom, looking at his jewellery tools and the little stashes of precious metals. He cannot summon the energy to carry on with the memorial daisy he has begun—silver and gold wire, wrought into a filigree pendant with a tiny diamond at the centre. It was to be his most ambitious daisy yet.

Jimmy's friends rally round, but his health is poor, and he struggles with deep depression. His doctor suggests reaching out to family—letters and phone calls. Jimmy thinks about it and decides, yes—it's a good idea.

He starts writing to his great-niece Phoebe, with whom he's long been friendly. They correspond about Phoebe's first garden; he sends her tips on growing. She sends him pictures of the results—ferociously verdant sweet peas pulling at the weak fence panels, riotous cabbages that threaten to take over the paths. She knows he was out in Egypt during the war, so she sends little films of her attempts at Arabic dance. He sends back suggestions—try a joggly eye for the belly button, he advises—and posts some of Dulcie's pretty scarves to use as accessories. The connection helps. The letters fly to and fro.

One day, Jimmy makes a decision. The box of family photos in the dormer has been weighing on his mind. He spends hours annotating the pictures—names, dates, little stories to bring them to life. Through the mists of time, Aunt Maud's odd sentiment floats back: "We all hold the keys to our family memories, don't we? But for some of us, Jim, that's our special job."

When he's done, he sends everything to Phoebe.

Dear Phoebe,

says his letter.

I hope you will accept these photos and memories of Dulcie's family and my own Ruggles family. I know you've shown interest in family history. I would like it if you owned these legacies. One day perhaps you can pass them on.

You might enjoy researching some of the people. I've annotated the photos for you.

They've meant a lot to me and Dulcie; they've rooted us in our lives. Understanding where we come from helps us understand who we are.

With my love, Uncle Jimmy.

As he writes, he thinks: *She's a custodian—someone who'll care for those pictures, and somehow even for the people in them.*

Phoebe receives the suitcase, and it starts her on a journey that can only be described as wondrous.

In the end, Jimmy's greatest act of resourcefulness isn't in fixing a tank or in crafting a floral masterpiece. It's in mending the broken threads of family history, ensuring that the lives he touched—and the life he lived—will not be forgotten.

Afterlife Encounters
Jimmy and Dulcie: visited 2022

"Can you get a sense of where Jimmy is?" asks Inessa, as we meditate on his photograph. I sense that he's somewhere bright, but he's not moving. He seems heavy, either with sorrow or something else, but there's also a warmth about him that feels encouraging.

Considering that Jimmy had no spiritual beliefs, he's done well after his death. Inessa identifies that he's in the soul-realm. Here, he spends time reflecting on his life and purifying himself of emotional burdens. He's almost all the way through this part of his journey, but has slowed down in the final mile.

Inessa finds that he's burdened by connections to illness—which appear as something like stones—and they drag him back, slowing his progress. Overarching him is an immense grief and loneliness. "Ah, poor Jimmy. He still doesn't understand that Dulcie is alive," exclaims Inessa. "He thinks she's gone forever, whereas she certainly is not."

Jimmy can't let go of his grief and will need our help. Inessa begins cleansing Jimmy's soul of burdens, while I send warmth and affection to kindle a lighter mood within him.

Meanwhile my heart goes out to Jimmy. How sad. I had hoped he and Dulcie had found one another long ago and were travelling through the spirit-realm hand in hand.

As a man of ingenuity, vigour, and resilience, Jimmy tilled the soil of earthly life diligently—crafting, gardening, relating, helping—but left one corner untilled: his spiritual ground. Inessa sees him pushing such thoughts away with an almost fearful gesture—the message clear: *not for me*. In doing so, he missed an important part of his karmic intention for this incarnation. His soul had intended him to awaken to spiritual connection, but it didn't happen.

After death, he harvested the crops of his life—both fruitful and fallow. His genuine efforts to embrace earthly life caused him to develop multidimensionally as a personality and to strengthen as a soul. He was so strong, in fact, that he managed to plough onwards through the soul-realm, despite lacking spiritual knowledge. He kept moving against the odds. But eventually, with no spirituality to fuel his progress, he ran out of steam and halted—remaining there for several of our earthly years.

Inessa now searches further back. "Why was he to concentrate particularly on spirituality this time?" she asks. "It's as if he missed his way in a previous life and was given this one to make up ground."

After a time of quiet searching, the answer begins to emerge. In a previous incarnation, Jimmy had been a young Venetian woman whose soul sought spiritual awakening. She spent her youth in frivolous, coquettish pursuits—balls and pretty frocks—while her soul longed to begin its work. Sadly, before this could happen, the young woman passed away in childbirth.

We smile at the similarity between this unknown girl and the flirtatious young Jimmy, but at the same time we note how sincerely he matured his soul during his existence as Jimmy Ruggles.

In life, Jimmy was courageous, tolerant, loyal. He developed a depth of fidelity and love his previous incarnation lacked, enriching his inner spirit immensely. He is now a bright soul with a promising future.

"It's very good indeed," confirms Inessa, "but he still needs to embrace spiritual thoughts, or he won't move forwards, and future incarnations won't go well."

We try to reach him with simple spiritual ideas, but I feel a repulsing gesture. "He doesn't like that," I comment.

"Yes," replies Inessa, "he's fearful. He can't trust."

An idea comes to mind: Jimmy loved gardening—why not send him a symbolic flower to tend? "This flower needs a special soil," I explain. "It needs spiritual soil. May I send you some of this soil?"

Yes, he agrees.

I form a rainbow arc between us, its colours curving from one soul to the other. I send just a few ideas, and he seems content to receive them. Inessa confirms: the strategy has helped him make a start.

Meanwhile, she studies him. "How has he come so far," she wonders, "burdened by illness and sorrow, and with no spirituality?"

When I mention my spiritual reading group for the dead, Inessa nods. "That's how he kept moving. Beings carried strength to him from the words you read—strength that allowed him to go onwards. The spiritual readings you dedicated to him helped."

I am astonished. Jimmy barely heard these readings, much less understood their purpose. Yet they reached him in the spirit world. "Like gifts placed beneath a Christmas tree, we send our thoughts into the spirit-realm with someone's name upon them," says Inessa. "Jimmy unwrapped them in his own time."

Jimmy is lighter now, clearer, easier to reach. I ask him, "Do you remember me?"

Yes, he says. *You're Phoebe—I remember you.*

I explain what Inessa and I are doing—spiritual research shared through a book.

Good, he responds. *That's good.*

I ask permission to share his story. His reply is simple: *I want to help others. I want to bear witness that life continues. I am alive and still growing.*

It is a simple and profoundly heart-warming answer.

Dancing Through Doubt

A few weeks later, we revisit Jimmy. He has progressed, but one thread remains: Dulcie. Can we find her and connect them?

Dulcie remains elusive to my vision. Inessa confirms she is far ahead—beyond the soul-realm into the spirit-realm—and no longer tied to her earthly name. How can we call her?

Inessa suggests we look for the family angel that oversaw the marriage of Jimmy and Dulcie.

Happily, the angel still exists—a testament to the couple's enduring bond. Inessa asks: "Will it benefit Jimmy and Dulcie to reconnect?"

The angel answers, *Yes. They are meant to meet again. They will help one another develop spirituality; they are at a similar stage of readiness.*

Reaching Dulcie is easy through the angel. Dulcie responds with joy and readiness to help. But Jimmy, sunk in his long-held doubts about Dulcie's continuing life, cannot recognise her presence. No matter how close she comes, he cannot see or sense her. "He still cannot believe or trust," explains Inessa.

She thinks… then: "Music might help."

I recall a photo in the suitcase: Jimmy in a dinner jacket, Dulcie in an evening gown, caught mid-dance on a cruise ship. Their postures suggest to me that they could be performing a quickstep. Then I recall a popular quickstep tune from the 1960s—*A Walk in the Black Forest*. I play the melody inwardly and imagine them stepping to its rhythm. I hope it can bridge the gap.

"Excellent—it's helping," says Inessa. But Jimmy's doubts linger. It is hard to unlearn firmly held beliefs. Yet this is exactly what Jimmy must do.

"I think we'll leave Jimmy for a space. Phoebe, why not continue the work today—see if you can connect Dulcie to him," says Inessa.

Throughout the day I return to the image of Dulcie and Jimmy sailing across the floor. Slowly, something shifts. Jimmy begins to believe. First a question; then an answer. *Yes,* he seems to murmur, *yes, yes— it could be her...*

Suddenly I perceive the loveliest sensation—it's as if a broad smile spreads across Jimmy's soul. This smile of his lights up the dance floor. It's as bright as sunshine and his joy is palpable. Dulcie's warmth and love reach him, unlocking a part of him that has been closed for a very long time. There are some moments of exuberant dancing—lithe as anything they performed in youth. They whirl and turn, and I have the impression of radiant happiness streaming from their souls.

Author's impression of Jimmy and Dulcie as they find one another at last, through a quickstep in the soul-realm.
Media: Acrylic, crayon, chalk.

After the dance is done, they set forth on their journey towards developing spirituality, buoyed by the strength of their devotion. Just as Jimmy once offered, with love, those small daisy gifts to Dulcie, now she offers him sparks of spiritual light to place within the sphere of his soul.

It is as if Polly's wish is quietly fulfilled in their reunion. Light and Love are the substances through which they join together once more.

The Power of Love

This reunion is more than a meeting of souls—it is an act of transformation. Dulcie's love reaches across the spiritual world, a selfless gesture of service towards the man to whom she devoted her life. Jimmy's love, in turn, opens him to the possibility of something greater, beyond the physical.

There is a hint of reward too—the harvest of long fidelity. The dedication towards one another with which they lived has reaped a beautiful crop: support, companionship, and joy as they move onwards into the spiritual world and their future incarnations together.

Their story recalls one told in Veronica van Duin's *A Rainbow over the River: Experiences of Life, Death and Other Worlds*: a woman lost in darkness after death is awakened by the healing love of a former life-partner who travels from a distant spirit-realm to reach her. Love, when freed of ego and imbued with true selflessness, becomes a force for profound change.

Rudolf Steiner once said, "Love is an experience of the other in one's soul." To love deeply is to lay aside the self and allow another's joys and sorrows to arise within us. It is this gesture of laying aside that is transformative. "Love," adds Steiner, "is the most important fruit of human experience."

This is the love Jimmy and Dulcie share—a love that transcends death, strengthens them both, and prepares them for their future together.

I think of them often, dancing their way back to one another with broad smiles, and I can't help but smile back. That suitcase—Jimmy's final gift to me—is no longer just photographs and memories. It is a testament to the enduring power of love and the web that connects us across time, space, and spirit.

Turning the Page

If Ernest and Beatrice's tale was the scene of the crime—the enactment of family wounds—then Dulcie and Jimmy's story offers a new pattern. In their partnership lies a quiet answer to the family's long sorrows: love, tended with patience, ripens into devotion strong enough to heal.

The light that illumines one life casts radiance and shadow upon all the others it touches. It is partly up to us whether we choose to stand in brightness or in shade. The threads that bind us knot, twist, unravel, and reweave into fresh patterns.

Every soul makes its choices.

Every soul takes its path upon the earth.

13:

A BRIDGE BETWEEN WORLDS

"Grandpapa, what is dying?" asked Miriam.
"Beloved Miriam, I will tell you about dying," said Grandpapa.

"The rock blinked its stony eyes at the caterpillar and rasped:
When may I become like you?
The caterpillar wiggled his soft eyes at the cat and murmured:
When may I become like you?
The black cat winked her green eyes at her human and purred:
When may I become like you?
And the human turned her admiring eyes to her angel and asked:
When may I become like you?

"All turns of the wheel carry us onward, dear Miriam. Fear not our passing—for with every becoming, we climb a little higher."

The Maple Tree, Lorenzo Ebrio (2019)

Our meetings are now complete for the maternal line of my family, and what remarkable meetings they have been. They reveal not only personal struggles and legacies, but also profound truths about growth, healing, and the spiritual realities that shape families.

We are all irregular guests upon this earth, coming and going in pursuit of our karmic goals. Spiritual science holds that we can only redeem our faults and build on our strengths when we are in human form. Rarely do we fulfil all our aims in one life, which is why we continue onward, weaving new strands into the fabric of our existence.

None of the souls I have met emerges as a villain; none set out to cause harm. Most were kind, generous, and well-intentioned. Yet harm was still done, often inadvertently, to those they loved most. Circumstances sometimes pressed them into choices they would not otherwise have made—choices that rippled outward with unforeseen consequences. From this I learn that we are all, at different times, both perpetrators and recipients, both rescuers and the rescued. We are simply human.

And so, this book has become a karmic detective story. It begins with a wound—the loss of Eric—and continues with an emotional amputation—the quiet severing of trust between Ernest and Beatrice. These events form the first fulcrum of the narrative.

Yet only later does a second fulcrum emerge: the moment when deeper meaning becomes visible, when the hidden pattern behind these twin injuries begins to reveal itself through the story of Lily and Arthur. From that point, the narrative unfolds like a mystery being solved. The origins and repercussions of the two injuries flow throughout the book; they ebb and surge through time and across generations. Who caused these hurts? Why did they arise? What forces shaped the sorrows of which we read?

In the end, the answer to our Whodunnit is this: no one dunnit, everyone dunnit, and life dunnit. The perpetrator is not one person at all. The entire cast of family characters contributes to the wounding and healing, and life itself also plays its part. Eric was shattered by war. Beatrice was silenced by sorrow. Ernest was shaped by shadows he never fully understood. Each of them would have set out with hope, yet all ultimately foundered in ways small or large.

But healing also arose, through gestures and actions: forgiveness that released the past; a long-ago promise that lived deep in a heart; a devotion that survived loss and heartache; a chance piece of music that unlocked insight. Healing happened because awareness was brought to pain, and love flowed where it was most needed. This, perhaps, is the deepest truth of the mystery: that what is broken can be mended—not through penance, but through understanding.

This research has also taught me to look at lives that appear modest and see them as extraordinary. A mother who spends her days in service to her family, a man who elevates his craft to a gesture of care, or a woman whose worth is overlooked—such lives may seem ordinary, yet they carry profound spiritual weight. Polly, a seller of cows' heels and tripe, became a portal for the release of many souls after death. Jimmy, though avoiding spiritual thought in life, advanced himself through humour, loyalty, decency, and the quiet love he grew into. Lily, marginalised by her husband, yet deployed her talent for love in ways that echoed far beyond her own days. In each case, the soul left a mark, a spiritual fingerprint that defined it, unique and indelible.

Throughout these stories, I have used a light touch to suggest these fingerprints—a bookmark, a daisy, a painting, a catalogue. They are not literal possessions but imagined symbols that reveal each soul's orientation and leaning of heart. Such delicate ciphers embody the truth that a soul's accumulated gestures—modest acts, unrealised potentials, quiet good intentions—possess spiritual substance and enduring power. They carry forward as legacies, providing nourishment for the soul's growth and quiet inspiration for those who follow.

Music, too, becomes a subtle language of the soul: the tender introspection of Chopin, the consoling stillness of Schumann, or the bright candour of a music-hall tune. At certain moments in the book, these musical choices serve as small revelations—glimpses of self-expression, inner longing, or the beginnings of spiritual awakening. Alongside these motifs, the Birmingham Art Gallery threads its way through multiple lives as a threshold place where spiritual truths are offered, glimpsed, disregarded, or held for later discovery—and for a very few, they remain just out of reach. These recurring signs remind us that even within ordinary days, there is the potential for supersensible doorways to open onto the eternal.

One of the most profound lessons of this work is the great importance of building bridges to the dead. Historically, it was understood that the living supported the dead through prayers and remembrance. After the Reformation, such practices faded. Yet this study reveals that the dead still benefit from our thoughts, prayers, and intentional actions. After all, how many of the characters in this book would still be marooned without a helping hand from the living? Consciously offered love can achieve great things when we allow it to unfold from within us.

With a little faith and imaginative willingness, we can all reach across the threshold. Share your thoughts, read a poem, light a candle. Keep the dead in your heart. In this way, we keep alive the bonds between the living and the dead. We nurture shared paths and interconnected histories.

Saving Ernest

Was Ernest saved? It is an important question—perhaps the most important of all. And if he was saved, how was this achieved?

Ernest was brought to a place of imprisonment by his own emotional landscape. This is a common experience—one many of us may recognise. In a way, everyone in the book was a prisoner to their emotions, one way or another.

But Ernest was restored. Although his life wounds were deep, he came to understand that redemption lay in his own hands. As Sartre said, "Freedom is what we do with what is done to us."

During the latter part of his life—and continuing after death, supported by Inessa and me—Ernest began to work upon himself. Stepping forward bravely, his soul took charge of its own fate, beginning to review and rebuild itself. In his next incarnation, Ernest will have chances to move forward once more, and do all the things he wished he had managed to do in this life.

Significantly, Ernest was not just saved by his own labours, and those of Inessa and me—he was saved by the whole family working redemptively upon themselves, both in life and after death. Ernest, as a symbol for the family, reveals what is possible when good hearts and courageous souls, on both sides of the threshold, work together.

Emmie forgave Thomas; Lily never gave up hope of saving Eric; Marion held on for decades to be at Beatrice's side; Dulcie came back from the far reaches of the spirit-realm to help Jimmy. Everywhere we look, in this family saga, we find hope and trust, acts of generosity and gestures of grace.

We come to understand that this saga of *Saving Ernest* is not a sequence of isolated lives and events—tragic, funny, beautiful, loving—but a coherent moral education of a family soul. Authority yields to humility; beauty outlasts vanity; egotism gives way to selfless loyalty; and love reaches where intellect cannot go.

Within this education, chapters 11 and 12 become the book's redemptive heart. In the first, we discover the moment when quiet devotion reveals its power; in the second, we meet a story in which joy arises as the natural flowering of earthly tasks fulfilled.

The reader may witness sorrow, fragmentation, and even despair, but eventually the family soul—represented by Ernest—finds a restored balance, a reintegration, and a quiet upward impulse that offers deep reassurance and an invitation to hope. Souls that were lost are found once more. The descent into pain finds its mirror, by the close of the story, in an ascent into light. Wounding, loss, healing, reconnection—the wheel turns, and spiritual growth moves forward.

Ultimately, this book serves as both an anatomy of redemption and a symphony to salvation—expressed through the gesture of love. In this way, the family story comes full circle, poised to begin anew, and with a new family pattern as its template.

My own pathway through this research has been full of wonder, almost of revelation. But little of this would have been possible without the unwavering and expert support of Inessa. Her skills as a spiritual researcher opened a doorway for my family through which renewal and revitalisation were able to stream in. Life after life, the story continues to unfold.

Benediction

During the research and creation of *Saving Ernest*, I kept this quotation in the forefront of my mind. It's an inspiring message, which I now share with you:

> "There is a living and perpetual dialogue between the so-called dead and the so-called living. Those who have passed through the Gate of Death have not ceased to be present, it is just that our eyes have ceased to see them. They are there, in very truth... Our whole being can be infinitely strengthened when our consciousness is filled not only with the realisation of our firm stand here in the physical world, but with the inner realisation that comes to us when we can say of the dead whom we have loved: The dead are with us; they are in our midst."

> *Life Beyond Death,* Rudolf Steiner (1918)

Bonus Chapter:

A TRUE FAIRYTALE OF THE SOUL

"Let me stay longer, Nanny," pleaded Belle,
looking at the beach and the sunshiny sea.

"You can't stay, Belle, my dear, unless you've another one of
you hidden away—another Belle who can come home with
me and practice her piano," said sensible Nanny.

So they left, and that was that.

But for weeks afterwards, Belle had the feeling that there
might be another one of her, a little girl who could perform
Belle's chores while she herself played all day long
on the beach.

Widdershins, Lorenzo Ebrio (2018)

This chapter tells a different kind of tale: a shared name, carried by two unconnected women in my extended family. The name is no coincidence. The story shows how love and intention may flow outward, shaping futures we may not see but can trust to unfold.

Jimmy's Aunt Maud 1884–1967

1921: Pies and Lodgers

Once upon a time there was a fine woman called Maud Compton Ruggles. But everyone called her Aunt Maud, and she had a nephew called Jimmy who was as lively as a frog in spring.

Here they are now, large as life, in the kitchen of Aunt Maud's little house in Sparkhill, Birmingham.

Maud at her brother Fred Ruggles' marriage to Polly, 1912.

Aunt Maud is a wizard in the kitchen. Young Jimmy watches as Aunt Maud slaps the pastry down on the table in a puff of flour. She flattens and rolls it. She makes it stretch big as a cloud. Then she lifts the pastry into a pie dish. There. Down it goes. She pinches and shapes it. Jimmy watches with round eyes.

"What will you put in the pie, Aunt Maud?" he asks, anticipating his tea.

"You," shouts Aunt Maud. She wields her rolling pin, up, down, and chases Jimmy around the table. He giggles and laughs 'til his breath runs out.

Aunt Maud cooks pies on Tuesdays. Or rather, her oven cooks them, regular as clockwork. Out come the pies, crisp and golden. "The pixies have been busy again," says Aunt Maud, as she sets the pastries steaming on the table.

Pie-Tuesdays are Jimmy's favourite days.

Aunt Maud adores kiddies, and often says so: "Especially tasty little sweet ones," she adds. And she tickles them around their tummies until they squeal.

Her own two children, Katie and Robert, are as round and as merry as robins. On the other hand, Aunt Maud's husband Gilbert is thin as a miser and hungry as a lion, but he smiles like a saint.

Aunt Maud takes in lodgers to earn extra money so she can buy the family a holiday by the sea. The tenants, Clarence and Leonard, work as clerks in Birmingham. They're quiet as mice, but they eat like wolves, so Aunt Maud has to keep a tight hold on the pennies. She puts the pennies in the teapot on the dresser and tells the fairies to make them into gold. Of course, they only do that when they feel like it, she explains to Jim, who looks for the gold every Tuesday without fail.

Aunt Maud loves her place at the centre of her family. She thinks about them all as she stirs the mutton and onion pie filling. She's one of ten children, so there's nieces and nephews a-plenty to go round. She has a soft spot for young Jim. He likes fun as much as a puppy, and his curiosity never tires her.

She empties the meaty filling into the pie. On goes the lid. She crimps the pie edges and paints it with milk. Then it's into the oven where it sits and sizzles.

"I've mixed in rats tails and frogs' legs for you, Jim," Aunt Maud says. "They'll be all the stringier for cooking." Six-year-old Jimmy gulps. He hopes his aunt is joking.

Now, thinks Aunt Maud, dusting off her hands, *time for some fairy stories before tea.*

1946: Loss and Love

"Come in, my dear," cries Maud to her youngest sister Emma. They hug and kiss, and then a tear slides down Emma's cheek. Today is the funeral of their oldest sister Martha. Martha fell from a ladder as she painted her ceiling one day. She fell and hit her head, and that was the end of her. "Poor Martha," laments Emma. Maud nods. And because grief must be dressed for, Maud pins a white lily to her black jacket in memory of Martha, who had skin pale as alabaster.

Maud looks in the mirror and her own green eyes look back at her. Behind her, Emma slides her gaze over Maud's hat and smiles. Maud is the one for hats. She makes them big and beautiful, with her very own hands. She's clever with a needle and thread. Her hats sit atop many heads in the neighbourhood. Folks say they reflect the very personality of the wearer.

For Mrs Grainger, the greengrocer's wife, Maud makes a hat full of cherries that bob when Mrs Grainger walks and seem to say hello to all who meet her. For Mrs Smithers, the curate's wife, she makes a white hat that looks as brittle as frost. It seems to frown disapprovingly at children playing in the street. For Miss Bonnie, Miss Lovewell and Miss Carefree, she makes hats that brim with flowers and leaves, butterflies and bees. Those hats look as though they might giggle and gossip with one another all day. Yes, Maud's hats are legendary. Even young Jimmy had one, long ago, but he claimed that it was so naughty it only stayed on his head for a minute. Then it ran off, never to be seen again.

Maud places her own hat upon her head. It's a sad hat today, drooping downwards, but wondrous fine all the same, with velvet bows and ribbons. Maud loves clothes, and so does Emma. She and Emma feel like twins, they are so alike. They share their thoughts and dreams. They swap dresses and coats, and they wear hats that—just maybe—whisper secrets to one another now and then.

"How do you make such beautiful hats, Maud?" sighs Emma, as she places her own sad hat upon her head and imagines that it dabs tears from itself.

"Magic," says Maud.

But no magic can alter this sad day. Maud doesn't know what to think about death. It's a fact that people leave their bodies, but where do they go after that? She hasn't spent much time considering the question, but this loss brings her up short. Is Martha watching her now? The thought makes Maud polish her shoes vigorously, for Martha must not see scuffs marks from beyond the veil.

A handkerchief, thinks Maud to herself, as she gets ready. *Make sure you've got a clean handkerchief.*

"Two would be wise," says Emma.

There's a sudden smell of rich, sweet ginger. Maud swoops on the oven. "There, now, I nearly forgot!" she tuts. Out comes a batch of perfect biscuits. Each is a neat little heart. "For love," says Maud.

The kitchen table groans with the weight of food for the wake. Even with rationing, Maud has magicked up eggs and sugar, flour and butter. "Best ask no questions," Maud will say, with a wink, if anyone asks.

When Emma sees the feast, she exclaims: "Maud Compton Ruggles, you're a marvel!"

"Jackson's the name now, you cheeky girl," corrects Maud the marvel, primly. "I'm married with two kiddies!" Emma laughs.

"When did you do all that baking?"

Maud waves her hand airily. "Oh, the fairies did it while I slept." Emma isn't sure that Maud is joking, either.

Now the two women sigh and pick up their handbags. The wake will be at Maud's house in just an hour's time. Off they go to the church, arm in arm, trying to smile for the sake of Martha.

1967: Departure with Prayers

Maud is breathless. Her heart stumbles, beats fast and slow. She must lie down after hanging the washing or whipping a cake. The doctor's told her to take it easy but it's difficult when there's others to look after. So many people rely on Maud.

She's taken to praying that she'll be spared for a few more years. She yearns to be on hand to support her grandchildren. It's not that Maud has firm religious beliefs. She's not too sure that God exists. But she has a natural hopefulness. It leads her to think that there's a benign presence somewhere, wanting the best for everyone.

Maud prays to a presence she can only half-imagine—the sky, the trees, the wind, or simply kindness itself.

What she murmurs to herself is this: "By frost and snow, let me stay here now. Or by wind and rain, let me come back again."

She says the rhyme came from the wind in the trees. She repeats it often, fingers crossed. Yet her strength slips away, despite her will.

Have her prayers floated off unheard? she wonders. Well, if so, then her part is done. Around the bed her family cluster. Their voices are soft, but outside, the wind buffets and blows. The rain scuds across the roads and pavements. The streetlights make diamonds of the raindrops in the twilight.

Now hark—the room grows still. The wild wind softens its song, the rain falls in silver threads against the glass. Maud's breath dwindles, yet her spirit is held in the circle of her family.

She thinks: *Perhaps my prayers were answered in another way.* For love and gratitude shine in the faces around her, as she closes her eyes.

The sprites stoop, unseen, and bear her gently into the quiet beyond.

And the wind carries her prayer onwards, far beyond her knowing.

1994: Paris: Marvellous Maud

A Child Lying in a Cradle

It is many years later.

Listen.

The wind howls. It rattles the windows of the bedroom of Chloé Compton, my cousin. Here Chloé lies, weary as a traveller, because tonight she has borne a lovely little girl.

"Oh my," she whispers, "what a night for our baby to be born. Dear Leo,"—for that is her husband's name—"tell me about the rain."

"The rain is like diamonds, twinkling in the streetlights," replies Leo. He draws back the curtain and shows her the shining droplets beading the glass.

Chloé smiles. The weather—wild and triumphant—feels right to greet the baby's arrival.

She sleeps. Now, watch. The wind swoops down and carries a dream. The dream slips in the window as natural as the night air and settles upon Chloé's closed eyes.

This is what she sees.

A sprite, tall and slender with arms that branch this way and that, like a birch. In each of her many hands the sprite bears a gift for the child lying in the cradle. Love. Lightness of being. A broad smile. Radiant eyes. Rosy cheeks. And a spirit of creativity.

"Oh," says Chloé, "I thank you."

"Wait," says the sprite. "There is a condition. To keep your child strong, you must fill her life with stories, with enchantments and songs. Only then will she endure the illness that lies ahead."

Chloé listens and is sad, for her little girl is scarcely three hours old, and already she hears of illness.

"Fear not," says the sprite, fading slowly from sight. "To protect your child, you shall call her by this name…"

Chloé strains to hear as the sound is carried on wind and rain.

At the baby's christening, she finds herself speaking the name the storm had brought her. The name is Maud.

Silk the Colour of the West Wind, Beadwork Like Falling Rain

Tiny Maud Compton is frail. But doctors visit day after day, and her mother brings her draughts of strength every morning. Little Maud drinks down this vigour, and clings to life with fierce energy. She grows, improves, flourishes.

Held in Leo's arms, she gazes at the twilight sky. She smiles, cheeks round and rosy. Her crinkled eyes are green as emeralds. Her hand reaches towards the rising moon. She spreads her fingers like a star.

"She's a changeling," says Leo, laughing with delight.
"She's a miracle," says Chloé, sighing with love.
"She's marvellous Maud," says the wind, though only the trees can hear it.

Maud is enchanted by the fairy stories her mother tells. Madame d'Aulnoy, Charles Perrault—tales of diamonds and toads, of clever servants and enchanted birds. Maud draws princesses in bright gowns, sketches castles and horses, makes up songs for her mother to play.

As Maud grows, she learns to sew. She cuts and stitches, adds ruffles and darts, turns old clothes into new. Her friends say she has enchanted fingers. "How do you do it, Maud?" they sigh.

"Magic," says young Maud.

She finds work in a house of fashion. Dresses come home with her— silk the colour of the west wind, beadwork like falling rain. Her wardrobe grows until it spills from her flat into her mother's house.

It recalls a tale Chloé once read aloud: of a princess who had a dress for every star. She marvels at her daughter's galaxy of gowns.

Wherever Maud goes, people take to her. They call her Marvellous Maud. And she lives in contentment at the heart of her family, where she both gives and receives the deepest warmth of love.

Author's Note: The Shared Name

Though this tale is told whimsically, its foundations are true. Within my extended family there exist two women who share the names Maud and Compton.

The younger—known to me personally as Maud Compton—is alive today. The elder—Maud Compton Ruggles—bore Compton as her middle name and came to light only later, when I researched the Ruggles family.

Separated by four generations, the two women never knew one another, and the families were unaware of the strange coincidence.

Yet here they are: two Mauds, joined across time by a single, delicate thread—the marriage of my great-uncle Jimmy Ruggles to my great-aunt Dulcie Mallory.

Young Maud's name is unusual. Why does cousin Chloé choose it? "It came to me somehow and I just liked it," Chloé explains.

Did Chloé know of Jimmy's Aunt Maud prior to choosing her daughter's name? No, because the Ruggles family only emerged when I researched Jimmy's family just a few years ago.

As I make this discovery, I ponder its significance—perhaps there is a connection here of a spiritual type? I decide to bring the question to Inessa.

Afterlife Encounters
Maud: visited 2024

Searching for Maud

"It's odd, but I sense Maud the elder to be both on earth and in the soul-realm," puzzles Inessa. "But how can that be?"

Inessa finds Maud the elder doing well in the soul-realm. Maud is approaching the end of her task of reviewing her past life. Yet there is something unusual about this soul, as if a part of it is not present. Maud the younger is, of course, enjoying her Parisian life on earth.

"Maud the younger is not a reincarnation of Maud the elder," comments Inessa, "but there is a remarkable similarity between the souls." Both Mauds are warm-hearted, with cosy and charming personalities. Both are undeniably drawn towards fashion and creativity.

Contemplating Maud the elder, Inessa glimpses a previous incarnation for her, taking place in the latter half of the 1500s. She sees twins, a pair of soldier boys who are pleased with their lives, and proud of their smart uniforms. These twins later reincarnated as Maud and Emma in the late nineteenth century.

"They liked their uniforms very much," smiles Inessa.

"Already in touch with a love of fashion!" I reply, amused.

When they came back as Maud and Emma, they continued where they'd left off, turning to dressmaking and millinery as both hobby and passion.

The boys lived in a German-speaking area—perhaps Austria or Prussia. Soldiers were not consistently attired in those days—when I look up Prussian and Austrian soldiers of this era, I find pictures of men dressed in an odd mish-mash of domestic and military garb—armour mixed with flamboyant hats and britches for example. Surely they didn't go into battle like this, I wonder? They would be as conspicuous as peacocks—no wonder Inessa indicates that these boys died young!

"They would certainly have stood out on a battlefield, dressed in such a fashion," laughs Inessa, when I show her the historical pictures. "But I can see that war didn't kill them; rather, some sort of illness."

What of Maud the younger? "It appears as if the two Mauds are very closely linked," confirms Inessa, "and yet they are different people in different times." After more searching, she finds some answers.

"I can see that Maud the elder's soul, at her death, split into two," Inessa begins.

Although rare, this is not unknown to spiritual research. In Maud's case, one piece of her split soul was large, and one was small. It appears that the small piece, when it incarnated again, was not expecting to survive for long — it simply sought a brief return to earthly life, and that alone would have fulfilled its impulse.

And yet this soul *did* survive. How did that happen? The little soul's survival is thanks to young Maud choosing to reincarnate in a place where medicine was advanced enough to save her life. "The small fragment of soul, seeing its possible destiny, strove to incarnate somewhere that would enable it to live," adds Inessa. "This is a resourceful soul, very determined."

"Why would a soul split like this?" I ask. I discover that souls occasionally divide and incarnate as two souls. One of the souls might then pass away quickly. By so doing, strength is added to the larger part of the soul that awaits its own turn to reincarnate.

"A short incarnation of one part of the soul may add experience and vital capacities to the main part of the soul, when they are reunited," clarifies Inessa. "And any incarnation, however short, can provide a soul with a significant boost, due to the potential to receive maternal love."

She can see that Maud the elder prayed with such fervour that she infused into her pleas the energy to seed a new incarnation. Lacking a firm belief in God, Maud yet prayed to an idea of kindness, beauty and love, and her prayers were answered. A little piece of her soul broke off, and returned to earth early, entering the 'same' family, in the broadest sense. The fragment of soul carried back to earth the older Maud's love of family as well as her desire to nurture. The ripples from the older woman's life dispersed into her young namesake, and inspired the web of love which now surrounds the youthful Maud.

This twenty-first century Maud Compton, so determined to live, beat the odds of an early death and grew into a full, ensouled human being in her own right.

To think, I would never have discovered this tale had not the shared name come to my attention!

"What about the name?" I ask, finally. "How did Chloé Compton come to choose that?"

"Yes, the name is most interesting," answers Inessa. "Your cousin's surname, Compton, drew towards that arm of the family the small piece of soul formerly belonging to Maud Compton Ruggles. During the young Maud's gestation, Maud the elder hovered around the parents, trying to look after this tiny soul prior to birth. I can see that she cared very much for this little soul and wanted to protect her. Due to Maud the elder's proximity, your cousin Chloé was able to pick this name out of the surrounding ether, and that is how the names came to be shared."

Reflecting on the Mauds' Journeys

What shines through this story is the rare bond between two women, joined not by time or memory, but by soul. Maud the elder, who prayed so fervently to remain with her family, had her prayers answered in a way she could never have foreseen. And Maud the younger now carries, within her own dreams and passions, the echo of her elder's existence. Though they are distinct, their likeness is striking: two lives, separated by generations, yet touched by the same thread of warmth and creativity. In a way, the elder Maud did not leave her family at all, but found her way back in a new and unexpected form.

Questions and Contemplations

This tale leaves me with many questions. How much can human longing shape the course of destiny? How often might souls interact in such profound and unexpected ways, lacing their journeys together across countless eons? And how do we, as descendants—or even as forbears—perceive and nurture these hidden bonds?

As I delve into these spiritual connections, I feel admiration for Maud the elder's determination and devotion—these qualities continue to resonate generations later. Maud the younger, with her vibrant energy and creativity, stands as a testament to the strength and beauty of human love—and to the unseen forces that guide us all.

And So, Onwards

Every book must have its closing, and this one comes to rest here.

That it should end with Maud feels right, for her tale is unlike any other I have discovered: startling, tender, and filled with wonder. It shows how love may cross thresholds and remake itself in ways beyond imagining.

I wish you well if you, too, set out to seek your beloved dead.

For they wait for us, and they walk beside us still.

Phoebe Tallis, 2025

EDITORIAL REFLECTION

Saving Ernest is, at heart, a work of spiritual detection—a search through time for the hidden sources of wounding and the quiet gestures that heal them. Beneath its surface of family biography lies a moral and psychological investigation: a tracing of cause and consequence through the generations, an anatomy of what spiritual science calls the 'education of the soul'.

What begins with a single wound—the wartime loss of Eric—unfolds into a widening circle of damage suffered and understanding gained. The book's early chapters examine the visible fractures of family life: the disappointments of marriage, the silences of grief, the unspoken rules that harden into habits—all these patterns of behaviour we witness, as readers, passed on from one generation to the next. Yet as the narrative deepens, it reveals a tale as old as the human story itself—the descent into fragmentation gives way, at last, to an ascent toward wholeness. In this sense, *Saving Ernest* forms a chiasmus of the spirit: its beginning and end mirror each other—hope descends into despair but rises once more to compassion and insight through the gesture of love.

Through the author's collaboration with spiritual researcher Inessa Burdich, these family stories become something much greater than memoir. They become a living laboratory of the soul, showing how consciousness can reach across the threshold between the living and the dead to perceive the unfinished work of those who have gone before. Each rescue performed by Inessa and the author, each act of recognition, becomes an experiment in what the author calls *consciously offered love*—a bridge between worlds built not of emotional sentimentality but of objective understanding.

The detective motif, introduced early in the book, gains depth as the chapters unfold. What starts as a search for *who caused the pain* evolves into an inquiry into *how love restores*—and *how responsibility is shared* among all who belong to the story. By the end, the revelation is both humbling and liberating: everyone participates in the woundings and the healings, everyone carries responsibility, everyone both hinders and helps. The family becomes a microcosm of humanity's shared evolution. Here, fault and forgiveness are entwined, and growth depends upon the courage to see ourselves in one another. And here, too, consciously offered love proves capable of shifting even long-entrenched patterns.

Across the book's tapestry runs a pattern of moral education: dominance, egotism, and emotional coolness are slowly softened by sacrifice, compassion, and devotion. Each generation, in its faltering way, takes one more step toward knowledge and integration, until the soul of the family—personified by Ernest—begins to recover its balance. What begins in loss ends in restoration—not as a final victory, but as a continuing act of grace.

Ultimately, *Saving Ernest* invites readers to look at their own families—their inheritances, their wounds, their quiet kindnesses—and to recognise in them the same divine economy of fall and rise. It suggests that redemption is not a matter of doctrine but of gesture: the small, conscious acts of love and forgiveness that redeem both giver and receiver. In tracing the unseen threads woven between generations, the book reveals a truth both intimate and universal—that every family, in its own way, is a school of the soul.

Geoffrey Bartlett-Thomas, Editor, 2025

END NOTES

Epigrams

The epigrams bearing the name Lorenzo Ebrio are fictitious. They offer a lightly drawn frame for each chapter—part homage, part imaginative lens.

They were written in conscious companionship with my late husband, a writer and inveterate observer of the everyday comedy of life. His humour, warmth, and quicksilver turns of phrase continue to live in these pages. These fragments were crafted with love—and remain, like his best works, tender, perceptive, and uncannily true to human nature.

Names, Dates, and Locations

In this book, personal names, dates, and locations may have been changed, for reasons of privacy and sensitivity. These changes do not affect the truth of the events described, nor the spirit in which the stories are told.

Note on Photographs

Most of the images in this book come from my family's own archive, lovingly preserved and shared through generations.

Some photographs include faces now unknown to us. Every effort has been made to present these images respectfully and within their historical context. These people remain part of the family story and are reproduced here in gratitude and remembrance of all who played their quiet part.

Acknowledgements and Thanks

Grateful thanks to: the early readers of my manuscript – Jenny, Rosemary, Pam, Steve, Susanna; to my editor, Geoffrey, for his endless patience in guiding me through the process of writing a 'faction' book of some complexity; to Gillies for his many hours of reading the manuscript aloud, his unstinting enthusiasm for this project, and his unwavering belief that I could write a book which I considered unwrite-able; to Inessa, for the chance to work alongside her in spiritual investigation and build a pathway of help to my family.

To those kind souls over the threshold of death without whose support I could not have written this book: thank you. My appreciation to Jimmy, for heeding the call and for the suitcase of photographs; likewise to all who have generously shared their lives and inner gestures of soul with Inessa and me; and to Penny for inspiring me to investigate Eric and, later, her whole family.

I acknowledge with deep gratitude the forces that have accompanied me during the creation of this book. Inspiration has walked alongside me during its writing, and some ideas arrived almost fully formed for me to translate and express. I received these experiences as gift and blessing, and honoured them to the best of my ability.

And to Lorenzo, my deepest thanks for your unfailing support with my storytelling—you are always in my heart.

About the Author

Phoebe Tallis was born into a family of Welsh storytellers, where truth and tale were woven together by memory and imagination. Her professional life has carried her through art, healthcare, writing and contemplative enquiry—four vantage points from which she has explored creativity and the inner life.

Following the death of her husband, she undertook a deeper study of Rudolf Steiner's work and a new kind of research across the threshold of death, guided by her collaboration with Inessa Burdich. Saving Ernest is the fruit of that work—a book shaped by love, humour, and revelation, written in the voice of a seeker who knows that even the smallest story can open a door.

About the Spiritual Researcher

Inessa Burdich is a spiritual researcher, therapeutic consultant and educator whose work unites scientific training with supersensible enquiry. A former chess champion, she was educated in physics, psychology, and business. She later turned her disciplined attention toward the inner sciences of consciousness, following the spiritual research methods of Rudolf Steiner.

For more than twenty-five years she has taught internationally, guiding individuals and groups in meditative practice, self-healing work, and spiritual development. Her approach is distinguished by precision, clarity, and compassion—exploring how consciousness itself can become an instrument of perception and transformation in both the earthly and spiritual realms.